MW00857245

From Selma to Montgomery

On March 7, 1965, a peaceful voting rights demonstration in Selma, Alabama, was met with an unprovoked attack of shocking violence that riveted the attention of the nation. In the days and weeks following "Bloody Sunday," the demonstrators would not be deterred, and thousands of others joined their cause, culminating in the successful march from Selma to Montgomery. The protest marches led directly to the passage of the Voting Rights Act of 1965, a major piece of legislation, which, 95 years after the passage of the Fifteenth Amendment, made the practice of the right to vote available to all Americans, irrespective of race. *From Selma to Montgomery* chronicles the marches, placing them in the context of the long Civil Rights Movement, and considers the legacy of the Act, drawing parallels with contemporary issues of enfranchisement.

In five concise chapters bolstered by primary documents including civil rights legislation, speeches, and news coverage, Combs introduces the Civil Rights Movement to undergraduates through the courageous actions of the freedom marchers.

Barbara Harris Combs is Assistant Professor of Sociology and Southern Studies at the University of Mississippi.

Critical Moments in American History

Edited by William Thomas Allison, Georgia Southern University

The Assassination of John F. Kennedy
Political Trauma and American Memory
Alice L. George

The Battle of the Greasy Grass/Little Bighorn
Custer's Last Stand in Memory, History, and Popular Culture
Debra Buchholtz

Freedom to Serve
Truman, Civil Rights, and Executive Order 9981
Jon E. Taylor

The Battles of Kings Mountain and Cowpens
The American Revolution in the Southern Backcountry
Melissa Walker

The Cuban Missile Crisis
The Threshold of Nuclear War
Alice L. George

The Nativist Movement in America
Religious Conflict in the 19th Century
Katie Oxx

The 1980 Presidential Election
Ronald Reagan and the Shaping of the American Conservative Movement
Jeffrey D. Howison

The Fort Pillow Massacre
North, South, and the Status of African Americans in the Civil War Era
Bruce Tap

The Louisiana Purchase
A Global Context
Robert D. Bush

From Selma to Montgomery
The Long March to Freedom
Barbara Harris Combs

The Homestead Strike
Labor, Violence, and American Industry
Paul E. Kahan

From Selma to Montgomery

The Long March to Freedom

Barbara Harris Combs

Routledge
Taylor & Francis Group

NEW YORK AND LONDON

First published 2014
by Routledge
711 Third Avenue, New York, NY 10017

and by Routledge
2 Park Square, Milton Park, Abingdon, Oxon OX14 4RN

Routledge is an imprint of the Taylor & Francis Group, an informa business

Library of Congress Cataloging in Publication Data
Combs, Barbara (Barbara Harris)
    From Selma to Montgomery: the long march to freedom/
    Barbara Combs.
    pages cm.—(Critical moments in American history)
    1. African Americans—Civil rights—History—20th century.
    2. Civil rights movements—United States—History—20th century.
    3. Civil rights movements—Southern States—History—20th century.
    4. Civil rights workers—United States—History—20th century.
    5. Civil rights workers—Southern States—History—20th century.
    6. United States—Race relations—History—20th century.
    7. Southern States—Race relations—History—20th century.
    8. Suffrage—United States—History—20th century.   I. Title.
    E185.61.C715 2013
    323.1196'073075—dc23
    2013023396

ISBN: 978-0-415-52959-4 (hbk)
ISBN: 978-0-415-52960-0 (pbk)
ISBN: 978-0-203-08144-0 (ebk)

Typeset in Bembo and Helvetica Neue
by Florence Production Ltd, Stoodleigh, Devon, UK

Contents

Series Introduction		vii
List of Figures		viii
Acknowledgments		ix
Timeline		x
1	Introduction	1
2	One Moment in Time	22
3	Portrait of a Nation	51
4	Everyday People	78
5	Aftermath	110
	Documents	139
	Notes	178
	Bibliography	205
	Index	217

Series Introduction

Welcome to the Routledge *Critical Moments in American History* series. The purpose of this new series is to give students a window into the historian's craft through concise, readable books by leading scholars, who bring together the best scholarship and engaging primary sources to explore a critical moment in the American past. In discovering the principal points of the story in these books, gaining a sense of historiography, following a fresh trail of primary documents, and exploring suggested readings, students can then set out on their own journey, to debate the ideas presented, interpret primary sources, and reach their own conclusions—just like the historian.

A critical moment in history can be a range of things—a pivotal year, the pinnacle of a movement or trend, or an important event such as the passage of a piece of legislation, an election, a court decision, a battle. It can be social, cultural, political, or economic. It can be heroic or tragic. Whatever they are, such moments are by definition "game changers," momentous changes in the pattern of the American fabric, paradigm shifts in the American experience. Many of the critical moments explored in this series are familiar; some less so.

There is no ultimate list of critical moments in American history—any group of students, historians, or other scholars may come up with a different catalog of topics. These differences of view, however, are what make history itself and the study of history so important and so fascinating. Therein can be found the utility of historical inquiry—to explore, to challenge, to understand, and to realize the legacy of the past through its influence on the present. It is the hope of this series to help students realize this intrinsic value of our past and of studying our past.

William Thomas Allison
Georgia Southern University

Figures

1.1	Communication channels	12
2.1	Register to vote poster	23
2.2	Adoption-innovation curve	28
2.3	John Lewis being beaten on Bloody Sunday	36
2.4	Edmund Pettus Bridge	38
2.5	Bloody Sunday and Turnaround Tuesday March routes in Selma, Alabama	39
2.6	Selma to Montgomery route along Highway 80	46
3.1	George Wallace stands in schoolhouse door	68
3.2	Sheriff Jim Clark abuses power	69
5.1	Percentage of registered voters in black voting-age population, 1960, 1971, 2008	119

Acknowledgments

I want to thank my mother and father, Ruby Mae and Joseph Harris, Jr., who were the first ones to tell me the Selma story. This book is dedicated to them.

I appreciatively acknowledge that I could not have written this without the love and support of my immediate family. I owe them a debt of gratitude that I can never repay. All I can say is a heartfelt thank you. So, I say thank you both to my dear, sweet husband Darrell, who is the wind beneath my wings and drove to Selma more times than he ever thought he might, and to our children—Jason and Breann—who were there every mile of the journey and always with a rousing chorus of "are we there yet?"

I owe a debt of gratitude to all of the people that I talked to and interviewed. Special thanks go to Rose Sanders and the members of the Bridge Crossing Jubilee Committee who, lest we all forget, keep the dream of freedom alive. Anne Knight at the Selma-Dallas County Public Library and Kathy Shoemaker at the Manuscripts and Rare Books Library (MARBL) at Emory University were particularly adept and helpful in my research. I am also grateful to countless friends and colleagues who provided me with invaluable feedback on drafts or other forms of moral support including Charles Reagan Wilson, Kirk Johnson, Willa Johnson, John Green, Shanesha Brooks Tatum, Amos Moore, Kirsten Dellinger and Noah Webb. Special thanks to Eleanor Green whose help and encouragement pushed me forward on the final stages of this project when the end was so close, but I could not find my way how to get there.

Finally, I say thank you to all of the nameless, faceless people who made up the Selma Movement. You were my true inspiration.

Timeline

1870	February 3: The Fifteenth Amendment, which granted African-Americans the right to vote, is ratified.
1920s	Dallas County Voters League (DCVL) formed in late 1920s.
1954	May 17: Brown v. Board of Education of Topeka, Kansas decision handed down.
1957	May 17: "Give us the Ballot" speech given by Martin Luther King Jr. in Washington, D.C., at the Prayer Pilgrimage for Freedom event.
1961	April: Justice Department files its first voting rights suit. The suit is filed in Selma, Alabama, and uses data collected from members of DCVL.
1962	November: Researching voting rights in the South, Assistant Attorney General for Civil Rights John Doar visits Selma.
1962	Bernard and Colia Lafayette marry.
1963	DCVL reinvigorated, and the group asks Student Non-Violent Coordinating Committee (SNCC) for assistance in registering black voters.
1963	February 1963: Bernard Lafayette and his wife, Colia, arrive in Selma, Alabama, where he assumes his position as director of SNCC Black Belt Alabama Voter Project and she works as field secretary.
1963	May 14: Sam Boynton, president of DCVL, dies, and a memorial service for him held at Tabernacle Baptist Church turns into a voter registration rally.
1964	July 2: President Lyndon Baines Johnson signs Civil Rights Act of 1964.
1964	July 6: SNCC Chairman John Lewis arrives in Selma, and leads a group of about fifty blacks to the courthouse to register to vote. The protestors are arrested.
1964	July 9: Selma Circuit Judge James Hare issues an injunction banning specific civil rights groups and organizers from any event involving the "assembly of three persons or more in a public place."
1964	December: DCVL appeals to the Southern Christian Leadership Conference (SCLC) and King to come to Selma and support the voting rights campaign there.
	December 10: King receives the Nobel Peace Prize in Oslo, Norway.
1965	January 2: In contravention of Judge Hare's injunction, and at the invitation of DCVL, Martin Luther King Jr. addresses a group at Brown Chapel in Selma.

1965	January 22: Led by F.D. Reese, teacher and President of DCVL, approximately 100 black teachers march to the Dallas County Courthouse and demand right to register to vote.
1965	Attorneys file an injunction to restrain Sheriff Jim Clark from his efforts to prevent African-Americans from registering to vote.
1965	January 23: Judge Daniel Thomas grants injunction restraining Sheriff Clark. Under Thomas' order, 100 are permitted to wait (in the alley) outside the Courthouse to be registered. Most days, applicants exceed this number.
1965	January 25: Sheriff Jim Clark assaults 54-year-old Annie Clark, and she fights back!
1965	February: Mass jailing of protestors continues. Most are charged with "parading without a permit."
1965	February 3: Malcolm X speaks to students at Tuskegee; SNCC organizers invite him to Selma, Alabama.
1965	February 4: In a non-inflammatory speech, Malcolm X addresses a group of largely student protestors at Brown Chapel. The daily marches are canceled for the day.
1965	Judge Thomas issues an order that enjoins registrars from using discriminatory tactics in the registration of voters.
1965	February 5: King's "Letter from a Selma Jail" is published as an advertisement in *The New York Times*. King is jailed on February 1; he is released February 5.
1965	February 10: Sheriff Clark pursues approximately 165 black teens and, through the use of cattle prods, a posse, and close pursuit in vehicles, Clark compels the youth to run for miles. Many are jailed.
1965	February 18: In nearby Marion, Alabama (Perry County), SCLC Project Coordinator James Orange is arrested on charges of disorderly conduct and contributing to the delinquency of minors for enlisting students to aid in voting rights drives.
1965	Protest marches in support of voting rights and to demand Orange's release spring up.
1965	About 500 join a night march in Marion. A state trooper shoots one marcher, Jimmie Lee Jackson. Following his arrest, Jackson is refused treatment at the hospital in Marion.
1965	February 26: Jimmie Lee Jackson dies from his wounds in a hospital in Selma, Alabama.
1965	March 1: Martin Luther King Jr. arrives in Haneyville, Alabama, as part of a four-county initiative in support of local voting rights.
1965	March 2: Memorial service is held in Marion, Alabama, for Jimmie Lee Jackson. SCLC's James Bevel suggests they take Jimmie Lee Jackson's body to Montgomery and deliver it at the steps of the Capitol.
1965	March 3: Thousands attend memorial service held in Selma, Alabama, for Jimmie Lee Jackson. Martin Luther King Jr. delivers the eulogy. March is discussed again.
1965	March 6: Approximately sixty white Lutheran ministers from across the state of Alabama participate in a march to the Dallas County Courthouse.

1965	March 7: Bloody Sunday.
1965	March 9: Turnaround Tuesday (also known as The Ministers' March).
	2,000 marchers set out from Brown Chapel to march to Montgomery. They are again confronted at the bridge, and King turns the marchers around.
1965	Later that evening, social worker and Unitarian Universalist, Reverend James Reeb, is beaten in Selma for his support of the voting rights movement.
1965	March 11: Reverend Reeb dies from his injuries.
1965	March 15: Memorial service is held at Brown Chapel (in Selma) for Reverend Reeb.
1965	President Johnson delivers televised Special Message to Congress entitled "The American Promise." Speech urges passage of a voting rights bill, and uses the words "we shall overcome."
1965	March 17: Federal Judge Frank Johnson clears way for Selma to Montgomery March.
1965	March 19: Lowndes County Christian Movement formed. Future County Sheriff, John Hulett, is its first leader.
1965	March 21: March begins in Selma, Alabama.
1965	March 24: The "Stars for Freedom Rally" organized by Harry Belafonte is held at the final march campsite on the grounds of City of St. Jude, a Catholic social services complex. Numerous stars perform boosting the morale of those in attendance.
1965	March 25: Marchers arrive in Montgomery, Alabama, and rally commences. The crowd swells to 25,000.
	Detroit housewife and movement volunteer Viola Liuzzo shot and killed.
1965	August 6: President Lyndon Baines Johnson signs the Voting Rights Act of 1965 into law.
1965	August 20: Jonathan Daniels, Episcopal seminary student and SNCC volunteer, is shot and killed.
1965	September 2: Court fines Sheriff Clark $1500 for February 10, 1965, actions, which were found to be in violation of the court restraining order.
1966	May: Lowndes County Freedom Organization (LCFO), which was the original Black Panther Party, is formed.
1966	November: Sheriff Jim Clark loses his re-election bid. Some credit the rise in black registered voters.
1966	LCFO sponsors seven African-American candidates for office. All lose. Later, LCFO merges with the local Democratic Party.
1967	Fall Elections: An estimated 10,000 blacks in Dallas County are registered.
2013	February 27: Shelby County v. Holder argued before U.S. Supreme Court.
2013	June 25: Decision issued in Shelby County v. Holder; Supreme Court invalidates Section 4 of the Voting Rights Act of 1965.

CHAPTER 1

Introduction

One moment in time can change the course of history. In his special message to Congress entitled "The American Promise," delivered on March 15, 1965, President Lyndon Baines Johnson acknowledged such. In person, before a joint session of Congress held at 9:02 p.m., President Johnson said,

> At times history and fate meet at a single time in a single place to shape a turning point in man's unending search for freedom. So it was at Lexington and Concord. So it was a century ago at Appomattox. So it was last week in Selma, Alabama.[1]

President Johnson spoke about the events of Sunday, March 7, 1965, which would come to be known as Bloody Sunday. On that day, a peaceful voting rights march ended in a violent, unprovoked attack against unarmed civil rights demonstrators in the Black Belt community of Selma, Alabama. Oftentimes we think that such moments just happen; however, that is seldom the case. Selma and so many other watershed moments in history arise because of a confluence of factors, which occur at just the right time to bring about social change.

This book is called *From Selma to Montgomery: The Long March to Freedom*. Today, Selma, Alabama, is known for its important role in the Civil Rights Movement, but its history is much longer and more complicated than that one event. Selma, Alabama, is also the site of Confederate General Nathan Bedford Forrest's last major battle.[2] Forrest, the Confederate general that Union General William T. Sherman termed a "devil" and once said "[should be] hunted down and killed if it cost 10,000 lives and bankrupts the [national] treasury," would go on to become the first Grand Wizard of the Ku Klux Klan.[3] Montgomery,

Alabama, also has an entangled history. Incorporated in 1819, Montgomery, Alabama, is the capital city of the state and served as the first capital of the Confederate States of America. Conversely, Montgomery is also the location of the successful Montgomery Bus Boycott, a seminal event in the modern civil rights struggle. Today, Montgomery's city seal is a six-pointed star, which contains the words "Cradle of the Confederacy," "Birthplace of the Civil Rights Movement," and "City of Montgomery."[4] Selma and Montgomery are places certainly; however, freedom is an amorphous concept, with different markings pre and post emancipation. Post emancipation, it was difficult to reach accord about what freedom would mean to and for America's formerly enslaved citizens.[5] Yet despite the uncertainty about what form freedom takes, what it looks like, and when it has been attained, mankind's pursuit of freedom is never in doubt.

FREEDOM—A DEEPLY HELD AMERICAN VALUE

Freedom is an entrenched American ideal. Early European American colonists, immigrants, came to the "New World" in pursuit of religious freedom. Many immigrants still come to the U.S. today on that same quest. The early settlers' yearning for freedom inspired them to fight in the Revolutionary War for American independence. Sparked largely by the Industrial Revolution and the Louisiana Purchase, which made opportunities for landownership available to white settlers, soon the mass quest for economic freedom began in earnest in the United States. Of course, these "crusades" for freedom were often at the expense of the Native American indigenous population of the United States and the growing slave population trapped into captivity in a foreign land. The westward expansion of Native Americans through forced removal efforts like the Trail of Tears did not silence the cries for freedom from other disadvantaged groups such as women and those fighting for the abolition of slavery. With some notable exceptions, during the Gilded Age (the period from Reconstruction to the turn of the century), America saw enormous growth that attracted more people to the area. World War I and later the Great Depression threatened to cripple the country, but these challenges also reaffirmed the American value of freedom. America would market itself as the symbolic icon of freedom—at home and abroad. In his 1932 bid for president of the United States, Franklin Delano Roosevelt made a campaign pledge to pull the country out of depression and give Americans a "New Deal."[6] In many ways, Roosevelt's New Deal programs changed the way Americans viewed their government. During this era, the concepts of freedom, liberty, and democracy became increasingly linked and intertwined.

FREEDOM AND AFRICAN-AMERICANS—WHAT IS FREEDOM?

Perhaps no word is more synonymous with the black liberation movement in America than freedom. A brief examination of the cultural and historical usage of the word reveals its common utilization. Historian John Hope Franklin and his co-author title what many consider the quintessential work about the history of African-Americans, *From Slavery to Freedom: A History of Negro Americans.*[7] In April 1865 the War Department enacted the Bureau of Refugees, Freedmen, and Abandoned Lands, more commonly known as the Freedmen's Bureau. The Freedmen's Bureau existed from 1865 to 1872 and was established for the express purpose of assisting freed men and women by providing them with food rations, clothing, medicine, educational opportunities, and, in some cases, land.[8]

The word "freedom" was also common in songs. In *The Souls of Black Folk*, W.E.B. DuBois discusses the power of the lyrics "O Freedom." DuBois writes:

> Through fugitive slaves and irrepressible discussion this desire for freedom seized the black millions still in bondage, and became their one ideal of life. The black bards caught new notes, and sometimes even dared to sing,
>
> "*O Freedom, O Freedom, O Freedom over me!*
> *Before I'll be a slave*
> *I'll be buried in my grave,*
> *And go home to my Lord*
> *And be free.*"[9]

The song lyrics were a declaration that the singer was willing to pay the ultimate price for freedom—his or her life. Facing "trouble" during a 1961 demonstration in Albany, Georgia, SNCC member Bernice Johnson Reagon changed the lyrics of the traditional Negro spiritual "Over My Head" from "over my head I see trouble in the air" to "over my head I see freedom in the air," and instantaneously changed the mood of the moment.[10] At the height of the period of direct action, civil rights groups and activities directly incorporated the name freedom into their identity. We had Freedom Singers,[11] Freedom Summer, and the Freedom Riders.

Movement workers lived in freedom houses, and they sang freedom songs. Writing about the music of the era of the black freedom struggle, most commonly known as the Civil Rights Movement, Seeger and Reiser conclude: "Yet, with all its complexity it [the Civil Rights era] yielded to the power of the simple truth articulated by the African-American community: "We want to be free!"[12]

But what does freedom mean? What does it look like? What does it taste like? Earlier, World War I prompted discussion about freedom for blacks at home (in the midst of discussions about affording protection for freedom abroad). After the war was over, scholars like W.E.B. DuBois began to publicly link the ideas of European imperialism and racial injustice. In a 1919 article, which appeared in *The Crisis*, the official magazine of the National Association for the Advancement of Colored People (NAACP), DuBois outlines the supreme injustice and irony faced by returning black soldiers and encourages them to fight racial injustice at home with the same vigor with which they had fought it abroad. DuBois urges:

> We are returning from war! *The Crisis* and tens of thousands of black men were drafted into a great struggle. For bleeding France and what she means and has meant and will mean to us and humanity and against the threat of German race arrogance, we fought gladly and to the last drop of blood; for America and her highest ideals, we fought in far-off hope; for the dominant southern oligarchy entrenched in Washington, we fought in bitter resignation.
>
> *We return.*
> *We return from fighting.*
> *We return fighting.*
> Make way for Democracy! We saved it in France, and by the Great Jehovah, we will save it in the United States of America, or know the reason why.[13]

Similarly, World War II, a conflict waged largely against the same "threat of German race arrogance" of which DuBois spoke, prompted new discussions about the African-American freedom struggle, and on January 6, 1941, President Franklin Delano Roosevelt delivered his State of the Union address, popularly known as "The Four Freedoms" speech. As President Roosevelt spoke, Americans were eerily cognizant that the specter of world war was looming.[14] Uncertainty in the world contributed to Roosevelt's election to an unprecedented third term as president of the United States, and while the U.S. had not formally entered the war,

President Roosevelt grew increasingly certain that the wartime efforts of the country's allies, especially Britain, could not be sustained without U.S. support. In his remarks to Congress, the president extols the virtues of freedom (for which democracy becomes a pseudonym) and clearly states that aggressions in Europe pose a serious threat to democracy everywhere. His rallying cry falls just short of calling America to arms.[15] President Roosevelt advises listeners:

> The Nation takes great satisfaction and much strength from the things which have been done to make its people conscious of their individual stake in the preservation of democratic life in America . . . Certainly this is no time for any of us to stop thinking about the social and economic problems which are the root cause of the social revolution which is today a supreme factor in the world. For there is nothing mysterious about the foundations of a healthy and strong democracy. The basic things expected by our people of their political and economic systems are simple . . . In the future days . . . we look forward to a world founded upon four essential human freedoms: The first is the freedom of speech and expression—everywhere in the world. The second is freedom of every person to worship God in his own way—everywhere in the world. The third is freedom from want, which, translated into world terms, means economic understandings which will secure to every nation a healthy peacetime life for its inhabitants—everywhere in the world. The fourth is the freedom from fear . . . that no nation will be in a position to commit an act of physical aggression against any neighbor—anywhere in the world.[16]

Ironically, the democratic way of life underscored as being in danger in "every part of the world" was also unavailable to blacks in America.

The world embraced Franklin Roosevelt's Four Freedoms as key components of basic human rights. Winston Churchill incorporated Roosevelt's four enumerated freedoms into the Atlantic Charter, and later the United Nations Declaration of 1942 included the same ideas. The concepts also undergird the provisions in the Universal Declaration of Human Rights. But the language of the Four Freedoms speech did not just have impact abroad. President Roosevelt provided a clear elucidation of the basic rights of humanity, and these principles resonated with African-Americans in the United States. The Four Freedoms helped to give shape and focus to the demands of an amorphous long-existing black liberation movement.

Freedom is a metaphysical quest, and black people throughout history have been willing to lay down their lives in search of this intangible pursuit.

Blacks wanted to be free, and Roosevelt's statements helped clarify what freedom looked like across the world: it was freedom of religion, freedom of speech, economic freedom, and freedom from fear. During the post-World War II period, African-American demands began to grow louder, more insistent, and more organized. So what is freedom? Freedom is an enigmatic quest. Freedom is an internal and external battle. Freedom is often taken for granted. But perhaps the words of "civil rights icon and mother of the next generation of the movement," Ella Baker, best sum up this pursuit: "freedom is a constant struggle."[17]

The African-American freedom struggle that emerged in the 1950s and 60s was not new, but the Movement did appear to have a momentum behind it that seemed absent at earlier times. Larry Isaac writes about how movements diffuse through society. Among the means Isaac examines, he states, "collective action tactics [can] diffuse [movements] spatially."[18] Arguably, the growth of the Movement during this time was because movement networks and tactics were becoming more widely diffused throughout the country.[19] Doug McAdam's book, *Political Process in the Development of Black Insurgency*, establishes the critical role that networks and organizations played in the successes of the Civil Rights Movement.[20] As these networks grew, leaders emerged, and each seemed to grow more emblazoned. For example, Medgar Evers, the bold leader of the NAACP in Jackson, Mississippi, had fought overseas in World War II and returned to the U.S. "fighting." Evers and his brother, Charles, drew large crowds wherever they spoke. On May 31, 1959, Evers said, "We are dedicated to the cause of freedom and will continue to fight under God's laws without fear of consequences."[21] The fearlessness expressed by Evers and others in the face of adversity is a reminder that freedom is not free. On the road from Selma to Montgomery to freedom many people would pay the ultimate price, but the Movement would not be stopped. The pages of this book tell a part of that story.

THE SELMA CAMPAIGN

Selma, which means "high point," would become America's call to action in the long battle over whether to provide meaningful protection to the U.S. Constitution's Fifteenth Amendment grant of equal voting rights under the law irrespective of "race, color, or previous condition of servitude."[22] In the same way that the modified Union song, "Which Side are You On," became a staple in the Civil Rights Movement's repertoire of songs,[23] watching the carnage of Bloody Sunday unfold before them on their television sets would provide viewers in America and across the globe with all-important knowledge about the Southern freedom struggle. Exposure to the struggle African-Americans in Selma and across the South faced amounted to knowledge, which, according to sociologist Everett Rogers, is the first stage through which an innovation (i.e., new idea) passes before it is adopted by society.[24]

Cultural change does not just happen. The triumphs of the Civil Rights Movement are often lauded in history books; however, the moments we herald, such as the successful Selma to Montgomery March (hereinafter the "March") and subsequent passage of the Voting Rights Act of 1965, often come about as a result of a series of lesser-known battles, events, and circumstances that make the climate ripe for change. This book tells the story of the conditions that gave rise to the social change necessary to guarantee the voting rights protections granted to African-Americans almost 100 years earlier in the Fourteenth and Fifteenth Amendments. The book is also a cautionary tale that warns the reader that progress is not linear and that the battle for voting rights has been just that—an arduous, lengthy battle fought with blood, sweat, and tears. As is the case in any lengthy campaign, the long march to freedom has been lined with successes, defeats, retreats, and ambushes.

The March and the earlier ancillary marches (Bloody Sunday and Turnaround Tuesday, respectively) have been chiefly written about by historians, political scientists, and various biographers, and they provide a record of the incident and some of the circumstances leading up to the demonstrations. In *Protest at Selma: Martin Luther King, Jr., and the Voting Rights Act of 1965*, author David Garrow provides a detailed day-to-day account of the events collectively comprising the protest.[25] *Selma, 1965: The March that Changed the South*, written by Charles Fager, a former

Sidebar 1.1

The African-American Civil Rights Movement is a term with which many people are familiar; however, it is important to point out that this term has been used to describe various separate social movements underway throughout the black community for many, many decades. Perhaps a better umbrella term to describe these social movements is the black freedom struggle.

Whether we are talking about John Brown's Raid at Harpers Ferry in 1859, the Double Victory campaign in the World War II era, the boycotts of the 1950s and 60s, or the Black Power Movement, each phase of the freedom struggle has been marked by resistance and protest aimed at bringing about social change.

member of the Southern Christian Leadership Conference (SCLC) and participant in the Selma Movement, provides helpful behind-the-scenes insights into the workings of the campaign.[26] By beginning its discussion of the Selma campaign in 1963, Vaughn and Davis' book, *The Selma Campaign 1963–1965: The Decisive Battle of the Civil Rights Movement*, establishes an important and often ignored contribution to the discussion of the Selma Marches.[27] As the authors of *The Selma Campaign* extend the origins of the Selma Movement, similarly, significant contributions about two white martyrs for the Movement, Mary Stanton's book on Viola Liuzzo[28] and Charles Eagles' work on Jonathan Daniels, [29] make clear that the battle for voting rights protection did not end with the successful march from Selma to Montgomery or the passage of the Voting Rights Act of 1965 (hereinafter sometimes called "the Act"). Though all these examinations are insightful, they provide an incomplete picture of the social processes that created change as they fail to address how "social action and social movements take place and are influenced by multiple levels of reality . . . which in turn influence future action."[30]

Previous works on the Selma campaign privilege one "level of reality" over another, and while each part of the story is important, the sum of the parts does not necessarily result in a complete understanding of the social change. Further, such an approach minimizes the significance of the March and subsequent passage of the Voting Rights Act, and reduces both to a bookend of the modern Civil Rights Movement. Such a conclusion

Sidebar 1.2

It is helpful to analyze social interactions at both the macro (large-scale groups/social processes) and micro (intimate, face-to-face interaction) levels. Each can help in understanding the process of social change.

Macro-level interactions enable us to look at the larger social structure and observe trends and patterns in society. This structure is discernible through looking at institutions and how the various statuses and roles people play influence the patterned behaviors observed in society. Macro-level observations help us to understand what holds societies together and, conversely, what tears societies apart.

While micro-level analyses focus on the individual, not society, they too are helpful. Micro-level analysis allows us to look at small-scale, individual face-to-face interactions. The same patterned behaviors seen on the macro level can be observed at the individual level, too, and these can provide a window into social change.

is an error. Instead, this work offers a contemporaneous examination of a number of macro and micro factors contributing to the social revolution, which ultimately produces cultural change. This examination concludes that the story of the Selma Movement is not a black story. It is not a white story. It is an American story, and this book attempts to highlight the continuing nature of the struggle for freedom inside a democracy which, by its very nature, is contested.

> In its simplest form, democracy is government by the people. President Lincoln said that democracy was "government of the people, by the people, for the people."

History reveals that democracy in America has long been contested.[31] Therefore, history, biography, and historical sources are important to this work, but the way history is approached is more consistent with historical sociology than history.[32] A socio-historical examination has several benefits: 1) it incorporates the intellectual climate of the time in order to shed light on the social aspects of societal change; and 2) it analyzes the cultural and historical contexts present, which allows readers to gain a better understanding of how the two influence both individual human actions and group behavior. The value of this approach is that it recognizes that individuals are contextually situated in both time and space,[33] and it allows the researcher to analyze the import of structure (the patterned, ordered manner of social life) and agency (individuals' free will or ability to make their own choices unconstrained by society) in creating or curtailing social change. As a methodological approach, historical sociology has value because it recognizes that historical events impact patterns of change (or lack of change) in society. Therefore historical sociology provides an important balance between theory and empiricism and allows us to both deconstruct and reconstruct history.[34]

The theoretical framework employed here to understand how social change takes root is Everett Rogers' Diffusion of Innovations Theory.[35] Rogers describes an innovation as something (including an idea or practice) that the adopter perceives as new.[36] Rogers' theory is usually used to explain how technological innovations come to be accepted in society; however, this book argues that the theory is also appropriate for the study of social change. This focus on the Diffusion of Innovations Theory differs from the prevailing analyses regarding social movements and collective action that often rely on Marxist political/economic issues or mobilization-based theories.[37] Applying Rogers' theoretical model to an empirical case—the voting rights struggle—allows us to see what fits and also to critique and elaborate the model in order to build on it and expand its explanatory power to cultural evolutions.

Sidebar 1.3

A theoretical framework provides a kind of lens through which to see and understand an issue. The theoretical framework is not proof or evidence that something is or is not a certain way; it simply provides a means through which to test our understanding of what factors influence society, the people in it, and their behaviors.

Throughout this work a number of theoretical perspectives will be introduced; however, the principal theory used to try to understand and test what brought about the social change under examination in this book is Diffusion of Innovations Theory.

There are a number of reasons Diffusion of Innovations Theory is appropriate for the study of social change. First, at the height of the Selma campaign mere talk about voting rights for African-Americans in the Black Belt region was so dangerous and novel as to represent a social innovation. Second, diffusion is a cultural process, and understanding this process enables us to understand how society and its ideas evolve or change. As such, one of the key insights the theory offers is what conditions aid the spread of an innovation, which, in this case, is social change. Third, time is often an ignored[38] variable in social science research; however, Diffusion of Innovations Theory employs time as a central variable. When applied to the Selma Movement, this theory helps to explain how social change that appears to occur very quickly is really a slow process that occurs in stages, which assists readers to understand both the process of social change and the continuing presence of counter attitudes once innovations have been adopted. Additionally, "uncovering temporal shifts in the impact of segregationist violence thus helps to further challenge the commonly held view that policy determinants are time invariant."[39] A fourth and final strength of the theory is its explanatory power. Understanding the process of innovation and diffusion can help us understand present attitudes in society, including how some people who have adopted the social change will revert to their old ways of thinking, as well as how some laggards will change, while others never change.

Social change is a process which requires time. Specifically, it refers to substantial changes in society's ideas, patterned behaviors, and norms.

Two separate but related premises undergird this work. The first is that it is impossible to detach individuals from their environment.[40] Therefore, when we examine change on a national level, it is important not to discount the amount of change going on at the local level. Patterned social systems are produced and reproduced through human social interaction;[41] therefore, new ideas—social change—can spread in one place but not another. The second premise is that social relationships are affected by both time and space, and these time-space connections are foundational to understanding social change.[42] The base of these premises is the recognition that historical events take shape in a context that is influenced by time, place, and space as well as history. Time, place, and history require no detailed exposition; however, space—whether geographical or cultural in its context—deeply influences people's ways of thinking and knowing,[43] which in turn impact their propensity to adopt social changes. All social life is ordered over time and through space, and it is the situated character of our social lives that makes time-space key to understanding the nature of social interactions.[44] In this manner, time and space are bound and influence patterned behaviors.[45]

The events of Bloody Sunday ushered in the relatively swift passage of the Voting Rights Act of 1965, a radical social change that provided meaningful voting rights protection for America's African-American citizens on a level not seen in the country since Reconstruction. The Fifteenth Amendment prohibits states, and the United States government, from discriminating in voting on the basis of race and color, and Section 2 of that same Amendment gives Congress the power to enforce the grant with any legislation it deems necessary to do so. While Bloody Sunday is the critical moment of focus, the arc of history will be considered. Such an approach is consistent with the growing idea of the "long Civil Rights Movement."

Traditionally, the consensus among historians is that America's Civil Rights Movement began with the Montgomery Bus Boycott and ended in the mid-1960s with the passage of the Voting Rights Act of 1965. Recently, historians have begun to reframe the African-American struggle for freedom and popularize the concept of the long Civil Rights Movement, which extends the undertaking by including civil liberties struggles of the 1930s, and also expands the Movement's influence beyond the continental United States.[46] Historian Eric Foner goes so far as to venture that the birth of civil rights began with the Civil Rights Act of 1866.[47] By examining the arc of history, this book allows the reader to conceptualize the Selma marches not as distinct events but as: 1) a part of the larger Civil Rights Movement, and 2) a necessary precursor to the passage of the Voting Rights Act of 1965. Additionally, by developing an awareness of the gains and losses in the 100-year struggle for equal voting rights protection, one may develop a deeper appreciation for why some see the need for continuing protections for the franchise.

Adoption and diffusion of an innovation is neither a quick nor easy process. Rogers outlines five steps through which an innovation must pass before it gets adopted.

Figure 1.1. provides a visual representation of how Rogers' theoretical diffusion process operates. The image shows how Rogers' innovation-decision model relies heavily on communication channels for dissemination of the idea (i.e., innovation) through society for its ultimate rejection or adoption. These stages include knowledge, persuasion, decision, implementation, and confirmation,[48] and the chapters that follow analyze the extent to which the five stages in the innovation–decision process are present. The remainder of the book is laid out as follows. Chapter 2, titled *One Moment in Time*, begins with a necessary discussion of the Reconstruction Era Amendments. This is done in order to communicate the length of the journey for full voting rights, which is why the chapter includes a brief discussion of black suffrage from Reconstruction to the Selma Movement. This historical base also further augments the claim that affording full protection to the black franchise was a social innovation. Further, it establishes how knowledge of the injustices faced by African-Americans in the Black Belt, an area whose beauty is matched only by its lack, got communicated to the nation through mass media and explains the influence of this exposure. Chapter 3, *Portrait of a Nation*, provides a social, political, and economic portrait of the nation during the years leading up to the Selma Movement. This portrait of the nation undergirds the

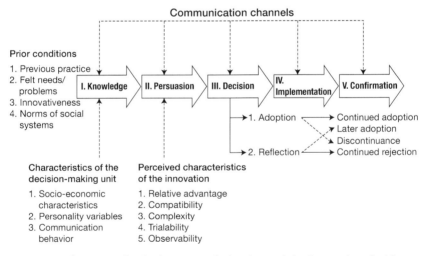

Figure 1.1 This image details the stages of adoption and the innovation-decision communication channel process.

Source: Everett M. Rogers' *Diffusion of Innovations*.

assertion that affording voting rights protection to blacks amounted to a social innovation. The chapter also establishes the breadth of knowledge being disseminated to the public about the Southern freedom struggle. As the chapter progresses, both social structure (macro) and social interactions (micro) are implicated, and, consistent with Rogers' model, provide support for his assertion that while the mass media is critical in the knowledge stage, interpersonal communication is important in the persuasion stage.[49] Chapter 4, *Everyday People*, discusses the often-ignored ordinary people who not only sustained the Movement but also carried this social innovation to the nation one person at a time. The chapter analyzes the vital role that formal and informal social networks played in the persuasion process and how these social networks influenced individuals' decisions on whether or not to adopt the innovation.

Chapter 5, the final chapter, *Aftermath*, provides information on the larger voting rights struggle and how it fits into the freedom struggle. Additionally, it discusses recent challenges to the extension of the Voting Rights Act, including several important legal battles. Debo P. Adegbile, Special Counsel of the NAACP Legal Defense and Educational Fund, Inc. (LDF), argued two constitutional challenges against Section 5 of the Act before the U.S. Supreme Court. Both challenges were brought during the tenure of America's first African-American president, Barack Obama. Adegbile and his team successfully defended the challenge raised in 2009.[50] The most recent challenge, Shelby County, Alabama v. Holder, was heard in late February 2013, and a decision (discussed later in this book) was rendered in early summer of the same year. In comments at a session sponsored by LDF held at the annual Bridge Crossing Jubilee Celebration in Selma, Alabama, on March 2, 2013, several months prior to the Shelby ruling, Adegbile advised those in attendance for the celebratory event about the need for constant vigilance:

> Immediately after the Voting Rights Act was passed and no longer was it easy to achieve discrimination in voting through vote denial the game changed but it only changed a little bit. It moved from denying African-Americans the right to register and participate at all to minimizing the ability of these new voters to have an influence in the political process by silencing their voices, by muting their voices, by chopping up their communities, by imposing rules that would not allow the chips to fall freely in the democracy, essentially by not playing by the rules of the game, and the Court has called this "pouring old poison in new bottles," and that's the consistent pattern that we have seen in the Voting Rights Act. It is because this is the pattern that Section 5 is so

> important because the law contemplates that that's the way the
> game goes down, and so it says we're not going to allow the
> people who seek to discriminate to have the advantage of being
> able to find a new way to achieve the same end. It says that
> when you change the voting rules, we're going to take a look.

Mr. Adegbile informed attendees that Shelby County, Alabama, and other jurisdictions could "bail out" of Section 5 by having a clean record of no voting discrimination for a 10-year period. According to a handout prepared by LDF entitled "Shelby County v. Holder General Q and A," over 190 jurisdictions have successfully "bailed out" of Section 5. In his observations, Mr. Adegbile goes on to state that both former presidents Ronald Reagan and George Bush extolled the virtues of the Act. Adegbile states, "Ronald Reagan called the Voting Rights Act 'the crown jewel of American democracy.' Right? So this is not a contested proposition in American life. It is one of the things that we hold up in our democracy."

The Selma campaign and passage of the Voting Rights Act are not just significant historical events; they have present-day import as well. The presence of federal voting registrars in the South following passage of the Act amounted to a quasi second-Reconstruction and helped bolster minority voter registration in the region, and just as the first Reconstruction came to an end, some voices argue that specific provisions of the Act amount to a "racial entitlement" and must come to an end.[51] But, the present is not untethered to the past, and while it is argued that protection for the black franchise amounted to a social innovation or cultural change, the freedom struggle is not over.

Selma resident and civil rights attorney, Faya Toure (aka Rose Sanders), remains as vigilant today about protecting black liberties, including voting rights, as she was in the 1960s. Soon after graduating from Harvard Law School, Toure and her husband, Alabama State Senator Hank Sanders, moved to Selma to work with civil rights attorney J.L. Chestnut. Toure was part of a group sponsoring the "Freedom Riders for Voting Rights Never Forget, Never Again Pilgrimage." In late April through early May 2013, participants in the pilgrimage toured across Alabama and Mississippi via bus in order to bring attention to the Supreme Court case of Shelby County, Alabama v. Holder, which challenges the constitutionality of Section 5 and other provisions of the Voting Rights Act. Toure spoke to Mississippi Public Broadcasting during a leg of tour:

> Some of us have forgotten the sacrifice so we are silent as the
> Supreme Court decides whether or not to declare Section 5
> unconstitutional. In Mississippi you had an African American

senator over one hundred years ago. It was all taken away
because we were not vigilant. We allowed the Klan and terror to
take away that right. We cannot allow that to happen again.[52]

Fellow Freedom Rider Hollis Watkins said he feared that if the Supreme
Court struck down Section 5 as unconstitutional, they would see the return
of voter intimidation tactics.[53]

The passage of the Voting Rights Act was a critical moment in history,
but we sit on the precipice of another such moment. To adopt Rogers'
language, at this juncture, the country has the opportunity to reaffirm or
reject its commitment to ensure strong protection for minority voting
rights. But history is more than a moment in time. It is the sum of who
we are. Throughout this book, consideration will be given to the role and
weight of history in the human experiences detailed on these pages, for
sociologist C. Wright Mills cautions us that history plays an important role
in each of our personal biographies.[54] For this reason, both our shared past
and the past we do not share in common with those who are different
from us (the "other") influence our present-day interactions and the
realities we create. Before concluding this chapter, it is only fitting to
examine our current "critical moment" and the role of history.

THE ROLE OF HISTORY

Most of the jurisdictions covered by Section 5 of the Voting Rights
Act are in the Southern states, and a number of those jurisdictions decry
this result as unfair. Rightly, these jurisdictions assert that race-based
discrimination in voting and otherwise can be found in locations outside
the South, too. However, the Southern past is a reality. In his book of
the same name, historian C. Vann Woodward writes about what he terms
"the burden of Southern history."[55] Woodward outlines the complicated
past of the idea of "southern distinctiveness." Southern distinctiveness is
a concept that, for various reasons and at different times, the North and
South each advanced.[56] Many Southerners appropriated the concept to
first popularize and then mythologize the Lost Cause;[57] while Northern
politicians, business leaders, diplomats and others intent on advancing the
concept of American exceptionalism used Southern distinctiveness to
constrain the moral failings of the nation to the Southern region.[58]
American exceptionalism was used to suggest that the U.S. was singularly
suited to be the keeper (and enforcer) of democracy across the globe,
but as Martin Lipset notes, this American exceptionalism proved to be a
two-edged sword.[59] Lipset explains: "American values are quite complex,

particularly because of paradoxes within our culture that permit pernicious and beneficial social phenomena to arise simultaneously from the same basic beliefs."[60] Slavery, the U.S. Civil War, and later the Civil Rights Movement ran afoul of the narrative of American exceptionalism, so the idea of Southern distinctiveness was once again employed, but this time to posit a view that the morally bereft South, which fought to maintain the institution of slavery, was different from the rest of the country.[61] In this manner, Southern distinctiveness was used as a tool in order to demonize the South and suggest that the social, political, and economic ills of the U.S. were the failings of one region and not the nation.[62] This narrative placed the South (and not the whole country itself) as moral wrongdoer, and it allowed American exceptionalism to persist.

Whether it is ideas about the South being more religious than the rest of the nation, the pervasiveness and distinctiveness of Southern hospitality and/or Southern cooking, or persistent representations of the American South as more racist than the rest of the nation, two things are true: "Southern distinctiveness" persists, and the American South has changed. Today, national surveys continue to note regionally based differences in social attitudes. For example, a 2011 Pew Charitable Trust survey revealed that, 150 years after the Civil War, the action is still "relevant," and deeply divisive regional differences can be noted on some questions.[63] The Pew Center report on the survey released April 8, 2011, notes,

> Whites who consider themselves Southerners have a more positive reaction to the Confederate flag than do other whites: 22% say they react positively when they see the Confederate flag displayed, compared with 8% of all whites and just 4% of whites who do not consider themselves Southerners.[64]

Additionally, in their 2005 article "Old Times There Are Not Forgotten: Race and Partisan Realignment in the Contemporary South," political scientists Nicholas A. Valentino and David O. Sears write, "[Southern whites] remain more racially conservative than whites elsewhere on every measure of racial attitude ordinarily used in national surveys."[65] These two realities—that attitudes in the American South often diverge from those in other regions of the country and that the American South is different than it was decades ago—underlie the dispute over the continuing need for "extraordinary" voting rights protections.[66]

On Tuesday, June 25, 2013, the U. S. Supreme Court handed down a landmark decision (Shelby County, Alabama v. Holder) that effectively gutted Section 4 of the Voting Rights Act of 1965.[67] Section 4 establishes the coverage formula for inclusion in the temporary preclearance

Sidebar 1.4

Of the three-tiered (strict scrutiny, intermediate scrutiny, and rational) system established by the court for dealing with constitutional issues, rational basis constitutes the lowest level of scrutiny requiring only that the enactment be "rationally related" to a "legitimate" government interest. Therefore, if a court determines that the legislature had a reasonable (as opposed to an arbitrary or capricious rationale) for enacting a statute, the statute should survive rational basis review.

requirements available through Section 5 of the Act, which the 1966 court termed an extraordinary measure appropriate for extraordinary times.[68] A majority of the 2013 Court felt that times were changing, and they held Section 4 as unconstitutional on the basis that the coverage formula it employed, which relied on data from the 1960s and 70s, was not rational in these "contemporary times."[69] The decision was much anticipated largely because during oral arguments it became clear that the seeds of social change were being sown, as one sound bite was privileged above all others and received repeated play in the media. That sound bite was of Supreme Court Justice Antonin Scalia equating Section 5 to a "racial entitlement."[70] Various legislators and others echoed the refrain of these change agents, and their message was carried through media outlets that disseminated the idea to the masses. Americans on both sides of the argument responded sharply to the notion of "racial entitlement."[71]

While there is little dispute that the South has changed, discord does exist surrounding the reason for those changes, and whether they are lasting changes. Chief Justice John Roberts wrote the majority opinion in the landmark case. In it, Roberts notes, "Our country has changed"; however, in a CNN interview following the announcement of the ruling, Representative Eleanor Holmes Norton responds, "Yes. The South has changed." She continues, "[but] guess why it's changed? It's changed because of the Voting Rights Act."[72] The historical record fuels doubts about a changing American South. During Reconstruction, the South changed due to continuing federal oversight of the region, and once that oversight ended, black gains rolled back too. This history implies that present-day concerns about the effect of such a rollback are not irrational, but rooted in a firm historical record that establishes such patterned behavior. In fact, in a press conference following the announcement of the Supreme Court's ruling, Attorney General Eric Holder states, "These problems have not been confined to history. They continue to exist. They are real. They are of today, not yesterday, and they corrode the foundations of our democracy."[73]

The deeply entrenched camps outlined by the majority opinion and dissenting opinion fit squarely into this analysis of what role history plays.[74] The majority held Section 4's coverage formula unconstitutional on the basis that Congress' 2006 reauthorization of the Act relied on data from 1975, which Roberts' opinion terms 40-year-old facts "not grounded in current conditions."[75] In many ways, the Court's recent precedent on this matter foreshadows the conclusion in Shelby County v. Holder. The Supreme Court's language in Northwest Austin Municipal Util. Dist. No. One v. Holder,[76] a 2009 Constitutional challenge to Section 5 of the Voting Rights Act, actually forecast this result. In that decision the Court criticizes the coverage formula stating that while "in 1966, the coverage formula was 'rational in both practice and theory'[77] . . . [c]overage today is based on decades-old data and eradicated practices."[78] Justice Ginsburg's dissent also relies on the historical record. Quoting son of the South, Dr. Martin Luther King Jr., Ginsburg states, "'the arc of the moral universe is long' and 'it bends towards justice,'[79] [but only] if there is a steadfast commitment to see the task through to completion."[80] But a leading member of the Judiciary Committee, Senator Charles Grassley of Iowa, opines that the high court's decision reflects "the positive impact of the Voting Rights Act and that the legislation was no longer needed."[81] These variations in the role of history leave little room for reconciliation.

It is widely conceded that the Shelby County decision will make voting rights laws harder to enforce, so where does that leave us? Civil rights advocates agree that the decision could have been worse. The Court could have struck down Section 5 altogether, but the holding in Shelby County v. Holder effectively hobbles the "strong medicine" of Section 5, and there is concerted agreement that it is unlikely the present Congress will agree upon a new coverage formula to enact. Additionally, while it is true that some things have changed in the American South, some things, some people, some jurisdictions have not. Writing for the dissent, Justice Ginsburg notes:

> Although circumstances in Alabama have changed, serious concerns remain. Between 1982 and 2005, Alabama had one of the highest rates of successful section 2 suits, second only to its VRA-covered neighbor Mississippi . . . In other words, even while subject to the restraining effects of section 5, Alabama was found to have "deni[ed] or abridge[d]" voting rights "on account of race or color" more frequently than nearly all other States in the Union.[82]

The flagrant abuses Justice Ginsburg note suggest a systemic problem. In an article for *Southern Spaces*, an interdisciplinary Internet journal on the American South housed at Emory University in Atlanta, Georgia, Steve Suitts, an Alabama native and vice president of the Southern Education Foundation, recounts an incident in Shelby County, Alabama. Suitts writes:

> Seven years ago, as I sat doing research at the historical society of Shelby County, Alabama, a county commissioner arrived, hailing the librarian and me, "Happy Martin Luther Coon Day!" he shouted.[83]

While the story Suitts retells is anecdotal, taken with the weight of the other data it offers a compelling picture that while some things have changed in all or parts of the American South, some things have not. The fact that an elected official in the very jurisdiction of the "contemporary South" that raised the current Supreme Court challenge felt free to make such a demeaning and derogatory racially based statement in the presence of both a stranger and an employee is telling. Narratives that postulate the nation's racial history as past ignore the weight of history. This is a grave error.

So what do we do with history? The weight of America's racial history cannot be forever borne by the descendants of former slaves and former slave owners, but we must also acknowledge that its shadow is still present.[84] If famed Southern writer William Faulkner is correct, and the past is neither dead nor forgotten,[85] those who know history are left with the two-edged sword of American exceptionalism of which Lipset speaks. In *Lies My Teacher Told Me: Everything Your American History Textbook Got Wrong*, sociologist James Loewen outlines the precarious role of history.[86] Loewen writes:

> More than any other topic, it [history] is about us. Whether one deems our present society wondrous or awful or both, history reveals how we arrived at this point. Understanding our past is central to understanding ourselves and the world around us.[87]

It remains to be seen whether the movement currently underway to mark America's storied racial history as past will catch hold. Only time will tell. If it does, there is a fear that history (and perhaps history teachers) will promulgate the wondrous part of America's history and forsake the awful. Both the wondrous and the awful are told in the pages hereafter.

Thus far, Section 5 of the Voting Rights Act has withstood several challenges, but the invalidation of Section 4 renders it unenforceable and increases the likelihood it will be challenged. The Act was amended in 1970, 1975, 1982, and 2006. In 1975, Congress added protection for language minorities, and in 2006, when the Act came up for review, Congress conducted a 9-month study, amassed a 15,000-page record, and determined that a sufficient enough record of discrimination in voting still existed to warrant the extension of key provisions of the Act for another 25 years. Consistent with Rogers' theory, some might call these reaffirmations confirmation. This book does not. Freedom is a constant struggle. When the Act came up for review, debate over the continuing need for the Act was both extensive and protracted. Key provisions of the Act were renewed, but little attention has been given to whether or not the protections afforded by the Fifteenth Amendment compel further reform to the Act.[88] In fact, recent court challenges focus on contraction of the Act, rather than its expansion. State-level attacks persist, too. Recent voting rights infringement claims (such as the treatment of Florida votes in the presidential election of 2000, threats of prosecution made against Prairie View A&M students in 2004, a stark rise in voter ID laws, felony disenfranchisement issues, and remedies needed to ensure Latinos and other language populations are fully able to exercise the franchise) are also examined in the final chapter.

CONCLUSION

Freedom is not a static concept. Additionally, it can vary widely by place such that narratives of freedom in the American South might look different than concurrent narratives of freedom in other parts of the United States. To those living in slave states during the era of slavery, freedom might look like the abolition of slavery, but soon after Reconstruction came to a close, an increasing amount of African-Americans began to equate freedom with full participation in the democratic process. Two things should be established. First, to be clear, the Reconstruction Era Amendments did grant protection to African-American voting rights; however, the point cannot be understated that protection for voting rights is not the same as enforcement of that protection. Second, protection for full voting participation by African-Americans was not the only obstacle blacks faced. African-Americans faced employment discrimination, segregation in public accommodations, lynching, disparaging attitudes, and threat of physical violence, including death. The advances of the 1950s and 1960s should not be forgotten, but neither should these cautionary words to future generations contained in one of the SNCC Freedom Singers' repertoire of songs: "freedom is a constant struggle."[89]

It may seem desecrating to end a book about a moment that is widely regarded as the high point of the American Civil Rights Movement on such a negative note, but to quote historian Hasan Jeffries' warning to Emilye Crosby cited in her article "Teaching Movement History," ending on a high note "would have meant overlooking valuable lessons about the perils of power, lessons that everyone committed to democracy should learn."[90] The Jeffries excerpt reminds us that freedom is not an event; it is a process, and to quote Bernice Johnson Reagon's song tribute to Ella Baker, "We who believe in freedom cannot rest until it's won."[91]

CHAPTER 2

One Moment in Time

It's been a long time coming
But I know a change is gonna come, oh yes it will.
Sam Cooke, *"A Change is Gonna Come"*

Things grow in the right environment, and by the mid-1960s conditions in the Alabama Black Belt were ripe for change. The soil of the area was rich with nutrients, and it had been watered with the blood of countless African-Americans. Something was ready to bloom. In his autobiography, *Black in Selma*, African-American civil rights attorney and activist J.L. Chestnut wrote, "for one hundred years the Black Belt dominated state politics and the big landowners dominated the Black Belt."[1] Over that nearly 100-year reign, the conservative white landowners in the Black Belt region maintained control over the larger black majority through dominance and economic intimidation.[2] That was about to come to an end. Aided by Freedom Summer and the Freedom Riders, which allowed various temporal-spatial movement sites and people to be influenced by and come into contact with others, the Movement was rapidly diffusing now, and more and more Southern blacks refused to be content with the status quo.

Still, perhaps no single variable contributed more to bringing about social change in the Alabama Black Belt than the willingness of the area's youth—many under 12 years old—to stand up and fight for their rights. In *Marching for Freedom: Walk Together Children and Don't you Grow Weary*, author Elizabeth Partridge, writes: "[H]undreds of kids in Selma . . . met and sang and marched and were jailed over and over again in the struggle for federal law ensuring every American the right to vote."[3]

Figure 2.1 Sometimes crudely drawn and sometimes elaborate, posters were one of the means used to communicate knowledge about the voting rights movement.

Source: Library of Congress, Prints and Photographs Division, [LC-USZ62-135368]

The youth and young adults of SNCC also played a vital role in changing the Southern social and cultural landscape, and while the triumphs of these young people are widely heralded, it is important to note that their sacrifices did not come without a cost. SNCC worker Annie Pearl Avery notes that incidences of ulcers were so common among SNCC workers that the malady came to be known as the "SNCC disease." Yet despite the jailings, beatings, economic threats, and possible loss of life, voter registration efforts continued regularly throughout the Selma campaign, even though voter registration applications were only accepted twice a month.

The Selma campaign alone did not change things. According to the *Oxford Handbook of Southern Politics*, "the political dominance of the Black Belt conservative white minority did not end until passage of the Civil Rights Act of 1964, the Voting Rights Act of 1965, and long-delayed legislative reapportionment."[4] The Selma campaign was, however, a critical step in the journey for equal voting rights protection for all Americans. This chapter outlines the moment in time that gave birth to the political reforms that changed the landscape of Southern politics after a nearly 100-year struggle.

A CHANGE IS GONNA COME

In December 1964, the now classic Sam Cooke song, "A Change is Gonna Come," was released. The song became emblematic of the Civil Rights Movement.[5] In the preceding decade, blacks had made some hard-fought gains, and white Southerners opposed to those advances were fighting back. In the shadow of the long battle for civil rights, it seemed that change would have to come or continued conflict would be certain. Two debates surrounded each option. First, a number of civil rights victories calculated to systematically chip away at desegregation bolstered cries for change from both white conservatives and civil rights protestors, but the opposing sides differed on what that change would be: a return to the segregated status quo, or continued economic and social advances for African-American equality, including protection for the franchise. The second debate surrounded the role of violence in the Movement. By 1964, riots had erupted in Northern cities, and more violence would come, and while in the South non-violence was still the stance adopted by many Movement people, civil rights veteran Ruby Nell Sales makes it clear that this preference was often a rational choice as much as it was a philosophical one.

In 1965, 17-year-old Sales was a college student at Tuskegee Institute in Tuskegee, Alabama. In an interview for the PBS series, *Eyes on the Prize*

II: America at the Crossroads 1965 to 1985, Sales poignantly discusses her non-violent evolution. She states:

> [W]hen I came to Tuskegee I had come from a background of non-violence where I did not have a clear understanding that there was a possibility that people would hurt each other . . . So I went to that demonstration [in Lowndes County, Alabama] with a great deal of naiveté and [without] a sense of what people's limits were. So when we got to the . . . capital in Montgomery and we were surrounded by police and dogs and horses and we were singing, "Come by here, Lord. Come by here." Well, coming from a Baptist background and . . . a religious background and this whole sense that we were bred on that, that right would ultimately win out and bad would be punished, when we were singing, "Come by here, Lord. Come by here," part of me expected at that point that the sky would literally open up and we would be rescued from the, from the dogs and from the, from the horses and, and from the violence. And when that didn't happen I think I went through a religious crisis at that point. I began to understand that there were things that existed in the world that I had not been prepared for and I began to understand that people would, in fact, kill you, [and] I had not been prepared for that reality, that there were people in the world who would kill you simply because you were Black, that they didn't even know [you] but that they would hurt you simply because of how you looked.[6]

Despite facing danger at the hands of angry white Southerners, Sales learned that non-violence served a utilitarian function, too.

The civil rights workers could not arm themselves enough to beat the entire South, or even just the white South opposed to their gains. The demonstrators were not suicidal, either, so they continued to fight but employed non-violent tactics. But if conflicts (in the form of organized protests and demonstrations) and other forms of direct action were to continue, some in the Movement began to question the continued utility of non-violence in the face of an adversary willing to use brute force. Still, as widespread media coverage of the Movement grew, the repressive nature of life for blacks in much of the Alabama Black Belt contrasted sharply against media images of the group's "civil" responses to the brute force and inhumanity all too quickly doled out by hard-line segregationists, law enforcement personnel, and their cronies. On the poles, each camp (the civil rights advocates and the segregationists) seemed deeply entrenched and committed to their ideas and ways. It would require a shift in the middle—what Everett Rogers terms the "early majority"[7]—to determine which way the country would go, and the deciding ground for this battle would be fought in Alabama, the Heart of Dixie.

Selma, Lord Selma

Selma, Alabama, sits in the Alabama Black Belt,[8] which is part of the larger Black Belt area of the country. The Black Belt is a geological region that includes parts of Virginia, the Carolinas, Georgia, Alabama, and extends into the Delta region of the Mississippi. During slavery, the Black Belt was the epicenter of a labor-intensive plantation-style agricultural system, which primarily grew tobacco and cotton.[9] The work was hard. The hours were long, and the soil was rich. The region gets its name from the black clay and topsoil prevalent in the area, but lore says the name comes from the blood of former black slaves and sharecroppers said to cover the region. The legacy of slavery is still present in the Black Belt, which is home to some of the poorest people in the nation.[10] The Black Belt also has another distinction: many of its jurisdictions are majority African-American. In fact, in *The Race Beat: The Press, the Civil Rights Struggle, and the Awakening of a Nation*, Roberts and Klibanoff write, "In many black belt counties, the black population outnumber the white, but whites remained in political control by tightly limiting the black vote."[11] According to the book *At Canaan's Edge*, Tuskegee professors called Lowndes "a problem county."[12] After the abolition of slavery and grant of the franchise to blacks, the presence of potential strong minority voting blocks made such areas particularly threatening places for whites seeking to retain their position in a changing society.

Today, the City of Selma's website boasts itself "the queen city of the Black Belt."[13] The dichotomy reflected in this modern-day moniker, "queen city of the Black Belt," has existed for some time. In *Ready for Revolution*, Stokely Carmichael (aka Kwame Ture), former leader in SNCC and the Black Panther Party, describes the county seat of Dallas and "gateway" to the Alabama Black Belt town and its black residents thus:

> A sharecropper is a tenant farmer who has to give up part of each crop for rent and other incidentals. The system of sharecropping existed before slavery, but after slavery the Southern model became particularly cruel and often resembled another form of servitude.

> Selma was a different place [from the Mississippi Delta]. Very different. No less oppressive or brutal, but so very different. For one thing, I really liked that African

community. See, if I say that racism in Selma was as ruthless, the segregation as complete as any I yet seen, but that the black community was more together—psychologically and culturally a proud community—than many I'd seen, it must certainly sound like a contradiction. But that was the Lord's truth. Could be that the strength was a consequence of the severity of the racism, or that the oppression was so severe because of the cultural strength of the Africans. Or both? Whatever the case, many movement people have said that Selma people were the "most African" blacks in the South. I could see exactly what they meant. The community was poor and economically oppressed, true. But it was also self-contained and self-sufficient with businesses (small but our own) and black professionals, and strong in black religion and culture, with even two tiny church-affiliated colleges, Lutheran College and Selma University.[14]

Like Stokely Carmichael, long-time Selma resident, Sam Walker, describes Selma as possessing a unique spirit. When asked why the voting rights campaign was waged in Selma, Alabama, Walker responds:

Well, Reverend Bevel answered that question for me. He said he tried this same strategy in Greenwood, Mississippi, and the people were too afraid.

. . . Yeah, yeah, he said they came to Selma because see the people in Selma they were already trying. They didn't invite Dr. King to lead them. They invited Dr. King to help them. They had already been engaged, intensely engaged with the local authority here. You know? So the people here were willing to try, and the people in those other places were afraid to try.[15]

This complicated place known as Selma, Alabama, is what journalist Charles Cobb calls, "the starting point of what is perhaps Alabama's most famous civil rights moment."[16] With a black majority in the county, Selma, Alabama, seemed a great place to elect blacks or those sympathetic to the black plight, but *Selma to Montgomery*, a pamphlet published by the National Park Service states, "[In] 1961 only 156 of the county's 15,000 voting age African Americans were registered to vote." By late 1965, the times were about to change.

Places, even places that are closely situated, may produce different results. Selma, located in Dallas County, is only one county away from Lowndes. "Negroes" comprised 80 percent of the population of Lowndes County, but in early 1965 not one was on the voting rolls in Lowndes.[17]

In *At Canaan's Edge: America in the King Years*, Taylor Branch writes, "Not for twenty years, until . . . the Selma voting rights movement one county to the west, did Negroes even discuss the franchise."[18] The last attempt anyone could recall by a Negro in Lowndes County to register to vote had been in 1945, so on February 28, 1965, when visiting pastor Reverend Lorenzo Harrison from Selma, Alabama, spoke at the Mt. Carmel Baptist Church (in the Lowndes County town of Haneyville, Alabama) and dared to mention the franchise for blacks, the Ku Klux Klan surrounded the church and shouted that "they'd get the out-of-county nigger preacher before sundown."[19]

Part of the aim of this work is to elucidate why critical change happened in Selma and why it happened at this particular moment in time. The variables of time and place have been largely ignored in previous works, but in this examination they are central to analysis of the social change under study. To that end, Rogers' Diffusion of Innovations Theory is employed. According to Rogers' theory, social change (i.e., the adoption of an innovation) has five steps: knowledge, persuasion, decision, implementation, and confirmation.[20]

The adopter categories break the population down into unequal quintiles, which include innovators (2.5 percent), early adopters (13.5 percent),

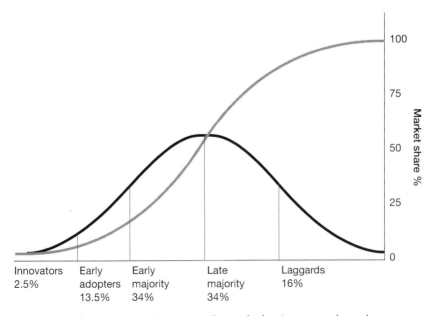

Figure 2.2 Adoption-innovation curve. Rogers' adoption curve shows how new ideas spread across segments of society.

early majority (34 percent), late majority (34 percent), and laggards (16 percent).[21] Rogers outlines five adopter categories.[22] Innovators are the visionaries who carry new ideas to the masses. They come in the first stage to communicate the idea to the masses. Early adopters are those who, once the benefits are clearly established, are said to "leap" on ideas. The early adopters are a crucial category. Because their adoption of the change (together with the innovators and early majority) constitutes 50 percent of the total population, they can potentially carry all-important knowledge about the innovation to the rest of the population, who will make a choice to adopt or reject the innovation. The late majority includes groups that Rogers describes as more skeptical; this group comprises conservatives and those who hate new ideas or are averse to risk. Finally, the laggards are the holdouts; this group has a very traditional epistemology and seldom changes its ways of doing things and knowing things. In Rogers' theory, the rate of adoption of an innovation is normally distributed and resembles a bell curve. On one end of the curve we have radical white conservatives intent on maintaining the status quo and black oppression; on the other we find liberal human and civil rights activists intent on increasing black liberties. In both cases, their minds seem relatively fixed, which is why the Selma campaign represented a battle for those in the middle.

Selma proved to be America's call to action in the long battle for voting rights protection for its African-American citizens, but as Diffusion of Innovations Theory evidences, only a percentage of America (not even a majority) would be necessary to effect the sought-after social change. Even talk of African-Americans exercising the franchise granted under the Fourteenth and Fifteenth Amendments was objectionable to the Southern white power structure, but growing mass media coverage exposed those outside the South to the struggle of blacks in the poorest region of the country.[23] Still, the weight of history was on the side of the South, and so the battle to persuade others to protect the black franchise would not be easy. This section begins with a brief sketch of the state of the Southern black franchise from the Civil War through to the Alabama voting rights campaign of the 1960s.

The End of the Civil War and the Black Vote During Reconstruction

When the Civil War was over, parts of the South lay in ruins, and the greatest economic resource of many Southern states[24]—its slaves— was declared free, but African-American emancipation did not occur in a single act. Instead, freedom was not an event, but a process.[25] The Thirteenth, Fourteenth, and Fifteenth Amendments to the United States

According to an 1872 article entitled "The State of the South 1872" which appeared in *The Nation*, "The total loss of the rebellious States by the war [was] $5,262,303,554."

Constitution, popularly known as the Reconstruction Era Amendments, collectively sought to deal with the Negro problem and move the country past the conflict.[26] For the next 12 years, the South found itself under "Reconstruction," which included Northern occupation and radical social change.

Reconstruction was a difficult, sometimes violent, and often patchwork campaign laden with successes and defeats.[27] Many large black-minority voting blocks joined together with white Republicans to elect officials.[28] A significant number of African-American representatives were elected during this period, too.[29] In states like Mississippi and South Carolina, there were even some black-majority voting blocks present, but Reconstruction was incomplete and would end too soon to transform much of the American South, which was still deeply entrenched in its separatist traditions and unequal ways.[30] As a result, Reconstruction brought about some temporary changes in Southern society, but these were not adopted widely.

Southerners resented the post-Civil War gains made by African-Americans, so when the Compromise of 1877 ended Reconstruction and removed federal troops from oversight in Southern capitols, this allowed Southern states carte blanche to create impediments (poll taxes, grandfather clauses, literacy tests, physical and/or economic intimidation, etc.), which significantly weakened the black franchise, especially in the South. At the time of the Compromise of 1877, the Fifteenth Amendment had only been ratified for 7 years. Hundreds of years of denial of the black franchise followed by 7 years of the grant of the vote would not prove long enough for this social change to take root across the land.

The Black Vote from the End of Reconstruction through the Civil Rights Era[31]

Time is an important dimension in the Diffusion of Innovations Theory, and as we examine the Selma campaign it is important to note that it is not only the Movement of the 1960s that must be taken into account, but also the broader long Civil Rights Movement referenced in Chapter 1. In the minds of black and white citizens alike, the franchise came to be synonymous with freedom—literal and figurative. As Reconstruction drew to a close, and in the early years after it, numerous restraints were instituted to curtail black progress and reinstitute a social order, which limited blacks' ability to advance.[32] These limitations included the institution of Black Codes and Jim Crow laws,[33] curtailment of the ability to register to vote, and limitations on the exercise of the franchise. The effect was a nullification of the rights granted under law. Many Alabama Black Belt counties maintained tight restraints on the civil rights of blacks, including barriers to the black vote. Among others, these restraints included poll taxes, party primary elections limited to whites, vouching for character, and literacy tests.

Post-Reconstruction, the law afforded Alabama blacks the right to vote, but, over time, the norms and customs of the area restrained its exercise.[34] Lowndes County provides a good example of the tension created between law and custom. In 1865 in Lowndes County, adjacent to Dallas County (where Selma is located), historian Hasan Jeffries writes, "[L]egislators supported a proposal to enfranchise black men, believing that they could control their votes."[35] However, the passage of Reconstruction Era Amendments changed the perspective of Lowndes County's white residents about granting the franchise to African-American men. With the passage of the Thirteenth Amendment, suppression of the black vote became the order of the day.[36] Jeffries writes, "In 1900, Lowndes County had more than five thousand registered black voters. A half dozen years later, the county had only fifty-seven."[37]

In the first half of the twentieth century, The Great Migration and World War II profoundly influenced African-American pursuit of the franchise.[38] Annie Pearl Avery grew up in Birmingham, Alabama, but she describes the influence of her trips to visit relatives in the North on her later decision to participate in the Civil Rights Movement:

> That might have been part of it. Just thinking in hindsight that might have been part of what it was because it's a funny thing being a slave. Once you have been free, you don't want to go back to be a slave no more: if you see what I'm getting at. When I came back into that situation it [accepting the status quo] wasn't what I thought I wanted to do.[39]

The Dallas County Voters League (DCVL), a small group of African-Americans committed to fighting for the franchise, was formed after World War II.[40] The seeds for the Selma voting rights movement were sown in those years. In the early 1960s the group revived and began to hold regular classes to help register people to vote.[41] Building on the base established by DCVL and others, SNCC developed programs in Dallas, Wilcox, and Gadsden counties.[42] Bernard Lafayette was the initial director of SNCC's Alabama Voter Registration Project. In late 1964, after SNCC's efforts had been underway about a year, DCVL made the courageous decision to contact Dr. Martin Luther King Jr., President of the Southern Christian Leadership Conference (SCLC), to request the group's help in the voter registration efforts already underway by SNCC.[43]

Civil rights activists were pleased by the passage of the 1964 Civil Rights Act, but disappointed because it would do little in the area of voting rights. Civil rights advocates clamored for new voting rights legislation.[44] The appointment of independent federal examiners was sought.[45] The threat produced by the black franchise is summed up in a scene from the movie, *The Long Walk Home*. In the movie, Odessa Cotter, a black domestic boycotting the buses in Montgomery asks her boss, a reluctant supporter of the protest, the following question: "What about when we start voting Ms. Thompson? And when we do, we are going to put Negroes in office."

By early 1965 most of the leading civil rights organizations—including SNCC, the National Urban League, NAACP, and SCLC—had all made voting rights for Negroes their priority, but there was no accord about what location would be the proving ground for this agenda.[46] The Civil Rights Division of the Justice Department was litigating almost seventy separate voting rights cases all across the intransigent South.[47] These cases, brought under the Civil Rights Acts of 1957 and 1960, respectively, included three in the Alabama counties of Sumter, Elmore, and Perry.[48] With the exception of Elmore, each was a Black Belt county. In each case, the Department of Justice's findings pointed to patterned and systemic denial of the franchise by means that included violence, intimidation, and foul play.[49] In nearby Dallas County, organized registration efforts were underway. Dallas County also had Sheriff Jim Clark, a staunch segregationist determined to stop black voters.[50] These antecedents made Selma, Alabama, an excellent contender from which to build a national voting rights campaign for blacks, but it was Bloody Sunday—a vicious encounter spurred by the death of a local Perry County man named Jimmie Lee Jackson that thrust the voting rights struggle in Selma into the national limelight.

The Death of Jimmie Lee Jackson

Jimmie Lee Jackson was the first official casualty of the Selma campaign, and his death triggered the Selma to Montgomery March.[51] Others had died for the cause of civil rights, but Jackson, a former member of the armed services, youngest deacon in the history of his church, and a devoted son and grandson, was someone the community could rally behind.[52] Jimmie Lee Jackson was no stranger to civil rights activities. He had tried to register to vote on five separate occasions, and on February 18, 1965, Jackson and his family (mother, sister, and his 82-year-old grandfather, Cager Lee) attended a rally and night march in Marion, Alabama[53] protesting the jailing of civil rights activist James Orange.[54]

The Movement was diffusing. Although the February 18, 1965 meeting and demonstration were in Marion (in nearby Perry County), the connections to the Selma campaign were express. C.T. Vivian, one of the featured speakers that evening, was expressly invited to speak about an encounter he had with Sheriff Jim Clark of Selma two days earlier.[55] The night march commenced after the meeting at Zion United Methodist Church in Marion attended by almost 500 people. The marchers seemed strengthened by the meeting and the fellowship of other marchers, but while there was an air of hope, there was also recognition of an inherent potential for danger.[56] Those in attendance at the Marion march must have been aware of the dangers, but hundreds attended.

Local police and members of the Alabama State Trooper force, led by Al Lingo, were waiting for the protestors,[57] and just as the protestors set off to march to the courthouse, someone shot out the streetlights and broke the media cameras.[58] In the darkness, panic ensued. The marchers fled, but police (auxiliary forces as well as state troopers) and angry white citizens pursued them.[59] NBC news correspondent, Richard Valeriani, describes the scene that evening:

> Chuck Quinn and I were covering the Selma events together and there was to be a nighttime march in Marion, Alabama. Nighttime marches were always dangerous, more dangerous than daytime marches and we were sending a film crew . . . I went to Marion and the crowd was particularly nasty that night and a lot of townspeople had gathered around, and we knew we were in for trouble right away because people came up and started spraying the cameras with paint. And then they'd insist [we] put the cameras down. Luckily there were Alabama Highway Patrolmen there, I say luckily because if there had been no semblance of outside uh, security, we would have been at the mercy of the townspeople I think. But we knew it was tough, so it was very tense and we were all very frightened . . . that was the night that Jimmy[60] Lee Jackson was shot. And I guess in the excitement somebody walked up behind me and hit me with an ax handle . . . he hit me here [pointing], drew blood which required stitches . . . But before I left a state trooper walked up took the ax handle away from the guy who hit me, threw it on the steps of city hall

and said I guess you've done enough damage with this tonight. But did not arrest him, and then somebody walked up to me, a white man walked up to me and he, he said "uh, are you hurt, do you need a doctor," and I was stunned, and I put my hand on the back of my head, and it was full of blood. And I said to him, "yeah, I think I do, I'm bleeding." And then he thrust his face right up against mine and he said, "Well, we don't have doctors for people like you."[61]

Around 9:30 p.m., Jackson and his family fled to Mack's Café, a nearby restaurant.[62] Inside the establishment, the police struck Jimmie Lee Jackson's mother with a club, and he came to her defense. In the struggle, Jackson was clubbed by one officer and shot in the stomach by another.[63] Jackson was unarmed, but the officer alleged Jackson was trying to take his gun and was shot during a struggle over it.[64] Jackson was arrested and denied medical attention in Marion. Later he was taken to a hospital in Selma that served blacks. That hospital was approximately 30 miles away. Eight days later, Jackson succumbed to his injuries in a Selma hospital.[65]

Across the Black Belt, crowds attended various services for the slain martyr. On Sunday, February 28, 1965, James Bevel of SCLC addressed a capacity crowd assembled at Brown Chapel in Selma, Alabama. The entrance to Brown Chapel bore a banner over it that read "Racism Killed Our Brother."[66] James Bevel urged the crowd to take their grievances to the state capitol.[67] Bevel went on to contrast the biblical story of Esther with the plight of blacks in the South.[68] Quoting Esther 4:8, Bevel said, "Charge her that she should go in unto the King, to make supplication unto him, and to make request before him for her people." Bevel told the crowd: "There is a decree of destruction against black people in Alabama, but we cannot stand by any longer and see it implemented . . . I must go to the King! . . . We must go to Montgomery and see the King!"[69] The King was famed Alabama governor George Wallace.

In the black community, the response to Jimmie Lee Jackson's death was swift if not decisive.[70] A symbolic march from Selma to Montgomery was planned in Jackson's honor. The FBI learned about the march through planting bugs in a local church. The FBI also learned about possible splinters (some were advocating violence) in the Movement through the same bugs. The original march plan involved carrying Jimmie Lee Jackson's body to Montgomery and presenting it to Governor Wallace. While plans to carry Jackson's body were abandoned, the 54-mile march to commence on Sunday, March 7, 1965, was not abandoned. The day would come to be known as Bloody Sunday.

Sidebar 2.1

George Wallace is one of Alabama's most iconic figures. His political career is a mystery to many. At times he was a fierce segregationist. Later in his life, he was an apologetic integrationist who asked for forgiveness from those he offended.

In Wallace's first bid for governor of Alabama he received and accepted the endorsement of NAACP, and he lost badly. Defeat did not sit well with the ambitious Wallace. He ran again, and won. In his 1963 inaugural address as governor he pledged "Segregation forever" in Alabama.

After four failed attempts to run for president, he was re-elected to an unprecedented third term as governor of Alabama.

Throughout the life course, people do change. This book is about social change. However, Wallace's ideological shifts often seemed more politically motivated than ideologically based.

Bloody Sunday

The people were ready to march.[71] They were committed to march for Jimmie Lee Jackson, for themselves, and for future generations, and they wanted the world to see and resolve to join their fight against racism. In the days before Bloody Sunday, Martin Luther King Jr. attended meetings in New York and Los Angeles; a weary King elected to return home to Atlanta to preach a sermon at the church he pastored there, so he would not be in Selma for the fateful Bloody Sunday march.[72] King was a great leader, and the media would miss him, but he was only the figurative head of the Selma campaign. In King's absence, leadership for the march was in the capable hands of Hosea Williams of SCLC and John Lewis and Robert Mants of SNCC.[73]

A critical mass showed up for the pilgrimage. Two hundred Perry County residents came, and an additional 400 marchers joined them.[74] After a meeting at Brown Chapel, a church located in the black section of town, which had become one of the headquarters for the Selma Movement, the marchers approached the bridge from Water Street, but what faced them on the other side of the bridge was not visible until they reached the bridge's apex.[75] The marchers advanced, but soon it would become clear that the demonstration would not proceed without challenge. In order to journey to Montgomery, the marchers would have to cross the Edmund Pettus Bridge, and there at the bridge law enforcement groups headed respectively by Jim Clark and Major John Cloud stood as a physical barricade blocking the demonstrators' goal. At the apex, police, mounted and on foot, as well as dozens of Clark's deputized posse could be seen at the other side. As the marchers boldly advanced, Major John Cloud ordered them to turn around. Hosea Williams asked for a "word" with Major Cloud, but the Major responded that there was nothing to talk about. John Lewis and others sent the word back through the line of marchers "to bow down in a prayerful manner."[76] John Lewis and Hosea Williams knelt to pray; at their urging, others knelt with them. Major Cloud told the marchers, "You are ordered to disperse. Go home or to your church. This march will not continue. You have two minutes."[77] Not more than a minute passed before the troopers charged.[78] Despite the protestors' non-violent stance, Cloud and Clark's men viciously attacked them. At the head of the line, Lewis bore the brunt of the initial attack. A large Alabama state trooper repeatedly struck John Lewis on the head with a club.[79] Lewis lay bloodied on the ground; his skull fractured.[80]

Selma resident Joanne Bland[81] was 11 at the time of Bloody Sunday, but she still recalls the day in gripping detail. Describing the scene on the bridge, Bland says:

Figure 2.3 SNCC Chairman John Lewis being beaten by police/possemen on Bloody Sunday. Lewis suffered a skull fracture.

Source: Library of Congress, Prints and Photographs Division, NYWT&S Collection, [LC-USZ62-127732].

> We were boxed in. . . . There was nowhere to go. I heard gunshots. We thought everyone was being killed. It's the screams I remember the most. People just screaming and screaming. The gunshot turned out to be tear gas. They were shooting tear gas canisters up in the crowds. All you could do is scream, and they were beating you . . . you couldn't outrun the men on horseback. The horses were scared too. They were kicking and rearing up. There was no place for us to go. People were being trampled by the horses. Blood was everywhere on the bridge, people were laying in the street as if they were dead and we couldn't even stop to see if they were alright. It was horrible. It seemed like it lasted an eternity . . . [Then]the last thing I remember seeing on the bridge that day was this lady. I don't know did the horse run over her? Did the guy hit her with the billy club and she fell? But I do know the sound of her head hitting that pavement, and I'll never forget it. It was just too much for me. I fainted, When I awakened, I was on the city side of the bridge.[82]

In her account, Bland reports that the aforementioned incidents happened right after the group kneeled to pray.

Clark and Cloud's point of attack was chosen with military precision. The Edmund Pettus Bridge, which overlooks the Alabama River, climbs to an incline. It is impossible to see one end of the bridge from the other. Instead, each end is only visible from the bridge's apex. In his memoir, *Walking with the Wind*, just before the marchers crossed the bridge John Lewis recalls seeing "a small posse" of armed white men near the Selma Times Journal building.[83] With the police in front of them and the river on either side, marchers had no choice but to retreat back to their point of origin, which meant going back past the small posse. As the protestors retreated, chaos marked the scene. The troopers beat the marchers using nightsticks (often striking them across their heads). Each blow sent up cheers from a small crowd of white spectators.[84]

The police dispersed cans of smoke, nausea gas, and tear gas into the crowd.[85] The items only exacerbated the problem: people grew disoriented; they could not see; they could not breathe.[86] The marchers fled on foot, but the police and mounted posse pursued them. The frenzied police and Clark's appointed posse chased some all the way back to their churches, trampling and beating many along the way.[87] Once there, law enforcement officials continued their assault.[88] Bland reports:

> Tear gas causes pain, irritation of the eyes, coughing, breathing difficulties, disorientation, and confusion.

Figure 2.4 Photo of the Edmund Pettus Bridge, which overlooks the Alabama River.

Source: The George F. Landegger Collection of Alabama Photographs in Carol M. Highsmith's America, Library of Congress, Prints and Photographs Division, [LC-DIG-highsm-07257].

> [We] couldn't make it home, but [we] made it to First Baptist Church. The police came in the church and they were looking for a girl in a red coat. The police started beating people again and ran us out of the church. . . . A woman fell down the stairs of the church. The police threw a man through a wall and he fell into the empty baptismal pool and broke both his arms. Then the police started shooting into the nearby homes. . . . It amazes me today that people didn't die. The magnitude of that violence was nothing like you see in the film [*Selma Lord Selma*]. They just showed a portion of it. The violence didn't end at the bridge. They went into the projects. It was all night long.[89]

Each of the major broadcast news outlets carried video of the attack.[90] Jim Clark's voice could be heard on many of the broadcasts, shouting orders to those under him—his posse—including "get those god-damned niggers. . . . and get those god-damned white niggers."[91] Many Americans were disturbed by what they saw.

The chaos challenged protestors' convictions. Annie Pearl Avery, a SNCC Field Secretary in Hale County, who reports having the distinction of being the only one arrested on Bloody Sunday, recalls her desire to keep moving. Avery states:

> Anyway, what happened is there was some people who had worked with us [SNCC] in Mississippi that were doctors and nurses that came in from the North to help us because sometimes we couldn't get treatment from the local people . . . I knew [the doctor and nurse] . . . they lived in New York. She said, "Annie Pearl, I don't know how to get up to the bridge." They

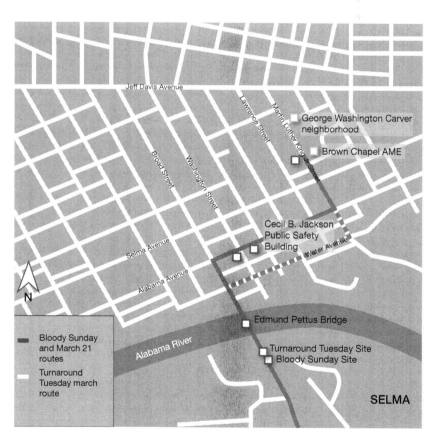

Figure 2.5 This map of Selma, Alabama, shows the route marchers took on Bloody Sunday and Turnaround Tuesday.

Source: Everett M. Rogers' *Diffusion of Innovations.*

were in a van with medical stuff, so I said, "I'll show you how
to get up to the bridge." But I said, "I got to get in the march,"
so what I said is "y'all drop me off, and then I'll jump in the
march, and then you'll know where the bridge is." So then I
jumped in the march, and I started moving forward, and I heard
something that sounded like gunshots. But it wasn't gunshots,
it was teargas, and there was a police line. They [the police]
was all along the side wherever we walked, and I was trying
to move forward and the police grabbed me. I don't know.
I should have been going in the other direction [laughter].
But my instinct told me to go forward, so I was trying
to go forward.[92]

The couple from New York remained in the vicinity to render medical
services to the injured. Peter Hall, a black lawyer from Birmingham came
and posted Ms. Avery's bond. Avery reports that from inside the jail she
could hear yells and screams coming from the direction of the bridge, but
she had no idea what transpired.

The evening news carried accounts of Bloody Sunday. News coverage
of Bloody Sunday impacted those watching. The Southern freedom
struggle was no longer a vague abstraction, but a reality, and those watching
were equipped with knowledge of its effects. Arguably, ABC News had
the most influence. The network interrupted the end of its Sunday night
movie to show part of the assault. Coverage came at the end of the film
Judgment at Nuremberg, which outlined atrocities committed by the Nazis
in World War II. *Judgment at Nuremberg* showed how Germans had ignored
or acquiesced to the horrors going on around them. Many people viewing
the coverage of Bloody Sunday thought they were still watching Nazi
Germany. The cautionary words at the end of the film seemed themselves
a call to action.

> ABC interrupted its broadcast of the 1961
> Oscar-winning film, *Judgment at
> Nuremberg*, which chronicled the war
> crime trials in Germany. The movie's
> message stresses what happens when
> ordinary people are silent in the face of
> evil, and its applicability to the peaceful
> protests going on in Selma was
> undeniable.

The decision to innovate is
an optional one, and it requires
the use of communication channels. There is little debate that
media coverage of the movement
influenced cultural change, but
Richard Valeriani agues, "I think
that television helped accelerate
the progress of a movement whose
time had come."[93] Intense media
coverage of Bloody Sunday helped
to bring the message of the protestors

—a message of social change communicated by a group of innovators—to the masses. Diffusion is a special type of communication, which can occur through either mass media or interpersonal channels, but while both mass communication and interpersonal communications with peers are important, it is personal communication that is most vital.[94] This is because according to Rogers' theory, interpersonal communications have trans-formative strength. The power of interpersonal communication is illustrated in Martin Luther King Jr.'s correspondence to clergy following the events of Bloody Sunday. From Atlanta, Georgia, Martin Luther King Jr. sent telegrams urging those who believed in justice to come to Selma; his telegram called for a march to Montgomery on March 9, 1965.[95] Dr. King's call went out to the nation, too. He urged people to come to Selma, Alabama, stating, "The tension is not between black men and white men . . . but between justice and injustice."[96] The next day, clergy and people from all over the U.S. boarded planes, got on buses, drove in cars and headed to Selma.[97]

Turnaround Tuesday

By the announced date of the second protest, March 9, 1965, Selma, Alabama, was flooded with visitors—both those sympathetic and unsympathetic to the cause. Many people came out to heed King's call; 450 were clergy. All the major civil rights organizations sent representatives to Selma, too. SNCC was already there, but after the assault on the Edmund Pettus Bridge, SNCC solidified its support of the march.[98] SNCC Program Secretary Cleveland Sellars said SNCC wanted the world, particularly certain whites, to know "we didn't intend to take any more shit."[99] Still, despite SNCC's long presence in Selma and the growing presence of other civil rights organizations, the press, the nation, and the world still saw Dr. Martin Luther King Jr. as the undisputed head of the cadre of groups.

On the morning of March 9, 1965, King and over 1,500 protestors assembled to set off on a purported pilgrimage to Montgomery—the symbolic site of freedom—where they would present their grievances to Governor Wallace.[100] King headed the line, but unbeknown to the protestors and other civil rights organizations present, King had struck a deal with the government. In closed talks, King promised to have the assembly turn back before they reached Highway 80.[101] The deal had been negotiated late the preceding evening, and even President Johnson was unaware of its particulars. According to phone recordings available at the Lyndon Baines Johnson Library, early on the morning of March 9, 1965, President Johnson spoke by telephone with special assistant Bill Moyers.

The same recordings demonstrate how Moyers assured President Johnson that King had agreed to halt the march at the location of the Bloody Sunday initial attack and that Governor Wallace, in turn, agreed not to call up the National Guard to halt the "symbolic" march to the bridge. King defended his actions by saying he did not want to violate a federal order restraining the march. The day commonly became known as Turnaround Tuesday.

The small city of Selma was filled with tension. Groups and individuals associated with the Movement grew more vocal about debating non-violence.[102] There was growing tension among the civil rights groups, too. These tensions included philosophical differences, financial issues, distrust, and jealousy. While King's secret negotiations raised the ire of some, making matters worse, an act of violence later that evening would turn attention away from internal dissent within the Movement.

When the march to Montgomery did not happen, King asked everyone to remain in Selma for a subsequent march to occur on an unnamed date in the future, and many agreed to do so. That night, three visiting white clergy (Reverend James Reeb, a social worker and Unitarian pastor from Boston, along with fellow Boston Unitarian ministers, Clark Olsen and Orloff Miller) ate at a black diner. On their way back to Brown Chapel, the three took a wrong turn and walked past the Silver Moon Café, a known racist hang-out. Without knowing it, the "outsiders" had crossed the intangible "color line" and found themselves in hostile territory. The three were pursued and badly beaten. Reverend Reeb, who had been struck on the head with a baseball bat, suffered the most serious injuries. Two days later, Reeb died from his injuries.

The nation was outraged by James Reeb's death, but many black residents of Selma reeled that while the country mourned the loss of James Reeb, it had not wept for Jimmie Lee Jackson.[103] Similar cries of injustice rose after the 1964 lynchings of white civil rights workers Michael "Mickey" Schwerner and Andrew Goodman. James Chaney, a young black man, was killed alongside Schwerner and Goodman, but Chaney's death did not illicit decries from the nation like the other two did. Regarding the deaths, Ella Baker is reported to have said:

> The unfortunate thing is that it took this [the deaths of Chaney, Goodman, and Schwerner] . . . to make the rest of the country turn its eyes on the fact that there were other (black) bodies lying in the swamps of Mississippi. Until the killing of a black mother's son becomes as important as the killing of a white mother's son, we who believe in freedom cannot rest.[104]

Now, less than a year later, President Johnson called Reeb's death "an American tragedy," but no mention was made of Jimmie Lee Jackson. The president phoned Reeb's wife and offered condolences. While Americans and the world responded dramatically to Reeb's death, the murder of Jimmie Lee Jackson, which sparked the march, drew few tears. No official government representatives called Jimmie Lee Jackson's family, but within days of James Reeb's death, President Johnson took to the floor of Congress and delivered "The American Promise Speech." While Reverend Reeb's death may have prompted Johnson's speech, Johnson pleased movement leaders near the close of his speech with the words of the movement and pledged to the nation: "We shall overcome."[105]

Until this point, both meaningful voting rights protection and the march seemed stalled. LDF had brought suits against Sheriff Jim Clark and Judge James Hare in order to stop the harassment tactics they used to discourage voter registration. The Fund also played a critical role in bailing people out of jail who were demonstrating, so that they could again return

---

Sidebar 2.2

Judge Frank M. Johnson was a crusader for justice. Born in 1918, the Alabama jurist went to law school at the University of Alabama where he was friends with future governor, George Wallace. Johnson was awarded two Purple Hearts and a Bronze Star for meritorious conduct in World War II. After his service in the Army, Johnson and his wife settled in Jasper, Alabama. The lawyer became politically involved, serving on future president Dwight D. Eisenhower's election campaign in Alabama. President Eisenhower later appointed him as a federal judge in Alabama. Judge Johnson's appointment came just before the Montgomery Bus Boycott.

Throughout his career, Johnson made many principled legal decisions that opened the door for civil rights victories in an era when Southern judges could not be counted on to do so. Governor George Wallace banned the Selma to Montgomery March. It was Judge Frank Johnson who issued the order that finally cleared the way for the Selma to Montgomery March to take place.

The courage of Johnson's convictions did not come without a price. Judge Johnson was constantly threatened and required round-the-clock protection for a period of 15 years. Later in life, but prior to his death, Frank Johnson received some of the honor he was due: Congress named the federal courthouse in Montgomery, Alabama, after him; then President Bill Clinton awarded Johnson the Presidential Medal of Freedom, and the same Alabama state legislature that had earlier called for his impeachment as a federal judge passed a resolution honoring him. Judge Johnson's decisions paved the way for many major civil rights victories to come.

to the demonstration line. On the evening of Bloody Sunday, LDF attorneys went to Montgomery, Alabama, to file a federal action in court to prevent the march from being stopped. Movement leaders were waiting for a federal judge to clear the route for the march. Prior to President Johnson's March 15, 1965 speech on the floor of Congress, the idea of a voting rights act had been languishing in Congress for years. The fateful speech accompanied the presentation of President Johnson's voting rights proposal to the legislative body. Impediments to the march continued to mount, but there was hope. In fact, fearful that federal Judge Frank Johnson might clear the way for the march, on March 18, 1965, the Alabama State Senate moved and said that Alabama could not pay to protect the marchers. Finally, Judge Johnson did lift the injunction, thus permitting the march. However, citing safety reasons he limited the number of marchers on the two-lane stretch of Highway 80 to just 300. President Johnson took over control of the Alabama National Guard and ordered them to protect the marchers. With the injunction lifted, the marchers prepared to march from Selma to Montgomery where they would take their voting rights grievances to Governor George Wallace.

Selma to Montgomery

In some ways, march delays aided in the diffusion of the idea by giving it time to spread across the country and throughout the world. As news about the march filtered through various communication channels— media and interpersonal—so too did people's commitment to the effort. On March 21, 1965, nearly 8,000 people traveled some part of the first leg of the journey from Selma to Montgomery.[106] Four thousand showed up just to cross the now highly symbolic Edmund Pettus Bridge.[107] But by court order, only 300 could march on the two-lane portions of Highway 80. The task of paring that number down to the 300 mandated by the federal court order on some legs of the journey would prove a logistical feat. Many of those who came to Selma helped to shuttle people and provisions back and forth from Selma to various march sites. One of those volunteers was a housewife from Detroit named Viola Liuzzo.

Despite fractures within the Movement, it was an unprecedented time of cooperation. An accord produced by singularity of vision seemed to rule the day. The Selma to Montgomery pilgrimage would take days, and the demonstrators would have to travel through hostile counties, such as Lowndes. To complete the trek, the protestors would require transportation, food, water, other provisions (like toiletries and tents), lodging, protection, medical attention, and emotional support. All but the latter cost money, but money was the least of their concerns. The journey from

Selma to Montgomery proved long. It was long in terms of distance—54 miles from Selma to Montgomery. It was long in terms of time—the journey would take five days and four nights, but that was nothing compared to the near 100-year struggle for meaningful voting rights protection. It was also long in terms of moral expanse for the country to travel. Disparaging attitudes about blacks had long persisted. In Harper Lee's classic, *To Kill a Mockingbird*, fictional character Atticus Finch cautions his child Jeb about the danger of those attitudes:

> As you grow older, you'll see white men cheat black men every day of your life, but let me tell you something and don't you forget it—whenever a white man does that to a black man, no matter who he is, how rich he is, or how fine a family he comes from, that white man is trash.[108]

Harper Lee's words, first published in 1960, were a precursor to changing attitudes to come. Freedom was a long way off, but it was in sight. On the journey to freedom, the demonstrators would suffer greatly for the cause. Some would even give their lives. Most suffered conditions including: sunburn; heatstroke; sore, blistered feet; torrential rain; exposure as they slept outdoors (sometimes uncovered); taunts; long waits (some waited up to 4 hours to join the March); accommodation in a cow pasture infested with red ants and another steeped in mud; unpotable water; gossip and innuendo; loss of revenue and jobs. Despite the conditions, the marchers continued moving.

Fueled by vitriolic hate, the character of the marchers was assailed on numerous sides. There were allegations of sexual orgies, abuse of drugs and alcohol, and constant claims of Communist involvement and other anti-American sentiments.[109] Some Southern newspaper accounts reported that "white women" and nuns were on the March to be used for the sexual pleasure of black men, and on the second day of the March, Alabama representative William Dickinson made similar claims in a speech before the House of Representatives.[110] Northern and national newspapers also reported such allegations. In *From Selma to Sorrow: The Life and Death of Viola Liuzzo*, author Mary Stanton writes:

> The national press, however, couldn't resist a good story. A rumor ran through Selma that a white girl had died of exhaustion after making thousands of dollars "providing comfort to the visiting clergy," and all the wire services picked it up. During the first week of May 1965, *Newsweek*, *Time*, and *U.S. News* carried features entitled "Kiss and Tell," "Charges of Interracial Sex," and "Orgies on the Rights March."[111]

Reports of the purity of white women being defiled by black men only served to fuel the ire of many opposed to black civil rights advances and contributed to fears about social change. On some parts of the route, angry crowds met the marchers. Some naysayers expressed doubt that the demonstrators possessed the fortitude to reach their goal. After all, in order to reach the capitol, the protestors would have to go through "Bloody Lowndes."

Such a visible act of defiance to the established social order of this Alabama Black Belt community took the kind of courage that few are ever called upon in their lifetimes to summon. In crossing Lowndes, many knew that they could literally be called upon to lay down their lives.[112]

Night-time held potential dangers, too. The marchers did not stay in deluxe accommodation. Instead, they camped out in the open elements. At great personal risk, a local black farmer agreed to let the demonstrators spend the night on his property, so the first night of the trek the group would camp out at David Hall's farm just 7 miles east of Selma and outside of Lowndes County. Two other black farmers agreed to host the marchers. After the first night at David Hall's farm, on March 22, 1965 the marchers

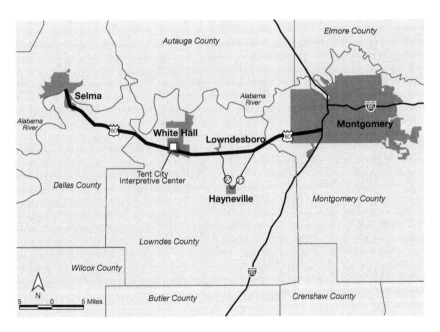

Figure 2.6 Map of Selma to Montgomery Voting Rights March route along U.S. Highway 80 (aka Jefferson Davis Memorial Highway).
Source: National Park Service.

camped inside Lowndes County at Rosie Steele's farm. Located 11 miles east of Rosie Steele's property, Robert Gardner hosted the marchers at his farm on the evening of March 23, 1965. The next night, the City of St. Jude Catholic Services Agency hosted the marchers on the complex's athletics field. Singer and activist Harry Belafonte arranged for a few of his friends, some of the biggest names in the entertainment industry, to entertain the marchers. It was just what the demonstrators needed. The marchers were not alone. The biggest names in the entertainment industry, change agents in their own right, supported them and the social change for which they fought. The "Stars for Freedom Rally" included Mahalia Jackson, Dick Gregory, Nina Simone, Sammy Davis Jr., Tony Bennett, James Baldwin, Joan Baez, Peter, Paul & Mary, and a host of others.[113] It also featured a rendition of "A Change is Gonna Come" sung by the SNCC Freedom Singers.[114] The music and words soothed tired feet and strengthened and encouraged everyone's resolve.[115]

The marchers entered Montgomery on Thursday, March 25, 1965; they were approximately 25,000 strong. As they approached the capitol, many observers heckled and harassed the marchers, but others demonstrated kindness to them. Selma resident Joanne Bland describes her favorite memory of the March:

> When we got to Montgomery we [had] just rode over. . . . the marchers had marched for days, but we rode over . . . These women in Montgomery were walking through the crowd saying "Hi, we're so glad you're here. Would you like to come home with me and eat a good meal and take a bath?" I swear we went home with one of those ladies like we had marched the whole way, and we slept in a bed all-comfortable, and she just spoiled us. We were clean. [Laughter] Why did she think we had marched all the way? She was so happy to see us . . . The fact that those women were marching through the crowd offering what they had to the marchers was just phenomenal to me. . . . In that day and time I don't think anyone from Montgomery could have come to Selma, and we'd have said, "Come in." You know? . . . We were hungry. Other people in the movement took people in [too]. We ate a whole lot of grits, greens, and bologna. [But] These people had a feast before us.[116]

That day, 10-year-old Bland learned about the kindness of strangers and fortified her belly and her resolve to fight for freedom.

The most compelling memory of the event was the mass movement of the protestors to the statehouse building. The group moved in concert.

Martin Luther King Jr. and his front line would arrive first. No one dared usurp his place. With King leading the way, they all marched together to capitol building. Almost in defiance, the Confederate flag flew over the building waving proudly, but the civil rights demonstrators did not seem to notice or mind. After jubilant speeches and a rendition of "The Battle Hymn of the Republic," eight representatives, including Amelia Boynton of Selma, were chosen to deliver a petition to the governor. The petition requested him to remove all barriers from voting, but the group was restrained from entering the building. After a stalemate, the governor's executive assistant agreed to carry the petition to the governor. Governor Wallace watched the scene unfold from his office, but he never came out to address the group. Content with their victory and aware of the dangers, the demonstrators agreed to leave Montgomery as soon as possible.[117]

Media outlets featured news of the March everyday, and as the information was disseminated, acceptance for the innovation grew. Diffusion of Innovations Theory helps to explain the influence a few powerful change agents can have on whether or not innovations are adopted. Rogers states, "Diffusion models portray society as a huge learning system where individuals are continually behaving and making decisions, not just on the basis for their own individual experiences, but to a large extent on the basis of the observed or talked about experiences of others."[118] The theory also possesses the explanatory power to elucidate how a few powerful change agents can stir the process of social change even in the absence of widespread adoption of the idea.[119] The marchers; countless logistical volunteers shuttling food, people, and incidentals; and the entertainers were all change agents bringing a message that it was time for a change. It was time for the country to provide meaningful protection for the black franchise.

AFTERMATH OF THE MARCH

At the end of the March, carpools carried many back to Selma. Unfortunately, the marchers' jubilation over the successful March was short-lived. One volunteer, a white housewife from Detroit named Viola Liuzzo, who had been transporting marchers, was shot and killed as she drove on the road that evening.[120] Mrs. Liuzzo's passenger, a black teen named Leroy Moton who worked with Mrs. Liuzzo providing transportation for the March, survived the attack by playing dead.[121] At the time of the attack, Moton and Liuzzo had just dropped off some people returning from the March when they were attacked in Lowndes County, Alabama.[122]

Once again, "Bloody Lowndes," the county Tuskegee University professors termed a "problem county," had lived up to its name.

Increasingly, civil rights workers knew the inherent risks in their involvement. This information was carried through the airwaves, television networks, and widely reported in magazines and newspapers. Additionally, Movement participants were part of independent, personal social networks that obtained, processed, and distributed Movement news. Movement knowledge abounded, and in the abundance of this knowledge, conviction grew. Influenced by change agents, individual actors became "persuaded" that their cause was just and that the time was ripe for change.

Conclusion

More than a month prior to Bloody Sunday, King asserted his belief that there were "millions of people of goodwill" throughout the white South.[123] King said,

> If the people of goodwill of the white South fail to act now history will have to record that the greatest tragedy of this period of social transition was not the vitriolic words and the violent actions of the bad people, but the appalling silence and indifference of the good people.[124]

When news of Bloody Sunday disseminated, thousands of good people answered King's call. They were everyday people who traveled from places including Detroit, Boston, Hawaii, California, and Germany, including almost 500 clergy from across the nation. But people of the South—black and white—responded, too, and they could potentially diffuse this new idea to others in their respective communities. Diffusion, however, does not occur without challenges; rather, it occurs in spite of challenges. Further, Rogers notes that even when a new idea is adopted, there will be laggards. Laggards may include traditionalists, holdouts (those people who refuse to adopt the change), and those late adopters who convert back to their old ways of thinking.[125]

Some call Bloody Sunday the day that changed America forever, and while the events of that fateful Sunday helped to usher in swift passage of the Voting Rights Act, the passage of a legislative act could not change people's hearts or immediately change the circumstances of African-Americans in the North or South. The Act was signed August 8, 1965. Less than a week later, rioting broke out in Watts.

Unrest continued in the South, too. In August 1965, young people in Fort Deposit, Alabama, asked for SNCC's help organizing a protest.

As a result of the protest, several were jailed. While being held in jail along with Stokely Carmichael, Jonathan Daniels, and others, on charges related to illicit voting rights efforts in Haneyville, Alabama, Willie Vaughn communicated his faith in the ability of people to change, and silenced the jail cell block when he said, "[H]ave you ever stood in the picket line and looked into the faces of your adversaries and watched them soften . . . ?"[126] Vaughn's words spoke optimistically about the future of race relations in the South, but upon release from jail just a few days later, one member of the group, Jonathan Daniels, a white Episcopalian pastor from the North, would give his life to save young Ruby Sales.[127] Daniels would be the last official martyr for the Selma campaign. He was killed just 14 days after passage of the Act.

"Selma" means high point, and, in many ways, the Selma to Montgomery Marches mark the high point of the Civil Rights Movement. In retrospect, many observers, including Georgia Congressman John Lewis, mark Selma as the beginning of the end. Selma was also America's call to action in the long struggle for Civil Rights. At the end of the March, King asks the rhetorical question, "How long will it take?" In a wave of optimism, he restates the question and then answers himself: "How long will it take? Not long." But after Selma, the Movement seemed to just fall apart.[128]

Popular notions about the Civil Rights Movement and the changes to the social structure that it prompted suggest that the country decided to do what is right. But the adoption of innovation is not always about doing what is right. Instead, Rogers makes clear that changes in social attitude (i.e., innovations) happen only to the extent that each adopter category perceives relative benefit to adoption of the change.[129] Innovators, including opinion leaders, change agents, and change makers, may be less concerned about doing what is "right" and more concerned about doing what is "right for them." Applying this idea to the atrocities of Bloody Sunday, Rogers observes, "Southerners saw on US television how they appeared to the rest of the world, and they did not like what they saw."[130] For some, that image was enough to effect change.

CHAPTER 3

Portrait of a Nation

The architecture of this work is rooted in the Temporal. Every human problem must be considered from the standpoint of time.

Homi Bhabha, *The Location of Culture (1994)*

The American South is often singled out as the locus of all of America's race problems. This focus on the South is not without merit. Southern culture, especially Jim Crow—the South's rigid system of repressive, anti-black laws intended to enforce strict racial (social) segregation through physical and mental intimidation and relegate blacks to second-class status—had operated like a caste system and restrained Southern blacks since the days of Reconstruction. In fact, a great deal of the early media attention on civil rights issues focused on "Southern" places and matters; however, survey research clearly reveals that in the first half of the twentieth century America had a "race problem," which extended far beyond the geographic borders of the bounded Southern states. Researching public opinion during this period, Paul Kellstedt notes, "American public opinion on race and civil rights . . . had a distinctly segregationist, nonegalitarian flavor to it."[1]

In the decade prior to the March, the stage was being set for social change in American society, but in order to apprehend the country's movement on the issue of race, it is important to understand national racial attitudes prior to the period of rapid social change under study. Indeed, such an appreciation has the potential to shift attitudes about the supposed rapidity of the social/cultural change examined here.

Culture is our taken-for-granted ways of knowing things and doing things, and it is highly symbolic in nature. It includes the language, habits, and norms of a society, and it can vary from time to time and from place to place. Yet, despite these variations, in the first half of the twentieth century, findings from national public opinion surveys conducted between 1942 and 1946 reveal that American culture was fairly homogeneous:[2]

> [A] 1942 survey revealed that only 41 percent of all Americans believe that black and white soldiers should serve together in the armed forces. Only 55 percent agreed that a black man could be just as good a soldier as a white man. Only 42 percent agreed that "Negroes are as intelligent as white people." The perceived differences between blacks and whites are hard to exaggerate, as only 36 percent believed that "Negro blood is the same as white blood." In addition to these strikingly prejudicial sentiments, the bulk of white Americans prefer to maintain [social] distance between races. Fifty-one percent claimed that streetcars and buses should be segregated. Fifty-four percent favored active job discrimination. Sixty-eight percent believed that white and black children should go to segregated schools. When it came to restaurants, 69 percent favored separate facilities, and fully 84 percent wanted segregated neighborhoods. These complex attitudes existed in an atmosphere of denial that race is a social problem worth addressing, as three in five Americans said that "Negroes are getting all the opportunities they deserve in this country."[3]

The survey results reported are "American" public opinion, not just "Southern" public opinion and suggest that white Southerners' attitudes on race relations were not decidedly different from those of their Northern counterparts. The following quote from Gene Roberts and Hank Klibanoff's Pulitzer Prize winning book, *The Race Beat: The Press, the Civil Rights Struggle, and the Awakening of a Nation*, may sum up the distinction best:

> He [Sander Vancour] loved the way [Harry] Ashmore defined the difference between the South and North: In the South, whites would say to Negroes, "come close, but don't go too high." In the North, whites would say, "go high, but don't come too close."[4]

Harry Ashmore was the executive editor of the *Arkansas Gazette* during the Little Rock crisis, and he wrote numerous editorials criticizing Governor Orval Faubus and appealing to the citizens of Little Rock to employ reason and allow school integration. Harry Ashmore's editorials earned him a Pulitzer Prize and the ire of white traditionalists. Sander Vancour, a new reporter to the "race beat," sought desperately to understand the Southern society on which he was being asked to report. One way to understand the

> Light diffusion is about the process that allows light to spread. Here a similar idea is examined—how does an idea spread or diffuse into society?

unknown is to compare it to something known. Ashmore's direct supposition about the distinctions between Southerners and Northerners appears to have resonated with Vancour. If white attitudes about blacks were changing, it had been a long time coming.

There is an adage that says nothing can stop an idea whose time has come, but the truth is, the mere passage of time alone is not enough for new ideas to be adopted by the larger society. Instead, the diffusion and/or ultimate adoption of new ideas by society relies heavily on human actors carrying the idea to the individual members of their social system(s) and persuading a critical mass to make a decision to adopt the innovation. Therefore, both the individual and the social system are central to diffusion. Individual actors are part of a larger social network with a reach that extends beyond the local, and so they are both local and global actors influenced by and influencing others at each level. The social relationships inside these networks are affected by time, space, and environment, and they cannot be easily disentangled from each other. The local is important, but so too is the national context. This chapter, *Portrait of a Nation*, focuses on the 10-year period prior to the March and unearths the broader environment in which the process of social change took place. It explains how increased communication channels (both personal and mass communication) helped spread knowledge about the black freedom struggle—local and global— and enabled individual actors to see and frame global matters as local, local matters as national, and the black freedom struggle as the human freedom struggle.

Freedom was the goal, and by the 1960s, free exercise of the franchise had become the literal and figurative symbol of black freedom. In her 1964 testimony before the Democratic National Convention in Atlantic City, New Jersey, Fannie Lou Hamer poignantly outlined the fervently held desire of many African-Americans "to register to become first-class citizens." The phrase "first-class citizens" became a mantra to Hamer.[5] The simplicity of her request contrasted starkly against the brutality of the denial she outlined and seemed to suggest that protection for the black franchise would only be possible through a shifting of attitudes. Rogers terms this kind of change in attitude "a social innovation." Social innovations are new ideas that diffuse successfully into the larger society.

The social innovation under examination is an essential part of the movement for civil and political rights for blacks, but "movements do not emerge in a vacuum"; instead, there is "larger political context in which social insurgency occurs."[6]

Because protection for the black franchise was a social innovation (i.e., new idea), it is useful to apply the tenets of the Diffusion of Innovations Theory to better understand its spread into the social system. This chapter outlines that larger political context which gave birth to the change in attitude necessary to implement and enforce meaningful voting rights protection for African-American citizens. The chapter explains how consensus for the social innovation was formed and reshaped across the geographies of time and space.

Time is an important variable in Rogers' diffusion process. Time is implicated in the innovation decision process, individual innovativeness, and the rate of adoption. The innovation decision process—knowledge to persuasion to decision to implementation to confirmation—occurs sequentially, but not instantaneously. Similarly, Rogers acknowledges that individual innovativeness is time sensitive as some people (and often categories of people) adopt ideas sooner than others. Finally, the rate of adoption is time sensitive, and while there is no formula for how much time is required for an innovation to take hold, it is established that one category of adopters follows another. The innovators are the first adopters; next come the early adopters, early majority, late majority, and laggards. Rogers describes this as a time-ordered sequence: the early majority adopts the idea after the early adopters but before the late majority. The first three adopter categories (i.e., the innovators, early adopters, and early majority) comprise 50 percent of the population, as do the last two—the late majority and laggards. People in each discrete adopter category often share common socio-economic factors, and in each category the rate of adoption tends to correspond to the perceived advantage that the group receives from adoption of the innovation.[7] However, perception of relative advantage (or disadvantage) can change, so once adopted, new ideas do not necessarily become a static part of society. The late majority can change its mind and revert back to its old ways of thinking (or new ways), and laggards often never adopt the innovation; therefore it is conceivable that social innovations can be abandoned after adoption.[8]

While time is an important variable in the adoption of innovations, the mere passage of time is not enough for new ideas to get diffused into the population; additional factors influence the rate of diffusion. First, society itself has a role in the rate of adoption of innovations. For Rogers, society constitutes a social system and comprises "a set of interrelated units that are engaged in problem solving to accomplish a common goal."[9] The rate of diffusion of new ideas into the social system is largely contingent upon the society's social structure, its norms, and its opinion leaders.[10] Within the established social structure, various groups tend to respond differently to the social innovation, but because people tend to communicate with those who are most like them (and influence those in their network), the responses (i.e., failure to adopt or propensity to adopt the innovation) of certain groups becomes somewhat patterned and even predictable. Finally, the norms of a social structure can promote or dissuade the adoption of innovations. Therefore, it is likely that because the normative social structure in the Southern states was to deny African-Americans the franchise, that structure acted as a barrier to impede adoption of the social innovation. Still it is important to note that opinion leaders, black and white alike—from across the nation, including the South—played a role in influencing others to adopt the idea of protection for the black vote and voters. These opinion leaders had access to communication channels and generally provided advice and support to the members of the social system. Opinion leaders' views are respected and therefore influential, and they helped awaken the nation.

Knowledge is the first element in the diffusion decision process. According to Rogers, knowledge is only "gained when an individual (or other decision-making unit) learns of the innovation's existence and gains some understanding of how it functions."[11] Opinion leaders provided a reputable knowledge base about the social innovation, and their information proves crucial to the decision-making process of individual actors. In an era where the Internet makes it possible to access information about an endless variety of topics almost instantaneously, it seems difficult to fathom a time where that was not the case; however, prior to the 1954 Supreme Court decision in Brown v. The Board of Education of Topeka, Kansas, relatively little about the condition of blacks in the Southern states was written about in majority presses—in the North or the South.[12] Instead, the story of black lynchings, repression, and domination was reserved to the black press.[13] The decade leading up to the March is crucial because it forms the knowledge/persuasion phase of Rogers' "innovation-decision process." During this period, major news outlets began to cover the black freedom struggle, and although several outlets insisted that the coverage be balanced,[14] mere coverage of the struggle put the "Southern way of life" on trial.[15] Prior to this widespread coverage, America seemed oblivious to its race problem. Therefore, mass media coverage of the struggle was crucial to adoption of the new idea (innovation) that the black franchise both deserved and needed protection, and during the knowledge/persuasion phase, coverage began to abound.

Post-Brown, Southern society was in danger of unraveling, and its most committed devotees made every attempt to hold the fabric of their society together by mounting concerted resistance to black gains. Deep Southern resistance to the impending normative structural changes to their society is best expressed by the title of Nigerian[16] author Chinua Achebe's 1958 work, *Things Fall Apart*. The title of Achebe's book is taken from the William Butler Yeats poem, *The Second Coming*. The key line of the poem says: "Things fall apart; the centre cannot hold." These pages tell the story of how, over time, the Southern way of life came under public scrutiny and began to fall apart. This public scrutiny was heightened by the Selma campaign, which influenced social change. In order to tell the story, attention is paid to the nation; however, specific emphasis is placed on the South, especially Dallas County, Alabama. As a final caution, this chapter requires readers' careful attention, as it is most helpful to talk about this perceived attack on the "Southern way of life" in thematic terms rather than chronological order. Further, to address the state of the nation in a chronological manner would embrace an idea that this book rejects: the idea that progress is linear. Instead, the story of the decade leading up to the March discusses the successes and defeats of the freedom struggle.

Introduction

In their own right, the civil rights acts of 1957, 1960, and 1964, were each sweeping pieces of civil rights legislation. The 1957 Civil Rights Act gave the Department of Justice the right to seek injunctive relief and otherwise intervene in voting rights violations in contravention of the Fifteenth Amendment. The 1957 Act also created the Civil Rights Division of the Department of Justice and the Commission on Civil Rights.[17] The 1960 Civil Rights Act gave federal courts the power to appoint voting referees to conduct voter registration; however, this could only happen after a judicial finding of interference with voting rights. The 1964 Civil Rights Act had minor voting rights provisions; however, it did contain sweeping legislation that outlawed various forms of discrimination against racial and ethnic minorities. The 1964 Act was a direct response by then President John F. Kennedy to ongoing civil rights protests seeking to integrate and open up public facilities including hotels, restaurants, stores, and other establishments. The bill survived the death of President Kennedy and a 54-day filibuster led by South Carolina Senator Strom Thurmond, but the bill that was ultimately passed was weaker than the one initially proposed. Separately and collectively, each did little to change the relative condition of disenfranchisement faced by blacks in the South.

History had demonstrated that preserving the condition of black disenfranchisement was the last and best way for Southern whites to retain their position of superiority and control over blacks. After passage of the Fifteenth Amendment granting the vote to racial and ethnic minorities, Southern blacks saw initial gains, but while the Fifteenth Amendment granted blacks the right to vote, the substantial presence of federal Northern troops helped to enforce that right. The end of Reconstruction largely marked the end of black gains. In fact, according to the Department of Justice's website section on Introduction to Federal Voting Rights, "by 1910, almost all blacks in the former Confederate states were effectively disenfranchised."[18] White Southerners regained control of Southern statehouses through a general climate of violence and intimidation.[19] This process of regaining control of the Southern states became known as Redemption.

The process of Southern "redemption" was so complete and effective that through much of the twentieth century, the Southern way of life and racial segregation became synonymous.[20] Blacks and whites in the North lived separate lives too, but Southern segregation was more caste-like and included the potential for violence for stepping outside those lines. Still, The Great Migration and two world wars allowed many people to see glimpses into societies that operated contrary to the "southern way of life."[21]

Black subjugation was trifold: social, political, and economic, but if the white power structure could retain political control, civil rights advances could be effectively contained or even curtailed. In the campaign for African-American civil and political rights, meaningful voting rights protection would be the deciding battle. Unrest about the social, political, and economic condition of the masses of U.S. African-Americans was not only rising in the South, but the North as well where millions of blacks who migrated "Any place that is North and West, and not South" came to realize that things were tough all over.[22] Frustration was mounting, and this was especially true of the young in the Alabama Black Belt and beyond who grew weary of accepting the status quo and discontented with the idea of waiting for a better tomorrow. Instead, they wanted to make a better tomorrow, today. To quote civil rights activist Fannie Lou Hamer, co-founder of the Mississippi Freedom Democratic Party (MFDP), many were "sick and tired of being sick and tired."[23] America itself was at a crossroads. Michael Harrington's The Other America reveals that the image of the affluent society that the nation worked to cultivate in the 1950s, was not possible for a large portion of the nation's citizens, but, in a nation divided, Northerners could claim superiority over Southerners, and poor white

Southerners could claim superiority over blacks. Blacks in the North and South would cry out for relief from the overlapping vectors of social, political/legal, and economic repression.

SOCIAL PORTRAIT OF A NATION

Social change is a process, not an event. Throughout much of the country, blacks and whites lived very separate social lives, and the Southern social structure in place pre-Brown provided neither the opportunity nor the desire to change that system. In truth, for many blacks fighting for civil rights, integration was not the aim—fair treatment and a better way of life for themselves and their children was the goal. The case of Prince Edward County, Virginia, illustrates this point. In 1951, black students in Prince Edward County, Virginia, staged a strike from school in an attempt to force the county to build a new facility for blacks. Instead, the county added additions to three already dilapidated buildings. Members of the Parent Teacher Association (PTA) at the impacted black schools invited the NAACP Legal Defense Fund to the area, and the NAACP lawyers agreed to represent the claimants but only if the group sued for the integration of Prince Edward County Schools—not equal facilities. Along with several similar cases from across the country, the Prince Edward County case became subsumed into one case, which collectively came to be known as Brown v. The Board of Education of Topeka, Kansas. The Brown decision was handed down in 1954, and soon afterwards schools in Prince Edward County Virginia closed, in a deliberate attempt to avoid forced integration. Some black students remained out of school for as long as 5 years. Both black and white fears about forced social integration of the races grew in the wake of cries for the dismantling of segregation.

The Supreme Court ruling in Brown overturned the long-standing precedent of "separate but equal" set in the 1896 case of Plessy v. Ferguson and threatened to dismantle the separate school systems prevalent throughout the South. Many Southern states were surprised by the decision and hailed the Court's ruling as interference with states' rights. News coverage of the case was carried across the nation. Almost a year prior to the decision, noted *Atlanta Constitution* publisher, Ralph McGill, cautioned the readers of his nationally syndicated column that "One Day it Will Be Monday."[24] Monday was the day the Supreme Court handed down its rulings, and McGill urged Southerners to consider peaceful integration or risk having it forced upon them. Among the largely staunch, conservative, white Southern power elite, McGill, referred to by outsiders as "the conscience of the South" was considered a radical,[25] and his position was

Sidebar 3.1

Brown v. Board of Education marks the first time social scientific evidence was used in a Supreme Court case. Two psychologists, Kenneth and Mamie Clark, provided expert testimony in the form of social scientific testimony that the system of 'separate but equal' engendered feelings of inferior status among African-Americans.

The Clarks conducted experiments on young African-Americans. These experiments came to be known as the doll experiments. In the doll experiments, students would be presented with various dolls. Some dolls had dark skin; some had white skin. Students were asked a series of questions about the dolls including which one was pretty, good, bad, ugly, etc. When asked which doll possessed positive attributes, many African-Americans chose the white doll over the black doll. The filmed results revealed some pain, which suggested that segregation had damaging effects on African-American children. A footnote in the majority decision in Brown evidences the import the Court placed on this social scientific evidence.

In subsequent years alternative explanations were posited for the Clarks' findings.

untenable. In many ways, McGill was practical in his realization that the Southern way of life, which had become code for segregation, separation, and degradation of blacks, could not remain forever. The Brown decision rocked the nation, but in truth, at the time of the Selma Movement some 11 years later, little had changed about the education, socialization, and integration of black children in the Alabama Black Belt. By 1965, even Southern states that remained resistant to integrated schools seemed resigned to the fact that federal government interference in such matters was certain.

The 1954 Brown decision marks a critical point in the knowledge-decision chain. Some jurisdictions implemented Brown; however, resistance to Brown, not its implementation, was the story the media followed most fervently. The dramatization of that resistance unfolded at Central High School in Little Rock, Arkansas. In *The Race Beat: The Press, the Civil Rights Struggle, and the Awakening of a Nation*, Roberts and Klibanoff write, "Little Rock was everyone's big story."[26] In 1957, when this story emerged, *The New York Times*, which had established a Southern bureau 6 years earlier, had a jump on all of the other newspapers and affiliates, and *The New York Times'* competitors scrambled to catch up with them.[27] But soon the media began to offer broader civil rights coverage. Again, this coverage, especially broadcast media coverage, had a great impact on some citizens. Years later, following the 1963 March on Washington, *The New York Times'* television critic, Jack Gould, would write, "[the] Drama of mass protests was brought to life in virtually every household in the nation, a social phenomenon inconceivable before the age of electronics . . . The gentle entrance and exit of so much petitioning humanity was an editorial in movement. Its eloquence could not be the same in only frozen word or still picture."[28]

So for years after the Brown decision, social discontent still remained. Everyone on various sides of the matter seemed sensitive to time. Moderates like McGill called for gradual change. Disenfranchised blacks called for change now, and the Alabama white power elite called for change "Never!" Even after Brown, the white power structure achieved some of its greatest successes at resisting black advancement by fighting racial integration in higher education. In the wake of rioting at the University of Alabama over African-American student Autherine Lucy's 1958 attempt to integrate the university, NAACP attorney Thurgood Marshall was asked if he thought a gradual approach to change was best. The future Supreme Court Justice responded, "The Emancipation Proclamation was issued in 1863—ninety odd years ago. I believe in gradualism, and I also believe that 90 odd years is pretty gradual."[29]

Additional segregation challenges followed Brown including the successful Montgomery Bus Boycott[30] and the 1960 Supreme Court ruling in Boynton v. Virginia declaring that segregation in interstate travel was illegal. These victories heightened hopes for widespread social change in American society, and in early 1961, the Congress on Race Equality (CORE) sought volunteers for the first Freedom Rides. The Freedom Riders were an integrated group of civil rights activists who rode interstate buses into areas of the segregated South in order to challenge the established social structure. Despite the advertisements' warnings of possible violence and prolonged incarceration, those eager to make a change responded.[31] On Mother's Day, May 14, 1961, just outside Anniston, Alabama, the promised violence materialized when one of the buses containing Freedom Riders was attacked and firebombed.[32] The Freedom Riders were met by more than a hundred Klansmen and attacked as they rushed off the bus to evade the flames.[33] Rumblings against non-violence began to grow in the wake of the attacks.

In many ways, the relationship between SNCC (formed in early 1960) and SCLC (formed in 1957) reflected the embodiment of the violence/non-violence debate. Some of the resistance to non-violence came not to the tactic as a philosophical policy, but to the appropriateness of the weapon in a battle where the toolbox of the enemy included violence, intimidation, and fear, but for others, non-violence made sense as a rational choice. Larry Isaac writes:

> A long tradition of self-defense, much more in tune with American culture, has been practiced for centuries in the black freedom struggle . . . While nonviolent activists in the movement would refrain from carrying guns, many still kept them in their homes. Even within what is often considered a classic period of the movement—1954 to 1965—typically characterized as a nonviolent monolith to movement at work in the South, there were important groups of grassroots citizens who armed themselves for self-defense as an alternative practice in the movement field.[34]

Similarly, SNCC member Annie Pearl Avery supported non-violence as a strategy, but often rejected personally embracing the philosophy. In fact, Avery indicates that she "never did attend a non-violence workshop."[35] Avery continues: "I came to adopt it [non-violence] as a tactic, a strategy to do because I thought it was worthwhile to get some things done, [so] I would go along with it. [But] every once and a while I'd backslide."[36] SCLC was largely a church-based organization run on Christian principles, and Christian doctrine teaches that when someone strikes you, you should turn the other cheek. African-American churches were the undisputed backbone of the black community as the church often served as its economic, political, educational, social, and civic center.[37] On the other hand, SNCC was a direct-action group which used a grassroots community approach to organizing. While SCLC focused on the black churches, SNCC leaders did dangerous organizing in communities throughout the Deep South. SNCC operated largely without media attention; SCLC's strategy was to use media attention. Together, the two organizations possessed great potential to reach most of the black community, and this made each group a threat to the Southern way of life.

Violence and unrest were erupting everywhere. On April 27, 1962, in Los Angeles there was an encounter outside a mosque between police and members of the Nation of Islam, which resulted in the death of a member of the mosque and the injury of several police officers and mosque members.[38] Later that year, on October 2, 1962, two people lost their lives during violent protests at the University of Mississippi by those opposing African-American student James Meredith's integration of the campus. The following year was also violent. On June 12, 1963, Medgar Evers, the popular and outspoken leader of NAACP in Jackson, Mississippi, was violently killed in front of his own home.[39] In *Parting the Waters: America in the King Years 1954–63*, author Taylor Branch reports: "The Evers murder came at the midpoint of a ten-week period after the Birmingham settlement when statisticians counted 758 racial demonstrations and 14,733 arrests in 186 American cities."[40] Later that year, on

November 22, President John F. Kennedy, the reluctant champion of the civil rights campaign, was gunned down while riding in a motorcade in Dallas, Texas. The violence and riots unearthed a symbiotic relationship between the rebellions and riots in the northern part of the nation and the social unrest in the South.[41]

Violence continued throughout 1964. Riots broke out in locations which included New York, New Jersey, Chicago, and Philadelphia. Northern blacks were upset about rising police brutality, employment segregation, housing discrimination, and the micro-aggressions that readily became ingrained into the fabric of Northern social relationships. Media attention focused on the inequities being suffered by Southern blacks, but little coverage addressed the fact that Northern blacks were suffering too. In each city, black residents living in largely segregated and crowded areas alleged police brutality, and on July 18, 1964, a 15-year-old black youth named James Powell was shot in Harlem by a white, off-duty police officer.[42] Eight thousand took to the streets. Fires were set, businesses looted, and windows broken. The rioting went on for 6 days, and it spread to the nearby Bedford Stuyvesant neighborhood.[43] As the unrest in Harlem and Bedford Stuyvesant began to die down, a new allegation of police brutality by a white police officer against a black person emerged in Rochester, New York. After 3 days, Governor Nelson Rockefeller called in the National Guard to quell the violence.

White backlash against black boldness mounted. Manifestations of this backlash included growing Senate opposition to pending civil rights legislation and burgeoning affiliation with white separatist groups. The same was true on the state level where on Independence Day 1964 Governor George Wallace traveled to Atlanta to join leaders from across the South in a rally in support of segregation.[44] The rally was an official event sponsored by the Grand Wizards of the Ku Klux Klan.[45]

The year of 1965 was equally full of social unrest. In early February, Malcolm X came to Selma and addressed a crowd at a mass meeting, but by February 21, 1965, the former leader of the Nation of Islam had been assassinated in Harlem. Five days later, Jimmie Lee Jackson died from injuries he received protecting his grandmother at a peaceful protest march in Marion, Alabama, held on February 18, 1965. The events of Bloody Sunday happened so soon after the deaths of Malcolm X and Jackson that black America did not have a chance to fully recover. Then, on the evening of Turnaround Tuesday, three white pastors who answered Martin Luther King Jr.'s call for those who loved peace to come to Selma, were violently assaulted there. James Reeb, one of the pastors, was repeatedly clubbed in the head. On March 11, 1965, Reeb died from head injuries he sustained in the beating. In stark contrast to the killing of Jimmie Lee Jackson, the nation mourned the death of James Reeb, which President Johnson called "an American tragedy."

The enumerated events and others not listed on these pages served to fuel social unrest across the nation. Once unleashed, that unrest could not be placated, even by the success of the March. In fact, despite the successful Selma to Montgomery March and subsequent passage of the Act, riots broke out in Watts just 10 days after President Johnson signed the Act; and rioting continued from August 11, 1965 through August 16, 1965. Then from July of 1964 through to March of 1968, rebellions erupted in a dozen major U.S. cities, including Watts, Newark, New York, and Detroit. These cities, largely populated by blacks, were burning.

POLITICAL/LEGAL PORTRAIT OF A NATION

During the period under examination, the social, political/legal, and economic structures of the nation acted as what sociologist Patricia Hill Collins terms "overlapping vectors of oppression." Disentanglement from the oppression required the dismantling of the separate, but related, structures. In addition to threatening the Southern social structure, Brown threatened the Southern political/legal structure, and while federal actions continued in the late 1950s, Southern resistance did, too. In 1957, President Eisenhower signed the Civil Rights Act of 1957. Southerners viewed this federal action negatively, and they cried out against perceived federal interference into state affairs.[46] Eisenhower's 1957 Civil Rights Act was "the first civil rights bill in 82 years" and gave precedent to federal intervention in civil rights matters.[47] As proposed, one of the aims of the 1957 Act was to increase the number of registered black voters, but opposition (largely from Southern senators) resulted in passage of a diluted version of the Act without the voting provisions.[48] Domestic matters continued to occupy President Eisenhower's attention throughout 1958 too. When Arkansas Governor Orval Faubus mobilized the National Guard of his state and used them to block the integration of Central High School in Little Rock, Eisenhower was forced to squarely confront civil rights issues. Amid Southern resistance, new federal civil rights legislation was introduced that year; however, it was not passed until 1960 when both parties were trying to cultivate the black vote.[49] Once passed, the Civil Rights Act of 1960 created the U.S. Civil Rights Commission and the Civil Rights Division of the Justice Department, and it instituted penalties for interference with anyone's attempt to vote or register to vote. As such, these acts were necessary precursors to providing protection for the black franchise.

The year that leaders in the American sit-in movement organized the Student Non-Violent Coordinating Committee (SNCC), 1960, was also the year of African liberation; countries including Zaire, Somalia, Dahomey, Upper Volta, Ivory Coast, Chad, Congo, Brazzaville, Gabon, Senegal, Mali, and Nigeria all gained independence from their European colonizers.[50] Algeria was engaged in a violent revolution. The anti-colonial struggle there began in 1954 and ended in 1962. French-Algerian author and psychiatrist Frantz Fanon wrote *The Wretched of the Earth* at the height of the conflict; in the book Fanon argues that only violence could bring about decolonization. In many ways, the Southern social structure served to effectively colonize African-Americans. President Sekou Toure of Guinea made the connection between the struggle of blacks in America for civil rights and the liberation struggles being fought by people of color in Africa. Toure said, "It is fundamental that you see the problem as exploitation . . . it is the entire [black] community that must be liberated."[51] Suddenly, SNCC members were beginning to see their plight as related to the condition of people of color across the globe and to align themselves with their causes. Then, in 1964, Harry Belafonte hosted a number of SNCC volunteers and Fannie Lou Hamer on a trip to Guinea, and the entourage was impacted greatly by the trip.[52] Ms. Hamer, who helped SNCC organize Freedom Summer and would become the vice-chair of the MFDP, argued that blacks visiting countries where other blacks run the government and industry was psychologically liberating.[53] James Forman said, "We went to Africa, we were broadening our struggle, we were going to become revolutionaries of the world."[54] The African freedom struggles inspired many African-Americans that the time was right for the liberation of people of color in America.[55] But in the U.S. the legal battle over segregation was being waged not only in the courts, but also in the hearts and minds of people.

Despite marked public Southern resistance, evidence was also mounting which suggested shifting Southern attitudes among some. The NAACP Legal Defense and Educational Fund had already mounted a legal attack on the system known as Jim Crow and begun to chip away at its foundation, and on January 11, 1961, administrators at the University of Georgia elected to follow a federal court order to admit "two Negroes"— Charlayne Hunter and Hamilton Holmes. A riot broke out at the university. Years earlier, a similar riot occurred when Autherine Lucy attempted to integrate the University of Alabama, and the school dismissed her, citing its inability to keep her safe.[56] Perhaps concerned that a similar fate would fall to Hunter and Holmes, a majority of the faculty at the University of Georgia signed a resolution calling for the students' admission to the university and condemning the violence.

One lesson that Brown unveiled is that, while many white Southerners might not be radically opposed to change, a number did oppose radical change; this was especially true regarding ending segregation and increasing black voting power. In early 1963, Bernard Lafayette, a member of SNCC, came to Selma to help strengthen the existing voting rights campaign there. In the 2 years that Bernard Lafayette and his wife were in Dallas County, 100 new black voters were added to the roll, and 2 years later, 2.2 percent of blacks in Dallas County were registered to vote; however, there were no registered black voters in nearby Lowndes or Wilcox counties.[57] The voter registration system in Alabama implicitly required the consent of the white power elite, and this had a chilling effect on black voting patterns. In addition to intimidation, applicants were discouraged from registering to vote, through the employment of restrictive hurdles such as limited registration days, the requirement to fill out an extensive voter application, literacy tests (of which there were over 100 versions), and the requirement to get someone to vouch for them. Excepting Mississippi, no state had a lower percentage of black voters on the registration rolls than Alabama.[58]

The year of 1963 proved to be a year of violence, and that violence often seemed to be a direct response to civil rights legal/political victories. After an almost 2-year silence on civil rights, President Kennedy announced his civil rights bill in a speech he delivered on June 11, 1963.[59] A few hours later, Medgar Evers was assassinated outside his home in Jackson, Mississippi. The remainder of the year would prove equally violent including the use of fire hoses against non-violent activists in Kelly Ingram Park in Birmingham, the 1963 Freedom Vote campaign in Mississippi, the bombing of Sixteenth Street Baptist Church in Birmingham and the subsequent killing of four girls. The year would conclude with the assassination of President Kennedy, on November 22, 1963.

While each black victory in the struggle often met with resistance, the threat of resistance did not stop the quest for freedom. By now, the parallels between the African liberation movement and the black freedom struggle were growing increasingly apparent, especially to members of SNCC, and while SNCC was globalizing the black freedom struggle, the Southern tactic was to localize it. These attempts at localization ardently argued that the federal government had no business interfering in affairs of individual states. One legal tactic Southern states used to make this argument was the doctrine of "states rights," a twist on the Tenth Amendment grant of authority to states.[60] States rights became code for the right of states to continue to impose racial segregation laws on their citizens, even when those laws were in contravention of the federal law. As part of the federal system of checks and balances, the doctrine of interposition allowed states to declare federal laws an invalid encroachment

Sidebar 3.2

The text of the Tenth Amendment states, "The powers not delegated to the United States by the Constitution, nor prohibited by it to the States, are reserved to the States respectively, or to the people."

In a traditional sense, we think of separation of powers as the division between the legislative, judicial, and executive branches of government; however, the Tenth Amendment addresses the important issue of the powers delegated to the federal government and those delegated to the states. During the Civil War, the issue of states' rights became a rallying cry among the Confederate territories that, prior to secession, argued for a weaker federal government and more state power/control.

on states' rights, and nullification allowed states to nullify or invalidate the federal mandate.[61] In an attempt to evade any race-related Supreme Court rulings with which they did not agree, Southern states including Virginia, Georgia, Mississippi, Alabama, and South Carolina adopted state resolutions of interposition and nullification.[62] King exposed this Southern tactic in his August 28, 1963 "I Have a Dream" speech delivered at the March on Washington. The legal maneuverings under these doctrines masked covert attempts to evade compliance with the law of the land and maintain the status quo.

For much of 1964, the attention of the nation and the world would focus on Mississippi. That summer, the bodies of Chaney, Goodman, and Schwerner, the three murdered civil rights activists, were found in Mississippi, and this heightened the call for legal protection for the black franchise. On Memorial Day of 1964, Schwerner addressed a crowd at Mount Zion Methodist Church in Philadelphia, Mississippi. He urged "the congregation of some 50 black men, women, and children to take the initial step towards achieving equal rights with white people by registering to vote."[63] Schwerner said, "you have been slaves too long. . . . We can help you help yourselves. . . . Meet us here, and we'll train you so you can qualify to vote." The civil rights workers were part of the Mississippi Freedom Summer project. This project had multiple foci: voter registration, literacy training, and the promotion of the MFDP, founded on April 26,

King specifically mentions Alabama in his "I Have a Dream" speech. He says, ". . . down in Alabama . . . with its governor [George Wallace] having his lips dripping with the words of interposition and nullification."

1964.[64] The three disappeared on June 21, 1964; their bodies were found 44 days later after an extensive search that consumed the attention of the nation. Spurred partly by the disappearance of Chaney, Goodman, and Schwerner, President Johnson signed the 1964 Civil Rights Act on July 2, 1964. Although Title I of the 1964 Act barred unequal application of voter registration standards, the legislation passed by substantially evading the issue of voting rights protection.[65] Southern conservatives relished that limited legal victory and reaffirmed their resolve to block African-American advances, especially in voting.

Black demands for equality were growing more insistent and more varied. MFDP sought not only to register blacks to vote, but to provide an alternative to the Democratic Party and elect black candidates. Blacks were shut out of the Mississippi Democratic Party meetings, and COFO (the Council of Federated Organizations, a coalition of the major civil rights organizations) and the spin-off MFDP sought to change that. The MFDP was open to blacks and whites. The group rose to national prominence late in 1964 when it attempted to unseat the all-white Mississippi Democratic Party delegation at the Democratic National Convention. Although the MFDP was unsuccessful in its attempts to unseat the delegates, through the use of media outlets its co-chair, Fannie Lou Hamer, brought the plight of millions of disfranchised blacks to the nation.[66] Using her plain-spoken way and endearing manner, Hamer recounted the specific details of her jailing, and the general violent response to attempts by blacks in Mississippi to register to vote, in her testimony before the Credentials Committee at the Democratic National Convention in Atlantic City in August 1964.[67] Her "televised" testimony influenced many viewers.[68]

Civil rights groups were hopeful that the presidential election would bring meaningful changes for blacks, and so in the summer of 1964, several civil rights organizations, including CORE, NAACP, LDF, SCLC, SNCC and the Urban League met to discuss the upcoming election.[69] Relations between the groups were strained. Multiple reasons can be proffered for the tension: jealousy between groups, a desire on the part of all to lead, and growing philosophical differences among the groups, especially SNCC which developed largely as a counter to the other groups. At this meeting, Roy Wilkins of NAACP proposed a moratorium on demonstrations.[70] There were several motivations behind the proposed moratorium. Wilkins and others feared that more demonstrations would get the conservative Republican candidate, Barry Goldwater, elected.[71] The Democratic Party had also threatened to discontinue its voter registration funding unless a moratorium on demonstrations was instituted until after the presidential election.[72] SNCC refused to agree to the détente; however, the organization's name was still listed as complying.[73]

Figure 3.1 On June 11, 1963, Alabama Governor George Wallace faces Assistant U.S. Attorney General Nicholas Katzenbach and stands "defiantly" in the schoolhouse door in an attempt to block the integration of the University of Alabama. Wallace's stance thrust him to national prominence and was the fulfillment of a campaign promise made by Wallace to block integration at the university. The stance, however, was largely symbolic as, soon after reading his proclamation declaring the sovereignty of the state of Alabama, Wallace returned to Montgomery, Alabama, and effectively opened the door for federal troops to escort the two black students (Vivian Malone and James Hood) into the building where they would both register for classes.

Source: Library of Congress, Prints and Photographs Division, NYWT&S Collection, [LC-DIG-ppmsca-04294].

Additionally, after the public deaths of Chaney, Goodman, and Schwerner, the same coalition group urged SNCC to end the Mississippi Freedom Summer project. By this time, SNCC was used to being disrespected by the other groups.[74]

During this period, several local segregationists would rise in power; some would earn national fame. George Wallace served in the Alabama State Legislature from 1947 to 1953. He would later serve as governor of the state of Alabama, and run in the presidential election of 1968. During Wallace's time in the state legislature, he was often described as a "political moderate," even on race relations, but that changed after Wallace lost his 1958 bid for governor to John Patterson.[75] The 1958 Alabama gubernatorial campaign occurred less than a year after the successful Montgomery Bus Boycott, and conservative Alabama whites were eager to preserve their Southern "way of life," which meant maintaining segregation and keeping blacks in their place. Patterson not only won his bid against Wallace for governor, he won by a large margin, and this stunning public defeat haunted Wallace.[76] Describing the loss, George Wallace is often quoted as saying, "I was out-niggered by John Patterson. And I'll tell you here and now, I will never be out-niggered again."[77] Patterson was endorsed by the Ku Klux Klan, and he campaigned on a promise to make race (specifically maintaining segregation) a front issue. Among other groups, one of Wallace's 1958 endorsements came from the Alabama NAACP.[78]

The Alabama Constitution prevented Patterson from running for a second term. George Wallace seized this opportunity and ran for the nomination, unveiling his new, modified conservative stance on race. In his January 13, 1963, inaugural speech, Wallace pledged to fight the specter of "tyranny," which Southern and Northern audiences alike read as code

Figure 3.2 Sheriff Jim Clark was determined not only to keep order in Selma, Alabama, but to maintain the status quo. His image—military style dress, billy club, cattle-prod, "Never" button, and gun—demanded attention.

Source: Library of Congress, Prints and Photographs Division, NYWT&S Collection, [LC-USZ62-135700].

for federal government interference in the matters of Southern states, and he triumphantly asserted, "segregation now, segregation tomorrow, segregation forever" would be the law of the land in Alabama.[79]

Along with George Wallace, Sheriff Jim Clark was another enigmatic figure of this time. Jim Clark was a portly man with a large belly who stood watching outside all SNCC and Dallas County Improvement Association (DCIA) meetings. According to Forman, many of those in the Movement called him "Big Belly Jim Clark."[80] Clark stood 6 feet tall. In 1965, he was 42 years old. Clark's image personified authority. In fact, after his death, an obituary in *The Economist* stated, "Clark dressed like a soldier."[81] He wore a sheriff's shirt and matching trousers, tie, and silver helmet. Clark wore a black leather belt around his waist with a .38 clipped to it. Additional accouterments included a nightstick, rope, and cattle prodder. Most days, two additional items adorned his shirt: his Sheriff's star pin and a white button with the word "Never!" written on it in black. Most of Clark's posse, many of which were members of the White Citizens' Council, dressed similarly: they wore army fatigues, carried ropes, cattle prods, and guns, and rode horses.[82]

Sociologist Erving Goffman discusses the idea of impression management. At its core, this symbolic interactionist perspective argues that people use symbols in order to convey ideas about themselves and thereby manage others' impressions of them. An individual's self-presentation not only manages how others view him or her; his or her presentation of self also influences how others act, interact, and react to the person. Sheriff Jim Clark's presentation of self and his very manner of comportment conveyed authority. Additionally, his cattle prod and gun were intimidating

---

Sidebar 3.3

Impression management is a micro-level sociological theory. It helps us to understand the process people go through to manage and control other people's perceptions about them.

Consider the choices you make in any given day—What will you wear? How will you comb your hair? Will you comb your hair?—Think about how those choices impact how other people perceive you, deal with you, or avoid you.

This theory suggests that an individual's self-presentation will influence how other people act, react, and interact with him/her. Based upon his dress, one may surmise what impression Sheriff Clark was trying to communicate.

regular accouterments, affecting how others might respond to him and how he intended for others to view him. By the mid-1960s, media coverage of civil rights conflicts was becoming increasingly common so there was also the question of how Sheriff Clark's image came across on national television.

By early 1965, the eyes of the nation were on Alabama, and it became clear that the battle for black voting rights protection would be waged in Alabama, not Mississippi. The legal groundwork for the battle had already been laid when, in 1961 and 1963, the Department of Justice filed two separate voting rights lawsuits for alleged infringements in the state.[83] Despite cries for voting rights legislation, President Johnson was moving slowly. He wanted to give the Southern states a chance to get used to the provisions of the 1964 Civil Rights Act, which included the formation of the Equal Employment Opportunity Commission.

ECONOMIC PORTRAIT OF A NATION

As the section on the legal/political portrait of a nation establishes, Southern conservatives began to combat civil rights court victories with legal maneuverings of their own. This coercive climate caused pressure to build. Now, the group perhaps most oppressed—poor, Black Belt, African-Americans—were willing to stand up and demand the franchise.[84] The bold act of these everyday people was certain to invite attack, yet they did it anyway.

Southern blacks constantly lived with the threat of violence, including economic, psychological, and physical backlash for any real, perceived, or fictitious affront against the social order, but in the post-Brown era, the oppressor's toolbox grew more complex. The Ku Klux Klan still perpetrated a great deal of the physical and psychological intimidation against blacks, but soon White Citizens' Councils emerged. Like the Ku Klux Klan, the White Citizens' Councils (later known as the Citizens' Councils of America) were equally devoted to maintaining the social separation of the races, but the latter group combated integration through more sophisticated means. Many Citizens' Councils followed the motto: "Why burn a cross when you can foreclose a mortgage?"[85]

Economic intimidation was one of the Councils' most effective tools, yet in spite of repression, segments of the black community in Selma and the surrounding Black Belt were willing to risk their personal liberty and fight for the right to vote. In the months prior to the March, White Citizens' Councils in the area sought to appeal to "the rest" of the black population of the area, and they published a full-page advertisement in

The Selma Times Journal, which read, "What have you done to maintain segregation?" About 3 months later, a more pointed advertisement appeared.[86] The second notice ran September 22, 1963, and it bore the names and institutional affiliations of its signatories. The header of this advertisement read, "A Declaration of Basic Human Rights and Principles." The second advertisement said the white population urges "reasonable" blacks to stop all the "outside agitators."[87] The use of the institutional affiliations was itself a form of economic intimidation.

In the wake of Brown, White Citizens' Councils determined to "make it difficult, if not impossible, for any Negro who advocates desegregation to find and hold a job, get credit, or renew a mortgage,"[88] but while individuals and groups such as the White Citizens' Councils employed financial means to maintain white domination over blacks, sometimes blacks effectively wielded this tool to combat black oppression and compel social change.[89] Economic pressure faced by the bus company and the downtown businesses in Montgomery brought the boycott to a successful close and compelled city officials to offer concessions.[90] Negative press surrounding the city's treatment of the Freedom Riders threated to harm economic development in Birmingham, Alabama's largest city.[91] But while financial pressure was effective, it came at a price. Medgar Evers' involvement in the successful boycott of businesses in Jackson, Mississippi, contributed to his death.[92]

Southern economic lack had an extensive history, and part of white Southern resistance to advancements for blacks stemmed from the fact that white members of the long economically disadvantaged South were scant willing to give up their relative position of advantage over African-Americans. Prior to the Civil War, most of the Southern wealth was attributable to slave ownership and slave labor, but despite the bounty of the land's promise, in the 1960s many Southern states had not regained the economic footing they retained prior to the war. Despite "Lost Cause" rhetoric touting the South's cause as noble and just, the shadow of war still loomed large. One hundred years later the words spoken by President Abraham Lincoln in his second inaugural address still seemed relevant:

> If we shall suppose that American Slavery is one of those
> offenses which, in the providence of God, must needs come, but
> which, having continued through His appointed time, He now
> wills to remove, and that He gives to both North and South, this
> terrible war, as the woe due to those by whom the offense came,
> shall we discern therein any departure from those divine
> attributes which the believers in a Living God always ascribe to
> Him? Fondly do we hope — fervently do we pray — that this

mighty scourge of war may speedily pass away. *Yet, if God wills that it continue, until all the wealth piled by the bond-man's two hundred and fifty years of unrequited toil shall be sunk* [emphasis added], and until every drop of blood drawn with the lash, shall be paid by another drawn with the sword, as was said three thousand years ago, so still it must be said "the judgments of the Lord, are true and righteous altogether."[93]

Lincoln's words seem to predict an economic devastation of sorts and suggest that this dearth may provide needed cathartic cleansing of the land, but the quote speaks of blood, too, and perhaps the blood of Bloody Sunday could provide that balm.

By the winter of 1963, white economic intimidation tactics in Greenwood, Mississippi, debased to the point where the white power structure there was willing to deny even base subsistence to those least able to defend themselves.[94] Poor people in the Mississippi Delta, many of whom were sharecroppers, did not have enough food to feed their families, and in the winter they routinely relied on federal assistance.[95] Citing excessive administrative costs, the Leflore County Board of Supervisors voted to discontinue food assistance for anyone not on welfare.[96] While the sharecroppers were poor, their labor as sharecroppers kept them from the welfare rolls. This action was taken in the summer of 1962 by a Board that was largely controlled by members of the area's White Citizens' Council.[97] By the winter of 1963, many families were starving, and initiatives to feed this population were literally blocked. In *Local People: The Struggle for Civil Rights in Mississippi*, John Dittmer writes:

> Among the first to respond were Ivanhoe Donaldson and Ben Taylor, black students at Michigan State University, who drove a truckload of food, clothing, and medicine down to the Delta during Christmas week. The two students were arrested in Clarksdale and charged with possession of narcotics; their cargo was confiscated. The "narcotics" were aspirin and vitamins.[98]

Eventually, relief did pour into Greenwood,[99] but the need was great, and it was difficult to insure that those with real needs were serviced. Ironically, the inhumanity of the Greenwood Food Blockade served to strengthen the resolve of the local people in Mississippi to be free of white tyranny and economic oppression. The vote became the symbolic proxy for freedom. Dittmer writes, "local people who pitched in to help with the distribution effort stayed on to become involved in the voter registration campaign."[100]

In the documentary *So the Whole World Could See*, filmmaker Harvey Richards films the efforts of SNCC volunteers, including James Forman, working on voter registration in the Mississippi Delta. By Mississippi Freedom Summer (1964), SNCC could rely on a dedicated cadre of local people, including the audacious Fannie Lou Hamer, as well as a steady stream of college students from various parts of the country.

Employment opportunities for blacks in the Mississippi Delta were severely constrained, but even in areas with relatively more industry, blacks faced employment segregation. That was the case in Danville, Virginia. Danville was a tobacco town on the border of North Carolina that had a black population of approximately 33 percent, but all blacks in the town were kept out of mill work, the most economically viable work in the area.[101] In the summer of 1963, residents of Danville held regular protests seeking desegregation of public facilities (including schools) and equal employment opportunities. The response in Danville was similar to the response in Birmingham, Alabama, which was happening almost simultaneously—mass jailings and fire hoses were used to dissuade the protestors.[102] Cries for equal access to employment in places like Danville, Virginia, become incorporated into provisions of the Civil Rights Act of 1964, but voting rights protection did not.

While in a Black Belt county, Selma was also the county seat of Dallas County, Alabama, and it had the distinction of having a relatively strong economy. The U.S. Air Force had a base just outside Selma, and in the early 1960s, it had a monthly payroll in excess of $600,000.[103] Most servicemen spent their money with Selma businesses, so, effectively, the U.S. government substantially supported Selma's businesses.[104] On June 7, 1963, the U.S. Secretary of Defense issued a directive stating that the Department of Defense would not tolerate racially discriminatory practices, but such policies were practiced by numerous Selma businesses. Additionally, black servicemen were not admitted to the USO (United Service Organizations) in Selma. SNCC officials in Dallas County asked the commander of Craig Air Force Base to ban his soldiers from shopping in Selma. When the local commander denied the request, SNCC Field Secretary Worth Long appealed to Washington. Both requests were denied.[105] Unfazed by this defeat, James Forman, Worth Long, and courageous Black Belt residents continued to resist the status quo. They staged lunch counter protests and marches, and they were arrested and beaten. Selma became "an important center of resistance."[106] On September 25, 1963, comedian and activist Dick Gregory

Craig Air Force Base was closed in 1977. It now operates as a civilian airport for nearby Selma.

came out to support the protestors. Later, author James Baldwin joined the students. Forman writes, "We needed a psychological victory—for the brave people who had already stuck out their necks, for the skeptical blacks in town and for ourselves—the organizers."[107] That "psychological victory" came in the form of "Freedom Day," which was held on October 7, 1963.

Historian Howard Zinn describes Freedom Day in an October 26, 1963, *New Republic* article.[108] Freedom Day was planned to correspond with one of the two days a month when the county courthouse was open for applicants to register to vote.[109] The event's slogan was "Freedom Now," and courageous African-Americans lined the street and stood in line to register to vote. According to Zinn's account, some "250 Negroes" stood in line while Clark and his posse "loomed" over them.[110] Sheriff Clark employed an intimidation tactic he developed early in the history of the Selma Movement. Clark had photographers take pictures of those in line, and he would regularly walk up to black applicants trying to register to vote and ask, "Does your employer know you're here?"[111] This question was a thinly veiled economic threat.

In the midst of this harassment and intimidation, Zinn reports that Justice Department men charged with the task of protecting the protestors were across the street in the Federal Building just taking their own pictures and watching.[112] The lines began to form at 8:30 a.m., and by noon over 300 "Negroes" were in line. Close to noon, Sheriff Clark confiscated all protest signs and arrested those carrying them. The signs bore various slogans including "Register to Vote" and "Vote Now for Freedom Now." The applicants stood in line from 8:30 a.m. to 4:30 p.m. without the benefit of food or drink.[113] In fact, anyone who attempted to bring the registrants food or drink was arrested.[114] Two SNCC members, Chico Neblett and Avery Williams, were attacked and arrested for their attempt.

Clark, the White Citizens' Council in Selma, and radical groups like the Ku Klux Klan, sought to contain early gains made by the Selma Movement, but momentum was building. According to Seeger and Reiser,

> In 1963, when Bernard and Colia Lafayette began a SNCC registration drive in Selma, fifteen thousand black adults were working and raising families there, but only 153 could vote . . . [however;] By September 1963, 2000 people went to the courthouse, [and] six hundred actually got registered.[115]

February 1, 1965, marked the fifth anniversary of the Greensboro sit-ins. More marches continued. In Perry County, Alabama, a local farmer, Albert Turner, led a Freedom Day. Others followed. Those who stood in line on Freedom Day showed real conviction and unity of purpose. Forman says,

> There would be other events called Freedom Day in various parts of the South, but there would never be one like that Freedom Day: the day when a century of Southern fear and terror—of night-riding Klansman, of the smooth talking but equally murderous, White Citizens' Councils, of vicious George Wallaces—when all these forces had not been able to stop the forward thrust of a people determined by any means necessary to be free.[116]

These freedom days were devoted to complete freedom from white subjugation in social, legal/political, and economic matters.

Conclusion: A Movement is Born

Despite opposition in Congress, the Civil Rights Act of 1964 was passed in November of that year, and leading civil rights groups made voting rights their primary focus. SCLC had long been committed to a voting rights campaign, but defeats in Albany and St. Augustine meant King could ill afford not to choose the next location wisely. The momentum of the whole Movement was at stake. After much debate, SCLC agreed to make Selma the location of its next direct action, and for voting rights to be the campaign's focus, but SCLC's presence and new commitment to Selma was met with mixed feelings, especially by SNCC.[117] Although each group was committed to voting rights for blacks, relations between SNCC and SCLC had grown increasingly tense.[118] There had long been disagreements over money, but the roots ran much deeper now. To many in the nation, Martin Luther King Jr. was the face of the Movement, but numerous SNCC personnel were openly distrustful of SCLC and, to a lesser extent, non-violence[119] as a tactic. The SCLC pattern of coming to a town, drawing publicity, and leaving had become all too familiar to SNCC. For their own safety and that of others, SNCC leaders often went covertly into areas of the Deep South to organize. This was a strategic and con-scientious choice that SNCC employed in order to protect the safety of local residents. For that reason, SNCC workers often shunned the kind of publicity King actively sought. So each group had the same ultimate goals, but they employed radically different tactics in order to achieve the communally desired end result. Additionally, for years, local leaders in Selma had been asking King to come into the area.[120] Now King agreed, but this was 2 years after SNCC had been hard at work in the extended

Alabama Black Belt region. It seemed likely that King would get credit for the work SNCC did, which itself was built on the foundation of the efforts of local people and groups. Still, as one SNCC worker stated effectively, it was clear that "[there was] a movement going on in Selma."

The Selma campaign had antecedent roots that went back for decades, but the Movement gained momentum in the wake of the social, political/legal, and economic unrest outlined. The threat of sanction was still great, but now each act of white aggression seemed to fuel black activism. By early 1965, a modified version of Diane Nash's direct action plan for Alabama was in place, and while the Vietnam War consumed President Johnson's attention, the attention of the nation was shifting to the Alabama Black Belt. This attention compelled President Johnson to act. In February 1965, President Johnson, a powerful change agent, issued a statement in defense of black voting rights.[121] This thrust the black voting struggle into a national limelight that it would not relinquish until passage of the Act.

Knowledge is the crucial first element in the decision-innovation process, and the heightened accessibility of information about the black freedom struggle available post-Brown from various sources significantly increased the chances of adoption of the innovation. The decade prior to the March saw the nation embroiled in conflict, and this conflict unfolded on the pages of national magazines, local newspapers, and television. The coverage exposed countless people to knowledge about the social innovation, and it fueled discussions about the condition of African-Americans, especially those in the Deep South. The direct action campaigns of organizations such as SNCC, SCLC, CORE, and others helped keep the social innovation in front of the public. By the time the events of Bloody Sunday occurred, many media observers were persuaded that the time for change had come.

CHAPTER 4

Everyday People

> *One day the South will recognize its real heroes.*
> *Dr. Martin Luther King Jr.*

It takes people to sustain a movement, and while the media is an important communication channel for the dissemination of information, as individual actors move from knowledge to persuasion to decision, interpersonal communication channels are most important.[1] This proposition supports Rogers' claims and is echoed over and over again in participants' discussions of their sustained involvement in the Movement. The decision-making process is social in nature, and more often than not Movement participants indicate that personal relationships and individuals, rather than the media, impacted their decision. Parents influenced children, children influenced parents, teachers influenced students, students influenced teachers, parishioners influenced clergy, clergy influenced parishioners, friends influenced friends, and the music influenced everyone. The narratives of those involved make it clear that this was not a children's movement, this was not a church movement, and this was not a movement of the elite or the downtrodden. This was a people's movement—everyday people. This chapter utilizes personal interviews and archival research to explain how support for the social movement under study and the ideological values it maintained gained growing acceptance in society through the efforts of everyday people (change agents) who communicated their personal support for the Movement to other individuals in their social network.

Many new ideas get diffused into the larger society through successful social movements. Tilly defines a social movement as "a substantial series of interactions between power holders and persons successfully claiming to speak on behalf of a constituency lacking formal representation, in the course of which those persons make publicly visible demands for changes in the distribution or exercise of power, and back those demands with public demonstrations of support."[2] Tilly's definition makes it clear that social movements require collectivities of people, and while the collective comprises individuals, it is the collective—not the individual—that compels social change. Social movements usher in change through a process that includes both interpersonal (face-to-face) communication channels and mass media channels.[3] This chapter focuses on the role of individuals in the decision process; however, because social persuasion is also involved, attention is paid to collectivities as well. When social protests are covered by the mass media, opinion leaders in organizations (such as pastors, principals, labor leaders, elected officials, presidents of clubs and auxiliaries, etc.) may use their personal influence to convey (and perhaps spin) the media message to their followers. In this process, organizations serve an intermediate function and provide formal structures for networks, avenues for communication. Organizations are important, but while Tilly's focus on collectivities is understandable, the supreme irony is that the definition pays little attention to the fact that each collectivity comprises individuals—many of whom are just everyday people who carry the message of social change to other everyday people. SNCC member Ruby Nell Sales outlines this process:

> Day to day we [SNCC members] would go around and knock on doors and talk with people . . . [We] were fully engaged because the community was engaged, and you could be walking down the street and someone would say, "Here comes a freedom fighter." . . . [I]t wasn't that kind of missionary style leadership. What was more important was engagement with people . . . So that often times what was more important than what you said to people was just to be present. To be there.[4]

Ruby Sales and countless, nameless others were there throughout the Alabama Black Belt and Southern region, and their presence made a difference by helping to bring about social change. This chapter outlines the process of social change in the Selma Movement and highlights the everyday people who helped to bring about that shift; it also highlights the important role of social institutions such as the family, school, and religion in the decision chain.

Teach Your Children Well

According to Social Learning Theory, children tend to imitate behavior they see; however, they only adopt those behaviors that are positively reinforced by others, such as parents.[5] Parents are a child's first teacher, and although learning in the family unit does not occur through a formal process, it is influential. Respondents' comments illustrate that many of them adopted their positive attitudes about participation in the Movement based upon the support and example of their parents. In this manner, even before (or in the absence of) mass media coverage of the African-American freedom struggle, parents and even ancestors served as an important source of knowledge about the Movement, which enabled children to move to the decision phase. Respondents describe a dynamic where the black community—school, church, home—formed a counter-culture way of life where children effectively learned the simultaneous acts of accommodation and resistance. Ruby Sales describes growing up in that counter-culture, specifically the black church. Sales states:

> Religion . . . was the ground that I stood on . . . [it] positioned us
> to stand against the wind. The winds of segregation, the winds of
> a society that by its very nature conspired to render us very, very
> small, and religion was the place that you stood . . . It moved us.
> It gave us hope. It was the repository of Black memory in a
> society that did not give us access to secular history. So it was in
> religion it was in the songs that were our memory, where you
> could go back and be connected to another generation . . . It is in
> that moment through song ["Way Down Yonder in the Valley So
> Low I Couldn't Hear Nobody Pray"] that I am able to feel
> something other than myself. I become a part of a community. I
> become a part of a struggle. Also listening to that song I thought,
> you know, freedom is a constant struggle.[6]

At later times during the freedom struggle Sales would question her faith, but reflecting on her upbringing in the black community she describes religion as something that connected her to the larger African community, which gave her both roots and wings. First and foremost, in the family unit Sales and those in her community learned how to survive, but they learned how to do so with a dignity that hundreds of years of slavery tried to eradicate from them, but could not.

The family may be a child's first teacher, but it is neither an uncomplicated educator nor a young person's only guide. As children grow, their relationship with their parents becomes more complex. Good parents want to keep their children safe, and yet they want them to grow strong and develop all the qualities necessary to take care of themselves; at times, these two objectives seem diametrically opposed. The duality Ruby Nell Sales outlines in her quote above illustrates the complexity and

Sidebar 4.1

W.E.B. DuBois was born in 1868, just a few years after the end of slavery. This noted African-American scholar was the first black to receive a PhD from Harvard.

DuBois was one of the founders of NAACP. He also taught at Atlanta University in Atlanta, Georgia, where he influenced countless new black scholars.

In his 1903 book, *The Souls of Black Folk*, DuBois prophetically writes, "The problem of the twentieth century is the problem of the color-line." His influence still resonates today, and, citing DuBois, many scholars argue that the problem of the twenty-first century continues to be the problem of the color-line.

sheer practicality of the conflicting lessons black parents instilled in their children. The culture Ruby Nell Sales describes is reminiscent of what noted African-American sociologist and scholar W.E.B. DuBois describes as "double consciousness."[7]

Ruby Nell Sales

In addition to her family, places had a profound impact on SNCC member and civil rights activist Ruby Nell Sales and the person she would become. Sales was born in Jemison, Alabama, and raised in Columbus, Georgia, and while there is no monolithic black experience, Ruby Nell Sales describes her childhood as somewhat atypical of the existence of many raised in the segregated South. Her father was in the military, and he was stationed at Fort Benning in Georgia, which was integrated at the behest of President Harry S. Truman. Fort Benning gave her a rare glimpse at an integrated society:

> As I think about growing up in Columbus, GA. I think about the duality—on the one hand being able to go on the army base which is where all of our business was taken care of by my family and that base was integrated—and then leaving the army base and coming to a segregated Columbus, GA, which was only 12 miles from the base. All of the movie theaters were located on

In 1948, President Truman issued Executive Order 9981, which outlawed discrimination in the armed forces and eventually led to the end of segregation in the military.

the army base, all of my doctors were at Martin Army Hospital or the old Fort Benning hospital, and the swimming pool was an integrated swimming pool. So that was one world, and then I came to Columbus, GA where my high school was not integrated. So, basically I grew up between these two worlds.[8]

The duality Sales describes seems to produce a sort of schizophrenic reality that she and her family had to learn to navigate in order to survive. Ironically, in their separate ways, both communities nurtured and inspired Sales. Sales and her family lived in the black section of town, and their neighbors included a number of other military families. Like Sales' father, many of these men had served in Korea. Some brought their Asian wives back to America with them, and these Asian women too were forced to live in the black section of town. Sales purposely interacted with these women, and their global experiences expanded her mind. The segregated black community and school she attended nurtured her and gave her the clear impression that she was somebody. Sales straddled these two worlds while growing up, and the duality seemed to make her strong and inquisitive.

After graduation from high school, Sales attended Tuskegee Institute in Tuskegee, Alabama, where she became part of a community of activists. Once again the people around her fueled her young mind. Everywhere Sales turned at Tuskegee, there was talk of the Movement and opportunities to get involved. Recalling her days at Tuskegee, Ruby Sales says:

When I came to Tuskegee, Tuskegee Institute and the faculty members at Tuskegee Institute had been very much themselves involved in challenging the segregation of Tuskegee in Montgomery, Alabama, so in some real ways the climate was there for that kind of participation. And we were very fortunate . . . to have a dean . . . who was very much committed to, to social change and encouraged the students and created an atmosphere that nurtured the kind of participation and involvement that later became very important at Tuskegee.[9]

Students were debating about the Movement, and their discussions raised Sales' consciousness. She read James Baldwin for the first time, and his works opened her mind. In response to Bloody Sunday, Gwen Patton, Tuskegee's first female student-body president, organized a group of students to march to Montgomery. Sales went. A number of younger faculty, including Dean Phillips and Jean Wiley, participated in the Movement activities with students, and as Sales and her friends hung out by the pond "to drink Catawba Pink [wine]," they talked about the Movement.[10] One student, Samuel Younge, had a particular influence on Sales and her colleagues.[11] Sales states, "And Samuel [Younge] got bit by the freedom bug, and if you knew Samuel—when he was bitten by something, he insisted that everybody else [get bitten]—he couldn't stop talking about it."[12] Sam Younge made a decision to fight for black liberation, and he encouraged Sales and others around him to do the same.[13]

Tuskegee cultivated a sense of personal and community obligation in its students. After receiving a medical discharge from the Navy, Younge enrolled in college at Tuskegee Institute. Along with a growing number of students at Tuskegee, Sammy Younge was a member of the Tuskegee Institute Advancement League (TIAL), a civil rights group comprising largely Tuskegee students.[14] On March 10, 1965, Younge, with hundreds of others, traveled to Montgomery, Alabama, to protest about the Bloody Sunday beatings. Later, he would travel to Mississippi to help register voters as well in the rural areas surrounding Selma.[15] On January 3, 1966, Sammy Younge was shot and killed by a white man as he tried to desegregate a "whites only" bathroom at Standard Oil Station in Macon County, Alabama.[16] He was 21 years old. Younge was a committed civil rights activist who gave his life to the cause, and the roots of his involvement can be traced back to Tuskegee and his early exposure to SNCC activists like James Forman and Stokely Carmichael. James Forman chronicles Younge's short life in his book, *Sammy Younge, Jr.: The First Black College Student to Die in the Black Liberation Movement.*[17]

While there was great support for students at Tuskegee to get involved in the Movement, there was also a structure in place that discouraged involvement, especially for women. Black schools of higher education often emulated the patriarchal patterns present in elite white society. One of the systems was the doctrine of *"in loco parentis."* The strict Latin definition for the term means "in place of the parents." Schools in the North and South used this doctrine to restrict student liberties; this was especially the case for female students. At Tuskegee, this took the form of parietals, which were strict campus rules governing student behavior, especially related to student comings and goings and dorm activity. Infractions of the rules usually resulted in harsh sanctions. Still, many students, including Sales, violated these traditions. Sales explains:

> Parietals still exist today, and there have been a number of student movements at various college campuses across the nation regarding these. Some of the student movements have sought to end parietals; others focus on extending student liberties under the parietal system.

[So] to go from that [old system], to make the radical move from that to going to Montgomery [to demonstrate], and also people going out into the county [to do Movement work] without any parental consent, and then coming into the lobby of the dormitory to make speeches—it really changed the social landscape at Tuskegee. In terms of what had existed for many, many years. Because suddenly there were students at Tuskegee that you couldn't control anymore. The boundaries were being collapsed. You couldn't keep someone like Gwen Patton [the student body president at Tuskegee] in that old system of getting your parents' permission to go downtown. I mean it was just kind of impossible.[16]

Sales' comments indicate that the students were changing Tuskegee, and Tuskegee was changing the students.

When summer came, Sales left Tuskegee and began to work for the Movement full time; SNCC assigned her to Calhoun County, Alabama, but by this time (summer of 1965) former boundaries had blurred, and Movement people worked very cooperatively across county lines. When young people in Fort Deposit, a small town in Lowndes County, Alabama, came to SNCC to ask for its support in a demonstration aimed at protesting at local storeowners' treatment of their parents, SNCC members in various counties joined the young people's cause. As sharecroppers, the youths' parents were required to deal with a particular store. The store's owner did business with the black sharecroppers; however, the storeowner failed to treat the African-American sharecroppers with even the least modicum of respect. The children of the sharecroppers represented a new generation, and they were intent on demanding that their parents be treated with dignity. With the support of SNCC, the students from Fort Deposit planned a bold, public demonstration in Lowndes County. "Bloody Lowndes" was not easy to organize, and Sales acknowledges that she and others were scared. They had every right to be. Black repression in Lowndes was well documented, and whites in Lowndes County maintained control over blacks through the twin vehicles of violence and economic intimidation.

About thirty people showed up for the August 14, 1965, demonstration, and, not surprisingly, the group met white resistance. A number of people, including Sales and Jonathan Daniels, a young white clergy student from New Hampshire, were jailed in Hayneville, Alabama. After a week in jail, the group was suddenly released. No advance notice was given, so there was no one available to pick up the demonstrators. As they walked through the town, they noted that it was eerily quiet—despite the fact that it was the middle of the afternoon on a bright Saturday in August. A segment of the group walked to a local store where Tom Coleman, an engineer with the state highway department and volunteer deputy, stood waiting inside the doorframe of the store with a shotgun. Coleman confronted the group and pointed his shotgun at 17-year-old Ruby Sales. In the midst of the encounter, Jonathan Daniels pulled Sales back, intentionally placing himself in harm's way in her stead. In so doing, Sales fell to the ground and Daniels took the bullet meant for her. As Father Richard Morrisroe, a white Roman Catholic priest from Chicago, and Joyce Bailey (another jailed demonstrator) fled hand-in-hand, Coleman shot Morrisroe in the back.

The sight of Jonathan Daniels' body flying through the air, the blood, the screams, and the confusion left Sales dazed. Tom Coleman tried to pursue the rest of the group, which by now had scattered in hiding. Finally, awakened by the insistent pleas of Joyce Bailey, Sales ran to safety. Later on, Sales came to believe that the group's release from jail after a week of substandard food and water and equally inhumane psychological treatment had been an intentional set-up. She says:

> When we got out of jail, — first of all, you have to understand that we were made to leave on our own word. We didn't even have bail, we didn't have anything. You know, that's a little weird that suddenly these people are gonna be gracious and say, "I trust you and you can go home." And nobody was alerted that we were gonna be leaving, and they wouldn't let us call anybody, and so we were turned out. It was afternoon. And the street was very eerie. There was a quietness over that downtown area that made us feel really, really eerie. You know, sometimes you get these little instincts and you push them aside.[19]

Despite constant threats and abuse at the hands of their jailers, the frightened group refused to give in to their fears, and to encourage each other and perhaps to keep their sanity, they sang freedom songs throughout their incarceration. The spirit of the group and the Movement they represented must have seemed undauntable to their oppressors, and it demanded action.

Tom Coleman was tried for Daniels' murder, and while the white press did not vilify Jonathan Daniels in the same manner as Viola Liuzzo (see Chapter 2), an all-white Alabama jury acquitted Coleman of all charges. But some in the Movement still refused to accept defeat. Ruby Nell Sales worked to ensure that neither Jonathan Daniels nor the black freedom struggle for which he gave his life was forgotten, and so she,

Gloria Larry, Willy Vaughn, and Joyce Bailey went on a national speaking tour to tell the world about "Bloody Lowndes."

Today, Ruby Nell Sales continues to work for human rights. She is the founder and director of SpiritHouse, a non-profit organization focused on community-organizing and spiritually based community-building, and she works avidly to keep the memory of Jonathan Daniels and Samuel Younge alive.

Although Sales recognizes the diversity of the black experience, she argues that many of her colleagues in the black freedom struggle all had the same type of parents, and that these parents instilled in their children the idea to fight for a better tomorrow, today. In addition to the example of parents, surrogate parents—often grandparents and other kin—inspired young people to get involved. Joanne Bland, one of the youngest participants in the Bloody Sunday march, argues that she became a part of the Movement due to the influence of relatives, specifically her grandmother.[20] Although Bland's grandmother could not read or write, she was a member of DCVL, formed in the 1930s by Sam and Amelia Boynton to aid blacks in registering to vote. Bland attended meetings with her grandmother, and through these meetings, the Movement became a part of her vernacular. Similarly, former Executive Director of the Albany Civil Rights Institute, Lee W. Formwalt explains how her father did not want her or his other children to go to mass meetings for fear of what "the white man" would do, but her grandmother took her anyway.[21]

The influence of parental figures on children is not uncontested. In a child's formative years, parents are the most important influence, but as children grow, the educational system and ultimately peers often replace parents in importance. SNCC member and Freedom Singer, Bill Perlman, was raised on the East Coast in a family he describes as "culturally Jewish" but not religious, and while Perlman learned about the Movement from his parents, his extended network of family, friends, and colleagues were also involved; the support of these informal communication channels helped move him readily "from knowledge to persuasion to decision." Perlman cites two major influences that inspired him to join SNCC—his family and James Forman, the Executive Director of SNCC. Bill Perlman states:

> Forman had come out to visit my parents at a house they had out on Long Island, and we went to a fundraising party for SNCC. I played the guitar and sang some freedom songs. Later he [Forman] called me to tell me that the group [the Freedom Singers] was looking for a guitarist, and they would prefer, he

would prefer a white guitarist, because he felt that there had been some criticism at the time (now mind you, this is 1965) of an all-black presence in the Freedom Singers, so um, I agreed.[22]

Despite Perlman's great reverence for James Forman and the work of SNCC, he argues that his family had the greatest influence on his decision to get involved with the Movement:

People often ask me how I got involved in the Civil Rights Movement and in political activism, and I tell them that in many ways it was sort of the family business. My mother was staff member of SNCC before I was.

She was in the New York office doing all of the mailings — the fundraising and all of the mailings . . . My cousin Joanie Rabinowitz had been a staff member of SNCC working in southwest Georgia with Charles Sherrod. Her father, Victor Rabinowitz, is a fairly well-known lawyer who was involved in many of the legal cases in and around the Movement for years . . . so I and my mother both go back to the International Labor Defense, American Labor Party, and my grandfather and great-grandfather were anarchists. It's a long, radical, political history.[23]

Perlman continues, revealing the paternal influences on his decision. He states:

He [my father] had at one time been a union organizer for bank tellers . . . It was a very political and activist family, so it was no, I didn't need to revolt against whatever to be in the Movement. If I would not have been in [the Movement] that would have been strange.[24]

His comments elucidate the influence primary reference groups such as families exert over an individual's decision whether or not to participate in the Movement.

It is expected that parents will have a profound influence on their children; what is less often stated is that the influence is reciprocal. Unlike Bill Perlman's family, Annie Pearl Avery did not come from "Movement people." While Annie Pearl's natural mother did not support her Movement efforts early on, she found "surrogate mothers" who did, including Ella Baker. By 1965, Ella Jo Baker, was in her early 60s but still active, very active in the Movement; the long-time grassroots organizer and civil rights activist had been influential in the formation of SNCC 5 years earlier, and she inspired other young people—especially young women—to do the same. Avery describes Baker and her influence:

> But anyway, it was young people in the Freedom Rides, and they started something, and it started snowballing. You know the Movement stuff just broke out everywhere. One of the reasons for that was you had people like Diane Nash who said they didn't want to wait 20 years to come from the back of the bus or to eat at a lunch counter. And Ms. Ella Jo Baker was one of the people who had the foresight enough to see this. And she was a part of SCLC, but they would not give her credit because she was a female . . . and so what happened was by Ella Baker doing this when SNCC was formed [she was] forming SNCC. But she wouldn't do it for us. I remember it was something I wanted her to help me do, and she told me, "I'm not gonna do it for you. You're gonna have to do it for yourself."[25]

Ms. Baker's maternal nature was comforting and inspiring, nurturing yet challenging. Annie Pearl Avery continues:

> Ms. Baker was really a driving force in the whole Movement. She came to every SNCC conference, every SNCC meeting. As a matter of fact, she had the foresight to see that the young people are the ones, matter of fact they should be the ones to carry it on. But we've got to prepare them for it. And she would be preparing us for it. We would be sitting at a meeting at 9 [p.m.], 10 [p.m.], 3 a.m. in the morning. When the meeting was over we'd go on to the watering holes, and she would be right there with us. She'd drink coffee and stuff and be sitting right there with us! I'd say, "What is this old lady doing out with us?!" But she was hanging for a reason, though. She was watching [after] us.[26]

While Avery's own mother challenged her participation in the Movement, Ella Baker encouraged it. Ella Jo Baker marched, so Annie Pearl Avery could march, and because Ella Jo Baker marched, Annie Pearl Avery did, too.

To the young people of the Movement, Ella Baker was their "fundi."[27] Fundi is a Swahili term that refers to one who passes on "knowledge through direct contact with people."[28] She visited them in jail. She encouraged them. She attended their meetings, and she acted as wise counsel, but despite her decades of Movement work, she never made the young people think that she had all the answers or that they were incapable of leading. Ella Baker did not try to wrestle the reins of leadership from the hands of the young; instead, she placed the reins in their hands. Among other capacities, in the early 1960s Robert (Bob) Moses and Charles Cobb both served as field secretaries for SNCC, and they were often in direct contact with Ms. Baker. In their 2001 book, *Radical Equations: Civil Rights from Mississippi to the Algebra Project*, Moses and Cobb reflect on Ella Baker's style. They write:

> [I]f you really want to do something with somebody else, really want to work with that person, the first thing you have to do is make a personal connection. You have to find out who it is you are working with. All across the South you could see that in grassroots rural people. That was their style. Miss Baker took this style to a sophisticated level of political work.[29]

Much has been said about the intergenerational and class struggles in the Movement, but people like Ella Baker were able to navigate the chasms, see the humanity in all, and bring that humanity out of people. Through wise counsel and example, Ella Baker showed others how to build a fellowship that crossed generations and social-class boundaries and transformed people.

Sometimes adult support for the Movement was tacit, and at other times it was expressed. Whichever the case, this "support" allowed the idea to diffuse through the society. Alabama native Samuel Walker outlines how the tacit support of his parents and teachers influenced his participation in the Selma campaign:

> During the Movement I was 11 years old and in the sixth grade. I had an older brother and sister that was very active in the Movement . . .
>
> They went to march almost every day, and so I was able to go with them to the marches. Yeah. That was one of the rules in my house was if I saw them out there, I could go with them, but I couldn't just leave school and go on my own.[30]

Sam Walker's parents expressly permitted his older siblings (one a high school senior and the other a sophomore) to march. Walker's parents' tacit consent for him to participate in Movement marches was based on concern about his young age, not a failure to support the marches. Similarly, the teachers at Walker's elementary school gave their tacit consent, as overt support for the marches could jeopardize their jobs and their personal safety. Walker continues:

> When they [my siblings] walked out of R.B. Hudson High School,
> they had to walk past my elementary school, which was Payne
> Elementary School, to line up at the church. So I would just go sit by
> the window and wait for them to come by the sidewalk, and when I'd
> see them, then I'd go. The teachers wouldn't try to stop you if they
> knew someone was going to look out for you. They wouldn't try to
> stop you. Then we would walk out and go join them.[31]

According to Walker, other elementary school children did the same thing.
In this manner, participation in the Movement was both learned and
supported inside the family unit. Further, in addition to the family unit,
the other important social institutions in the children's lives—the church
and the school—each supported the Movement too.

While tacit, the black teachers' support of the Selma Movement was
critical to its success. F.D. Reese, who served as president of both the
Black Teachers' Association (in Selma) and DCVL explains:

> In the mass meetings, now you have teachers at the mass
> meetings, too. Now you know. Now they're not separated. And
> then you're talking in the mass meeting and finding out what's
> going to happen tomorrow. Students are in there. Teachers are in
> there. Parents. So, we're all there. And then you say tomorrow . . .
> at a certain time we'd say we're going down to the courthouse.
> And so, when it was time for them [the children] to leave I just
> kinda, I mean I didn't say y'all get up and go, I just kinda
> [gesturing a head turning away from the students]. And when
> you look back half the class was gone. When the class was
> gone, I'd go.[32]

Reese explains the efficacy of the teacher's actions thus:

> Well you see . . . the point is that in the mass meetings parents
> were in the mass meetings, too. And so they were somewhat
> understanding. Talk about getting an education: You get
> education by being in the streets, too. That was an education for
> some of those students.[33]

In the mass meetings teachers, students, and parents obtained knowledge
about the Movement; however, the students were only able to move from
knowledge to persuasion to decision through the often tacit and sometimes
expressed consent of the larger community, including parents, "other-
mothers," clergy, and teachers.

More than Reading, Writing and Arithmetic: Teachers and the Movement

Soon, a large group of the African-American teachers in Selma took the bold step of explicitly supporting voting rights efforts, and it is no understatement to say that their audacity helped sustain the Movement. In an era of stark economic and residential segregation that both constrained employment opportunities for African-Americans and contained them in tight-knit, vertically integrated communities,[34] African-American teachers, clergy, and other professionals often held heightened prestige and influence in the black community, and despite the danger (especially for teachers in the public system) a number used their influence to educate others about the Movement. As opinion leaders, their ideas and choices held great weight in the community. The boldness of these educators inspired students and parents to make a decision to demonstrate, register to vote, or fight in other ways for expanded rights for African-Americans. Describing the precarious dual status occupied by black teachers during this era, Black Teachers' Association president Reese states: "Teachers teaching citizenship were not first-class citizens themselves."[35] Yet, on the other end of this duality, Reese recalls the respect and praise the black teachers' decision to walk out of school and march to the courthouse to demand the right to register to vote engendered among the black community:

> [The] Teachers' March was set for January 22nd [1965]. It would go right past the projects. They came out of Clark Elementary School. Parents were crying. Students were jumping for joy as they saw their teachers protesting and asking for the right to vote . . . [At the courthouse] we were jabbed down three times with a billyclub . . . We went to Brown Chapel to a heroes' welcome . . . We were the first group of teachers in the U.S. to demonstrate for the right to vote. This was January 22, 1965.[36]

Support for the voting rights struggle began to spread like a contagion, and soon after the teachers marched, the black beauticians and undertakers were inspired to march too.

Beyond Selma

Numerous social laboratories grew, where young people could learn the skills to challenge the social structure in a nurturing, safe environment; this group of social engineers included a number of faculty and administrators at Tuskegee Institute.[37]

Chapter 1 of this book details how time and place are important considerations in this work, and the location and history of Tuskegee Institute, founded in 1881 by Booker T. Washington,[38] amply illustrates the significance of these variables in the creation of an environment conducive to lasting social change. Tuskegee Institute was home to many veteran civil rights activists, including Charles Gomillion[39] who fought for the right to vote in the 1950s and won a Supreme Court victory.[40] Now, with Tuskegee's strategic location in Alabama between Montgomery and Birmingham—the location of two important Movement campaigns—many young people entered the campus with that experience of having participated in local movements. This bred a new and young crop of students who came of age during some of the most noted recent victories of the black freedom struggle. Tuskegee Institute not only had a long history of Movement work and an eager, involved student population, it also had current leadership who provided the kind of support that proved instrumental in allowing students to make a decision to participate in the Movement efforts without failing school on academic grounds or getting kicked out of school for violating parietals. Stokely Carmichael, the then-leader of SNCC, went to the campus to recruit protestors, and Sales and a friend joined him organizing in Lowndes County, Alabama. This picture paints a perfect outline of a community where students not only became informed about the Movement, but received the reinforcement to move readily from persuasion to decision, with the full support of their peers and superiors.

And a Child Shall Lead Them

The boldness of everyday people—educators, day laborers, maids, parents, and grandparents—inspired the African-American residents of Selma and the surrounding Black Belt counties, especially the youth, to seek more than just the franchise. Sam Walker, who was in elementary school when the teachers marched, states:

> We knew that—that voting was something for our parents; we understood that clearly, but see, when we marched as students we would always say we want our freedom, too. We want our freedom, too, because see we knew that we wanted to be freed of those things that we were being oppressed by. Back then they had the colored and the white water fountains, colored and white bathrooms, colored and white seats in the movie theater, so when you marched at 11 years old you felt you was marching for your freedom. So it was bigger than voting for us. It was our freedom. We wanted to be free from all those things we were being oppressed by.[41]

Sam Walker's comments illustrate that the children who participated in the demonstrations were not just playing follow-the-leader. They marched for parents who could not march, and they marched for themselves. They were committed, and their resolve came from their community and was nurtured in it.

Since the Birmingham Crusade, children were playing an increasingly significant role in the Movement. Media coverage of Birmingham contains some of the best-known images of the Civil Rights Movement, including indelible images of teenagers and young adults in Kelly Ingram Park being attacked by dogs and sheltering themselves from the blast of the fire hoses. The participation of young people in Selma was also documented in the media and discussed among other youth. Once again, the communication channels—media and interpersonal (face-to-face)—inspired other young people to get involved. Annie Pearl Avery states:

> I was willing to jump on board with Diane Nash, and these people who were Freedom Riders . . . Cuz when they started talking about younger people, I thought: I was young. I can do that.[42]

And she did.

Soon, Avery became engrossed in the Movement. The civil rights veteran describes herself as a "follower—not a leader," but Annie Pearl Avery's commitment inspired her own mother to participate. Avery recalls:

> One day I called home, and mom was in jail! That's how I found out. I wanted to speak to my mom, and my older brother said, "She's not here," and you know you always know where your mom is, right?
>
> And my brother said, "Mama is in jail. She's down there with Hosea Williams." I just said, "Okay" . . . My mother, she started marching with me, and she had my son with her.[43]

Three generations—grandmother, mother, and son—all marched together, but a "child" led the way.

And They Tell Two Friends, and So On, and So On

I'll Follow You

Prior to her active involvement, Annie Avery, a young, newly married wife and mother forced to drop out of high school, learned bits about the Movement through her social network. In the years following the successful Montgomery Bus Boycott, Alabama remained in the foreground of the Southern freedom struggle. In May of 1961, the Freedom Riders, a group of civil rights activists organized by the CORE, rode the public buses into the Deep South in order to challenge the system of segregation in public transportation over interstate commerce. The group was attacked and firebombed in Anniston, Alabama, and they faced an angry, violent mob in nearby Birmingham, Alabama. After that event, Annie Avery and her friends regularly gathered at the lounge in Birmingham's premier black establishment, the A.G. Gaston Motel, and discussed the Movement. Noted African-American entertainers and leaders in the Movement frequented the Gaston Motel and, through a chance meeting there, Avery received an invitation to travel to her first SNCC meeting in Atlanta, Georgia.

At SNCC headquarters in Atlanta, Avery gained additional knowledge about the Movement. The Atlanta trip served as a catalyst for Avery, and she moved quickly from knowledge to persuasion to decision. She began to work for SNCC, traveling to various places across the United States. Avery states:

> In Birmingham I didn't work with SNCC on a project because they didn't have a chapter there. So I worked with Alabama Christian Movement and the SCLC. I had no problem with what the name of it was. I just wanted to be doing something. And that gave me to opportunity to meet Dr. Wyatt T. Walker, who was one of my mentors. He didn't know it at the time, but he was one of my mentors, and what he did was he sent me out on a decoy demonstration. I didn't know nothing about no decoy demonstration, but [soon] I realized. It was a strategy they used, and one of my best friends, Betty, she said to me, "You going to jail?" And I said, "Yeah, I'm going." She said, "I'm not going to jail." Because see, jail was always associated with doing something bad. So, I decided I was going to go, and he sent me out on a decoy demonstration. See that demonstration was supposed to throw the people off. See what we did is they used to figure we would march once that day, and that would be the end of it, but see there was a bigger demonstration coming behind that one. I guess about 10 or 15 of us went on that decoy march, and later on Betty came in jail, and I said, "What are you doing here?" And she said, "I'm not gon' be out there by myself." I said, "You crazy!"[44]

These comments illustrate that while Betty was knowledgeable about the Movement and even willing to participate in it, her conviction to go to jail came about because the close personal ties in her interpersonal network were willing to do the same. The influence of this interpersonal communication channel moved her from decision to persuasion. These conclusions are echoed by Avery's reflections decades after the event. She states:

> When I think about it now, you know we talked about this thing when we became adults—you know much more mature adults, and she [Betty] said, "Chile—[I told you] I'm not gone be out there by myself."[45]

While the larger society had yet to adopt the social innovation, Betty quickly moved through the stages (from knowledge to persuasion to decision) because her interpersonal network did the same. These networks carried the message to the larger African-American community.

Spreading Through the Community (church, SNCC, etc.)

For a time, Judge Hare's July 1964 injunction (prohibiting groups of blacks from congregating for the purpose of discussing civil rights) effectively stifled many voting rights efforts in Selma,[46] and breaking the injunction was dangerous, so many local churches expressed reservations about getting involved. Discussing this involvement, Sam Walker states:

> Well. It was reluctant involvement [on the part of some local churches]. And so people had to be brought around to those viewpoints. Ultimately, a lot of people was brought around to those viewpoints, but everybody didn't come around at the same time; it took time.[47]

However, despite some reluctance on the part of the black religious community to get involved, the Movement relied on the black church, and in order to stay relevant to a new generation of black youth eager for change, the black church needed the Movement.

The musical tradition present in the black church helped to inspire those on the periphery of decision to commit. It informed the uneducated; it soothed the weary; and it raised funds for the cause. Bill Perlman, a member of SNCC's Freedom Singers, discusses these multiple objectives:

> When people talked about music and the Movement primarily the stories you get are people singing in jail on picket lines in places where you are threatened where you need courage and you need

> inspiration at um meetings etc., and from that point of view, the
> music was absolutely invaluable . . . There is something
> empowering and there is something exciting about the music,
> and also the sound of many voices singing it. There is a power
> there that I can't explain, but I certainly felt [it], and I think
> everybody else in that Movement also felt it, and I think
> everybody else in the Movement felt it and they used it to keep
> us going in really, really difficult situations.[48]

Music was not only used as a tool to strengthen those in the struggle, it
also became a vehicle to inform others about the black freedom struggle.
Bill Perlman continues.

> The other side of it was what the Freedom Singers did, and we
> were a much more rehearsed, more polished group, and we used
> the music both at rallies, meetings, things like that, but also in
> fundraising . . . We toured through the United States, through
> Canada . . . and [performed] in everything from people's living
> rooms to Carnegie Hall. You know, singing and telling the story of
> the Movement, raising the consciousness . . . stories that we
> would tell from the stage about happenings, these were things
> that no one had ever heard of. And the other side of it was raising
> their consciousness and the fact that the music was so emotional
> was getting them riled up and involved. You know the songs
> ranged from those that were sung in jails and in picket lines to
> those that made fun of Wallace and various other people down
> there and you know an entire range of things that educated
> people and brought people in and empowered and encouraged
> people to get involved.[49]

In this manner, the music of the Movement touched everyday people
across the nation and moved many further along on Rogers' information-
decision chain.

Interpersonal communication channels helped usher many local people
to the decision phase, but a large part of the country still needed to know
about the struggle, and the mass media was most successful in carrying
this message to the nation. In fact, King's strategy relied on powerful visual
images being communicated through mass media channels, and those
powerful images included scenes of brutality and scores of people peacefully
waiting in line to obtain the vote. But the whole strategy was in jeopardy
unless people were willing to stand in line. The mass meetings held at
local churches were crucial because they served to strengthen and
encourage people's resolve to labor for the cause. F.D. Reese states:

> You couldn't go to a mass meeting and not come out changed
> because all the folk around you could see how the change is
> taking place. The determination to make a change: those mass
> meetings they were tremendous. Those persons who were so
> nonchalant from the beginning, now in the mass meetings, you
> could see them: We'd have . . . handclapping, jumping up,
> making speeches. Yeah. That's right. It happened. Now I'm not
> saying everybody was changed because there were those who
> were there just to say that they were part of the crowd, but then
> again they were in that environment that really would put them in
> a position to actually be changed. And if nothing else for the
> moment, even if they did not mean it, it put them in a position to
> later be changed.[50]

Most meetings occurred at local churches and involved large segments of the black community. The communal nature of the assemblies helped usher attendees through the early phases of the diffusion process. Equally importantly, the mass meetings helped create a devoted cadre of committed followers who would form the critical mass of people needed to create compelling images of what *The New York Times'* television critic Jack Gould earlier termed "petitioning humanity."[51] As Roberts and Klibanoff ably argue in *The Race Beat: The Press, the Civil Rights Struggle, and the Awakening of a Nation*, news coverage of the Movement changed the Movement and helped awaken the nation to the plight of many of its African-American citizens. The images of people standing in line quietly, forcefully, and peaceably petitioning for their humanity had local, national, and global impacts. Again, F.D. Reese comments:

> Oftentimes we would talk to people, and they'd see you were part
> of the line or they saw you in this line in the paper, saw you on
> the news, and seeing some of your neighbors in line [would
> influence them]. And the neighbors some would say are you
> going to get in line today? This would encourage others to
> become a part of it, you see?[52]

Reese's comments elucidate the local nature of the protest. The Selma campaign was not a Movement led by "outside agitators," as white Alabama officials had claimed. It was a local campaign with global import, and once the campaign's message was effectively communicated through the media, people from all over felt compelled to come to Selma and fight for the cause of humanity.

Sidebar 4.2

Accurately or not, many Southern communities liked to assert that their "Negroes were happy," and would not engage in any of the widespread public protest activities growing throughout the South in the late 1950s and early 60s. Instead, these locals suggested that it was "outside agitators" who were responsible for stirring up trouble.

Martin Luther King Jr. framed a response to the outside agitators' argument in "Letter from a Birmingham Jail," which was published in *The New York Times* on April 16, 1963. King states, "Injustice anywhere is a threat to justice everywhere." King's words challenge and expand the traditional notions of community and are consistent with his ideas about the "beloved community," a brotherly society based on love and concern for mankind.

Ordinary People, Extraordinary Sacrifices

In his classic work titled *Local People: The Struggle for Civil Rights in Mississippi*, historian John Dittmer establishes that the struggle for basic human and civil rights for blacks in Mississippi was waged by local people who, over the course of many decades, fought numerous battles. The same was true across the Deep South, and the efforts of local people inspired many people across the region, the nation, and sometimes the world. The names of all the people who made great sacrifices in the black freedom struggle are too numerous to list or even know, but the remaining pages of this chapter introduce the reader to some of the extraordinary people who sustained the Selma Movement, including some local people, martyrs of the Movement, and women of the cause.

Local People

Despite discrete geographic boundaries that separated the counties, evidence suggests that people in surrounding locales worked collaboratively to maintain the Movement and in so doing they effectively expanded their local boundaries to include neighboring borders. In her book titled *In the Shadow of Selma: The Continuing Struggle for Civil Rights in the Rural South*, historian Cynthia Fleming provides an in-depth analysis of the civil rights struggle in neighboring Wilcox County. In the early 1960s, Wilcox County, Alabama, was known as a restrictive place for blacks, and its Sheriff, Lummie Jenkins, was part of the reason for this label. Sheriff Jenkins' reputation for suppressing the rights of the black residents of

Wilcox County was so heinous that some called Sheriff Jim Clark—the Selma lawman who famously opposed black voting rights by beating and arresting peaceful protesters—"tame" by comparison.[53] Despite its reputation, a brave Selma resident named James Gildersleeve and Bernard Lafayette of SNCC traveled almost 50 miles into Wilcox County to aid in voter registration efforts there.[54]

The strong, expanding sense of black community was not without fractures. For example, one of Fleming's most successful insights is the realization that despite stark poverty, the black population of Wilcox County was accentuated by class differences. SNCC organizer, Bernard Lafayette, noted these class distinctions in his 1963 visit to Wilcox County, which Fleming discusses. At Movement meetings Lafayette observed many hopeful and dedicated residents of Gee's Bend (one of the most culturally rich but poor black areas in the country) and a reluctant black middle class that "all too often . . . was resistant to change because it had a stake in the system as it existed."[55] This black middle class was still oppressed, but better off than most blacks in the area, which made some of them hesitant to agitate against the white power structure and risk losing life and/or property. Many residents of Gee's Bend attended Lafayette's early organization meetings in the area, and Lafayette was gladdened because he was said to have become frustrated with "middle class" blacks and their ways.[56] This comment points to some of the class-based distinctions in the Movement, but it also illustrates how Gildersleeve and others broadened their definition of who constituted their neighbor to reflect an expanding sense of black community among those in the freedom struggle.

In the decade prior to the March, voter registration and other civil rights efforts were ablaze throughout the rural South.[57] Residents in Wilcox, Dallas, Perry, and Lowndes counties were not only aware of each other's efforts, they supported each other. This expanded locality also provided some protection for in-county black residents as out-of-county agitators could be blamed accurately—for once—for stirring up trouble and then escaping back to their county of residence. These collaborative efforts among residents of various counties allowed the social innovation to stay alive.

In the fall of 1965, numerous black sharecroppers in Lowndes County were kicked off their land because they were bold enough to try to register to vote. For decades, white landowners in Lowndes County maintained black repression because, "Although the population was roughly 80 percent African American, no black resident had successfully registered to vote in more than 60 years, as the county was controlled by 86 white families who owned 90 percent of the land."[58] Sharecropping was a hard system, and the tenant farmers seldom came out even, let alone ahead, but it provided a place to live and something of a living. The audacious act of registering to vote could mean the loss of income, life and/or home. The black tenant farmers knew the risks, and they registered anyway. They were kicked off the land, but they were not defeated. An agency formed in their struggle, and the community organized to "house" the displaced sharecroppers.[59] SNCC raised funds and purchased the land. People in the surrounding communities provided food, water, clothing, and other items needed for survival. Despite constant attacks, including having shots fired over their heads with alarming frequency, they survived.[60] Soon, the Lowndes County Freedom Organization (LCFO), a precursor to the better-known Black Panther Party, was formed and continued to register black voters and push a slate of candidates in the upcoming election.[61]

In Dallas County, local leadership included one group known as the Courageous Eight: Mrs. Amelia Boynton, Mrs. Marie Foster, Mr. Ernest Doyle, Reverend John D. Hunter, Mr. James Gildersleeve, Reverend Henry Shannon, Mr. Ulysses Blackmon, and Dr. Frederick D. Reese. All were members of DCVL; following the death of Sam Boynton, this group of eight comprised its steering committee. In 1963 DCVL invited SNCC to Selma to help them in their voter education and registration efforts. By 1964, 2.2 percent of Dallas County's eligible black electorate was registered to vote, and while this number is small, it is directly attributable to the efforts of the DCVL and represents a much larger percentage of black registered voters than was on the rolls in surrounding counties. Threatened by the passage of the Civil Rights Act of 1964, Alabama Circuit Judge James Hare issued an injunction prohibiting meetings of three or more, but the eight members of the group (nicknamed the Courageous Eight but facetiously referred to as the Crazy Eight by their opponents) continued to meet. This is the group who defied Judge Hare's injunction and invited Dr. Martin Luther King Jr. to come to Alabama to launch his voting rights campaign.

Without detracting from the committed people who came from around the nation to help with the Movement, it is important to underscore that the intrepidity of local people was of a special brand. Local men and women participated in the struggle with their eyes wide open despite the "forces of intimidation and repression" they might face. Despite this environment, three African-Americans allowed the marchers to camp on their property, and their courage and contribution to the Movement cannot be overstated. Without lodging, the marchers would have had to be shuttled back to Selma and the other places from which they came, and the mere image of such caravans might have jeopardized the momentum of the idea's diffusion through society. Segments of the white media were intent on discrediting the March, including claims of sexual impropriety and other debauchery at the campsites. Still others claimed the protestors did not walk the whole way. But most importantly, the campsites simulated the mass meetings, and campers drew a sense of solidarity, encouragement, and purpose from the communal setting.

On the first night (March 21, 1965), David Hall allowed the marchers to camp at his property. The Hall farm site is located about 7 miles east of Selma. On the second night (March 22, 1965), marchers camped at Rosie Steele's farm, and on night three (March 23, 1965), they camped at Robert Gardner's farm. On the final night of the March there was a concert at the City of St. Jude, and at the invitation of the Catholic group, the marchers camped there. Each of them faced possible economic, social, physical, and/or emotional reprisal, and yet they made a decision to support the Movement. Their participation, despite the risk, served as a testament to their neighbors, and some would join the African-American freedom struggle because of their example.

Even after the successful March and passage of the Voting Rights Act, reprisals against blacks continued. Dozens of black sharecroppers in Lowndes County, Alabama, were evicted from the land they leased and forced to live in a Tent City erected on land purchased by SNCC for the purpose of housing the displaced population.[62] Some families were forced to live in the tents for up to 2 years, and the whole tent community was subject to constant harassment, including regularly being shot at by whites opposed to the population's efforts to register to vote.

Martyrs of the Movement

The media's influence on the Civil Rights Movement is well stated in Roberts and Klibanoff's book, *The Race Beat: The Press, the Civil Rights Struggle, and the Awakening of a Nation*; however, increased media attention alone was not enough to sustain the Movement or bring about social change. This section discusses five important martyrs for the movement: Jimmie Lee Jackson, James Reeb, Viola Liuzzo, Jonathan Daniels, and Sammy Younge. Each story is certainly important because of the ultimate sacrifice made by the individuals, but, to varying extents, their stories garnered media attention and propelled individual actors to make a decision. News of their deaths spread across various segments of the U.S. population, and as media outlets broke the stories to their followers, opinion leaders picked up the reports and carried them to their adherents.

In a 1944 work, sociologist Paul Lazarsfeld et al. outline the process of decision-making in a presidential election.[63] This seminal work states that communication, even media communication, is not one-sided, but follows a two-step flow. Lazarsfeld wrote at a time when many experts subscribed to the so-called hypodermic theory of media effects: a single dose of a media message is enough to influence a consumer. His work showed that the media message isn't enough; that people influence people, and so news reports flow to influential local opinion leaders (work supervisors, community leaders, ministers, elders, etc.) who in turn prevail on individuals and influence them in one way or another. Each martyr was an everyday person, and this book examines the dual influences of the media and their personal networks on their decision to fight—and ultimately lay down their lives—for the African-American freedom struggle.

Every martyr mentioned learned about the Movement through the all-important social networks they maintained. Jimmie Lee Jackson, who was shot at a night rally in Marion, attended the rally with his family, including his sister, mother, and 87-year-old grandfather. His intimate social networks not only embraced the Movement, they fought in the struggle. James Reeb was a social worker and former minister who moved his family into a black neighborhood surrounding the church where he served, and he immediately became immersed in the issues of the community and the people there.[64] Reeb was committed to the cause of equality, and he traveled to Selma from Boston with two fellow Unitarian Universalist minister friends. Viola Liuzzo's social networks—including her union affiliations through her husband and her involvement in the African-American freedom struggle in Detroit—will be outlined in more detail later in the chapter in a section on "Women in the Movement," and Samuel Younge's background has already been discussed. Jon Daniels, along with ten fellow students from Episcopal Theological School (ETS) in Cambridge, Massachusetts, traveled to Selma, Alabama, to participate in the second March.[65] Daniels traveled with like-minded colleagues, and they were all committed to the African-American freedom struggle. The group only intended to stay a few days, but Jonathan Daniels and another colleague requested and were granted permission from the administration to stay longer.[66] Daniels returned to seminary to take his exams, and then went back to Alabama to work in the struggle.[67] Jonathan Daniels' parents, his colleagues at seminary, instructors, and new-found community in Alabama all supported his involvement in the Movement, and this support gave him the freedom to make a decision to fight for the cause. None of these dedicated martyrs came to their conviction in a vacuum. Instead, each was firmly entrenched in social networks that allowed them to become early adopters and even innovators of the idea.

Their stories stress the overarching importance of personal communication in the adoption of the social innovation. The impact of the martyrs continued to be felt in death. Even after news outlets ceased reporting stories of their lives and deaths, opinion leaders and the people in their social networks continued to discuss the incidents. Their deaths caused ripple effects. For example, after the death of Sam Younge, SNCC staff began to advocate against the Vietnam War; SNCC membership could not imagine sending someone off to fight a war abroad, when America had a war still to fight at home.[68] Viola Liuzzo's story was debated on college campuses and likely in her children's schools where teachers and young people alike discussed her decision to go to Alabama and fight for the Movement and the propriety of it. The story of Viola Liuzzo still resonates today. What right does a woman have to leave her family? Others might argue the opposite. When James Reeb died, President Johnson called it "an American tragedy," and in his address to Congress he employed the words of the freedom struggle and twice told the nation: "We shall overcome." The strong language from this opinion leader increased knowledge of the freedom struggle and perhaps persuaded some of the rightness of the cause. While rightness is not a prerequisite in Rogers' theory, it does suggest a level of persuasion, which might ultimately usher some to a decision. Numerous opinion leaders carried the story to various segments of the U.S. population thereby increasing the potential for the story to reach saturation and a threshold number of people to adopt the innovation.

Women of the Movement

Women played a vital role in the Movement, for they were simultaneously protectors (of the community, the children, and the faith) and deemed worthy of protection. The larger black community would not only follow the virtuous women of the Movement, they seemed ready to defend them, even when these women proved willing, able, and capable of defending themselves. Gender disparities did exist, especially in organizations such as SCLC with deeply entrenched ties to the highly patriarchal church structure, but SNCC emerged as one of the premier civil rights organizations where women could play a decisive leadership role.[69] In 1965, Fay Bellamy Powell was a member of the United States Air Force working in Selma. Soon, Powell became involved in SNCC. Speaking about Movement women, Powell says, "Many of the women in SNCC sincerely believed it would be hypocritical to talk about fighting for the freedom of others and then allow yourself to be enslaved inside your organization."[70] As SNCC labored throughout rural areas in the Deep South, "strong women in those communities would rise up like cream rising to the top."[71]

Many Movement women were church ladies, too. It is alleged that numerous churches reluctantly became involved in Movement work because their largely female congregations insisted they did so, on threat of withholding money from the church. Even when Movement women left the church, the church was still in them. In the largely segregated South, the black church operated as the social, cultural, and political base for the community. Movement women sang the songs they learned in church, and they taught songs to the young. They inspired crowds at mass meetings, protest marches, and in jail. Soon, they adapted the church songs to the freedom struggle and added enough of a contemporary sound and beat to grip young and old in their rhythmic spell. Bernice Johnson Reagon, a song leader in the Albany Movement, explains the power of the music she learned in church:

> [Someone] looked at me and said, "Bernice, sing a song." I took
> a breath and started "Over my Head, I see Trouble in the Air." As
> I moved down the first line, I knew it would not be a good idea to
> sing the word *trouble*, even though I knew we were in trouble . . .
> instead I put in *freedom* . . . It was the first time I'd ever changed
> the text of a sacred song. It was the beginning of my
> understanding how to use what I'd been given in that body of old
> songs we had learned growing up in school and church.[72]

Reagon describes a "oneness" of the spirit, which the music invoked. The role of women in the Movement is only now starting to be heralded. In many ways, their role is, again, reminiscent of DuBois' "double consciousness" in that women were the seen but unsung heroes of the Movement.

Numerous local women who were never elevated to the national scene played a vital role in the African-American freedom struggle. In the Selma campaign, Annie Cooper was one such woman. Annie Cooper was born and raised in Selma, Alabama. She was the tenth child in her family. When she was 14, she left Selma to go to Kentucky and live with a sister. Later, she moved to Pennsylvania. She had been able to vote in both locales. In 1962, Cooper moved back to Selma, but she couldn't vote because she didn't have anyone to vouch for her.[73] She had out-of-town references, but the voting registrars in Dallas County would not accept out-of-town references. Soon, Cooper got a job in Selma and through those networks she began to hear discussions about SNCC's efforts to register people to vote.

She decided to join with others trying to secure the same right, and one day, she got in line on Church Street to register to vote. The line had about 300 people in it. The owner of the rest home where she worked surveyed the line to see if any of his employees were in it. Cooper stayed in line, but her friend (a co-worker) left. Ms. Cooper was fired for her efforts, and her co-workers rallied to her defense. Over forty co-workers signed a petition urging the owner to rehire her. After the owner refused, the group boycotted. Most of those who boycotted were also fired and summarily blocked from obtaining employment in other places. The economic duress had the opposite effect that those imposing it might have expected: some of the people who lost their jobs started attending mass meetings and marching to the courthouse regularly to try to register to vote.

On January 25, 1965, Annie Cooper had a fateful encounter with Sheriff Clark. The whole community seemed reinvigorated by Martin Luther King Jr.'s early January 1965 visit to break the injunction. King built on the efforts of SNCC and DCVL, and soon the demonstrators started regularly standing on Alabama Avenue in front of the courthouse to try to register. A group marched to the courthouse to register, and they were told they could not stand on Alabama Avenue anymore. Cooper had a prominent position in that assembly, which almost ensured an encounter with Clark. The assembly walked on Lauderdale Street by the steps of the courthouse. Wilson Baker, the safety director, was supposed to handle the marchers, but Sheriff Clark intervened. Cooper describes her encounter with the Sheriff:

> Seemed like Jim Clark just dropped out of the sky or some place . . . I had on a lot of clothes . . . I took the coat off and put it around my shoulders . . . Clark thought he was jerking me, but the coat fell. Then he grabbed me and started twisting my arm. I jerked a-loose from him and told him "Don't twist my arm." Then he hit me with the side of his arm on my neck. When he did that, I just lost control. I just started fighting him . . . He said to his deputies, "Did you see that nigger woman beating the hell out of me? Why didn't you do something about it? Y'all standing there see her beating the hell out of me." Four of his deputies they pulled me, and they wrestled me to the ground. When they wrestled me to ground, he got up with his knees in my stomach. . . . Then they turned me over on my stomach, and they handcuffed my hands. . . . and pulled me up off the ground. . . . they put me in the car. . . . when he got me away from the crowd then he hit me with a club, and blood was flowing everywhere.[74]

Cooper was jailed for the incident and initially charged with intent to kill, but even in a Movement dedicated to non-violence, her boldness invigorated others. News of 55-year-old Cooper's encounter with Sheriff Clark circulated throughout the community and images of the exchange were quickly broadcast through national media outlets. In a speech made at a mass meeting at Brown Chapel on the evening of her arrest, Dr. King praised her. The white establishment did not treat men and women differently. Women protestors had as great a chance of being jailed as male protestors and, as the story of Annie Cooper illustrates, the white power establishment was no respecter of age, either.

Not all of the women involved in the Movement were African-American, and Viola Gregg Liuzzo is perhaps the most famous of all the white, female Movement workers. Liuzzo answered Dr. Martin Luther King Jr.'s call for those who love justice to come to Selma, Alabama. Although accounts of the day called her a "housewife," Liuzzo was a mother, a wife, and an activist. The 39-year-old Detroit mother of five was accustomed to standing up and fighting for what she thought was right, even if it violated the conventions of the larger society. In 1949 she divorced her husband, with whom she had two children. The following year she married Anthony James Liuzzo, who was a Teamster organizer, and together they had three additional children. Circumstances forced Liuzzo to drop out of high school, and it was a decision that filled her with regret, so in her adult life she fought for reforms in the Detroit school system.

Liuzzo learned about the African-American freedom struggle through both interpersonal and mass media communication channels.[75] When her children were all in school, she returned to school in order to finish high school and then attended Wayne State University.[76] There, she met students who participated in Freedom Summer, and her knowledge about the Movement grew from this circle. Together, she participated with other like-minded persons in sympathy marches protesting for federal voting rights legislation. She also watched media coverage of the black freedom struggle on the television.[77] The First Unitarian Universalist Church, just two blocks from Wayne State University, had a firm commitment to social justice, and Liuzzo got involved in their activities too.[78] She attended a memorial service for James Reeb, the ordained Universalist pastor killed in Selma, held at the First Unitarian Universalist Church in Detroit.[79] This continued exposure fed her knowledge about the struggle, and when she saw continuing coverage of the Selma campaign on the news, Liuzzo felt compelled to go to Selma. Once persuaded in her conviction, Liuzzo could not be deterred. In fact, prior to leaving, Liuzzo's husband told her she could be killed in Selma. Liuzzo acknowledged this possibility, but she went anyway. To adopt Rogers' words, Liuzzo moved from knowledge to persuasion to decision.

In Selma, Liuzzo played an invaluable role by serving on the SCLC hospitality and transportations committees. Women were often taxed to fill these duties, but the significance of the tasks should not be diminished. Once the federal injunction was lifted, the March could commence, but the protest organizers needed substantial logistics support to keep people informed and shuttle people, food, and equipment back and forth from various locations. Additionally, while the order permitted the March to continue, parts of Highway 80 were only two lanes, and for safety concerns, the order restricted the demonstrators to only 300 people in these areas; yet there were thousands of local people who wanted to participate in the March and thousands more from across the globe who answered King's call. Liuzzo used her car to shuttle people back and forth to various destinations. She was killed while operating in this capacity.

Whites often responded to the successes of the Movement by employing violence, and the final day of the March proved deadly. Viola Liuzzo and Leroy Moton (a young black man from the Selma area who would carry an American flag through much of the March) set off for Montgomery to pick up marchers and return them to Selma. Not far from the Edmund Pettus Bridge, four local Klansmen spotted Liuzzo and Moton, and they began to follow them. Soon, a high-speed chase ensued down Highway 80. Near mile marker 111 in Lowndes County, Alabama, the Klansmen pulled up alongside Liuzzo's moving vehicle, fired inside and killed her. After the car crashed, the Klansmen checked the wreckage. Liuzzo had died immediately. Covered with Liuzzo's blood, Leroy Moton, her passenger, feigned death and survived.

Liuzzo and Moton were readily identified and targeted—likely, the mere act of a white woman in a car with blacks drew attention and suspicion, especially one with out-of-town plates—but so too were her alleged killers. Within 24 hours of the killing, all four Klansmen had been identified. One was an FBI informant. All four were taken into custody and prosecuted, but the Alabama courts convicted none. Instead Viola Liuzzo was vilified in the media and said to be a loose woman. Her participation in the black freedom struggle was painted as depraved, and she was termed an "outside agitator" who left her children to come to the South and stir up trouble. Even her husband's Teamster background was the subject of scrutiny and condemnation. FBI Director, J. Edgar Hoover, himself suggested that Liuzzo and Moton had been engaged in some type of illicit romantic act.

Justice was long delayed and substantially denied for Viola Liuzzo and her family, and much of the public scrutiny she faced stemmed from her gender. In language dangerously close to assertions that some female assault victims are "asking for trouble," questions circled about the propriety of her actions. The first defendant's trial was held in Hayneville, Alabama.

Matthew Hobson Murphy Jr., a Grand Klonsel of the United Klans of America, defended 21-year-old Collie Leroy Wilkins, the alleged triggerman. Murphy was masterful. He successfully painted the FBI informant as someone who could not be trusted (because he had broken his oath with his fellow Klan brothers), and he painted Liuzzo as a white woman who got what she deserved for violating the social norms of the South by being alone in a car with a black man. Wilkins' trial ended in a hung jury. The second trial had the same result. Eugene Thomas (the alleged driver of the car) was acquitted. William Orville Eaton died in 1966. None of the men were ever convicted on state murder charges, and the FBI informant was not even tried in state court. Later, a federal court would convict three of the men of civil rights violations and sentence them to 10 years in prison; however, Gary Thomas Rowe (the FBI informant) was placed in the federal witness protection program and granted immunity.

A popular adage states "the hand that rocks the cradle rules the world," and while this ideology is steeped in gendered ideals, it also reflects the intense importance and centrality of women—mothers, "other-mothers", educators, wives, activists, singers, friends, and parishioners—in sustaining the Movement. Ruby Nell Sales explains how the values the various people—but especially the women—involved in her upbringing inspired her to get involved in the black freedom struggle while she was in college. Sales states:

> So we were in a mutual process of figuring out ways that we could move forward our own lives because once again it was a simultaneous position of individual success and community development. But our success was inextricably tied to the community. We were not on a trajectory of self-ambition for our own selves, and so that was very, very important. For a black child, you were programmed to work for the community. So, it was no stretch to get involved in the Movement. That's what you had been told: "Oh Miss Sales, you're going to be a great lawyer to defend our people and to free our people." Well, if you're told that, it's no great stretch to be in the Movement, so these were the kind of messages that we were getting.

The women of the Movement played multiple roles, and they impressed upon future generations the importance of personal excellence, community, and family, but they were also women seeking freedom from the bondages of those traditional roles. Still, the primary concern of the women of the Movement was the liberation of black people.[80]

Conclusion

Everyday people and their networks were indispensible to the knowledge-persuasion-decision process in the Selma campaign. The formal and informal networks people maintained were key to sustaining the African-American freedom struggle and the mass protests that were dramatized on television and in newspapers. The mass meetings strengthened and encouraged the local people, and the image of local people "petitioning humanity" moved the nation. In this way, the two communication channels—one micro and one macro—are inextricably linked. The pages of history books are laden with stories of the courage of well-known Movement leaders, and their tales are important; however, the courage of everyday people like Jimmie Lee Jackson and James Gildersleeve sustained not only the Selma Movement, but also the larger Civil Rights Movement, of which the Selma Movement and its results would be the pinnacle.

There was a movement underway in Selma long before the early 1965 arrival of Dr. Martin Luther King Jr. or even the arrival of Bernard and Colia Lafayette of SNCC almost 3 years earlier. Instead, it was the people of Selma and the surrounding areas—young and old, working class and professional, male and female—who sustained the Movement, everyday people who made life better for people everywhere just by standing up and insisting on obtaining the rights granted them under the Fifteenth Amendment almost 100 years earlier. To paraphrase Dr. Martin Luther King Jr., these everyday people are the South's true heroes. It is time that they are recognized as such.

CHAPTER 5

Aftermath

The past is never dead. It's not even past.
William Faulkner, Requiem for a Nun, Act 1, Scene III

Fifty-four miles—a total of 285,120 feet walked over the course of 5 days. The Selma to Montgomery protesters walked through torrential rains, taunts, and cheers on a symbolic march to freedom. Montgomery, Alabama, was no promised land. In fact, upon arrival in Montgomery the demonstrators assembled at the foot of the Alabama State Capitol building, the original capitol of the Confederacy, just steps from where Jefferson Davis took the oath of office as President of the Confederate States of America over 100 years earlier. Dexter Avenue Baptist Church, where Martin Luther King Jr., served as pastor from 1954 to 1960 and strategized about the Montgomery Bus Boycott, stood less than 500 feet away, an eerie reminder of the intertwining legacies shared by blacks and whites in the region. So, the march to freedom was circuitous, but as scholar Alexander Keyssar warns, "Democracy . . . must remain a project, a goal, something to be endlessly nurtured and reinforced, an ideal that cannot be fully realized but always can be pursued."[1] This chapter outlines that pursuit. It focuses on the immediate, intermediate, and present-day impacts of the March in order to understand how the project of democracy in America has been and continues to be contested.

The right to vote is among the most cherished of American values. President Ronald Reagan once termed the vote "the crown jewel of American liberties," and said, "we will not see its luster diminished."[2] But the right to vote is not the same as the guarantee of protection for exercise of the same. The year of 1965 marked a critical moment, a turning point in the long African-American quest for freedom, but LDF Special Counsel, Debo Adegbile argues that "the [oral] argument [in Shelby County, Alabama v. Holder] the other day was [also] a critical moment. It was a crossroad in the movement."[3] Earlier laws passed in 1957, 1960, and 1964 provided redress for grievances through the same Southern judicial system that had effectively denied blacks equal protection under the law for hundreds of years. The Voting Rights Act sought to circumvent that ineffective process, and the events of Bloody Sunday helped usher in the swift passage of the Act. According to a 2005 report by the National Commission on the Voting Rights Act:

> Following the brutal attack in Selma, Alabama, by local law enforcement officers on civil rights demonstrators crossing the Edmund Pettus Bridge in March 1965, President Lyndon Johnson asked Congress to pass legislation *guaranteeing* [emphasis added] the voting rights of all citizens.[4]

In fact, "President Lyndon B. Johnson told his Attorney General, Nicholas deB. Katzenbach, to draft the 'goddamnest toughest' voting bill he could write, which Katzenbach proceeded to do."[5] President Johnson was enraged over the events of Bloody Sunday, and especially the killing of Unitarian Universalist minister James Reeb, which the President had termed "an American tragedy."

The preceding chapter discusses the significance of individuals on the diffusion of an innovation; however, the successful adaptation of an idea by the larger society is a social process that operates at the system level. When trusted opinion leaders adopt positive attitudes about the adaptation, it exerts a social pressure on the members of the system to adopt the idea too.[6] The social system will follow its trusted opinion leaders. Following Bloody Sunday, the voting rights struggle, which had been marked for over 100 years by a series of minor successes and vast retreats, reached a threshold or "critical mass." Rogers defines the critical mass as "a kind of tipping point, or social threshold in the diffusion process" when the idea (innovation) catches and spreads.[7] On March 15, 1965, when the opinion leader of the free world, President Lyndon Baines Johnson, took a stand on protection for the minority franchise in his nationally televised address before Congress entitled "The American Promise," he created such a tipping point, and the events of Bloody Sunday were the catalyst.

The events on the Edmund Pettus Bridge acted like a contagion, and support for the social innovation quickly spread. Bloody Sunday, America's call to action in the long march to freedom, occurred on March 7, 1965. Turnaround Tuesday happened on March 9, 1965; James Reeb was assaulted that evening. Two days later, on March 11, 1965, Reeb died of injuries he sustained in his attack. The evening of March 15, 1965, President Johnson delivered his address to Congress. President Johnson said:

> Many of the issues of civil rights are very complex and most difficult. But about this there can and should be no argument. Every American citizen must have an equal right to vote. . . . There is no duty which weighs more heavily on us than the duty we have to ensure that right.[8]

On March 17, 1965, President Johnson sent the matter to Congress. The successful Selma to Montgomery March commenced on March 21, 1965, and it ended on March 25, 1965. Later that evening, Viola Liuzzo was assassinated. After a May 23, 1965 cloture vote,[9] the voting rights bill was passed by Senate on May 26, 1965. Approximately 6 weeks later, the House passed its version of the voting rights bill, and on August 6, 1965, in a public ceremony attended by civil rights leaders including Martin Luther King Jr. and Rosa Parks, President Johnson signed the Voting Rights Act into law. Later in his life, President Johnson called the Civil Rights Act of 1965 his greatest accomplishment.[10]

Seemingly swift passage of the Voting Rights Act was not the only marker of the change in attitudes[11] that provided an ideological shift toward meaningful protection for the minority franchise grants under the Fourteenth and Fifteenth Amendments of the U.S. Constitution. Earlier civil rights legislation failed to address the intractable nature of the Southern legal system, so, arguably, in order to ensure those promises, the provisions of the Voting Rights Act included a level of government interference in state matters unprecedented since the days of the "First Reconstruction."[12]

Voting is a political right, not a civil right, and the First Reconstruction brought political gains for many African-Americans. During Reconstruction, African-Americans took advantage of their new rights and several blacks held office. Franklin and Moss report that between 1869 and 1901 two blacks served in Senate and twenty in the House of Representatives.[13] Surprisingly, the two senators were from Mississippi, and all the representatives were from former Confederate states.[14] But despite the fact that black representation in Congress occurred up to 1901, setbacks began as early as the presidential election of 1876.[15]

The presidential election of 1876 resulted in the Hayes–Tilden compromise.[16] In the election, Republican candidate Rutherford B. Hayes ran against Democratic candidate Samuel Tilden. Tilden received 250,000 more popular votes and appeared to win the electoral vote by one, but election results of four states, including three Southern states—Florida, South Carolina, and Louisiana—were in dispute.[17] The Constitution did not provide a means to resolve the matter, so a fifteen-person panel commission comprising eight Republicans and seven Democrats decided the final election results;[18] they decided on party lines, and gave the presidency to Hayes. The decision was subject to appeal; however, Democrats did not take advantage of the appeal process because the two parties struck an agreement.[19] The Republicans promised to withdraw from the South and increase funding for Southern improvements if the Democrats allowed the election of Hayes to stay. According to noted African-American legal scholar, Derrick Bell, "the demise of blacks as a political force proceeded rapidly thereafter."[20]

After the Hayes–Tilden compromise, African-American rights continued on a steady decline. In *From Slavery to Freedom: A History of Negro Americans*, Franklin and Moss write that, as Reconstruction came to a close, "the North grew weary of the crusade of the Negro."[21] Even prior to the official close of Reconstruction, two 1875 Supreme Court decisions weakened the effectiveness of the Fifteenth Amendment. In U.S. v. Reese,[22] the Supreme Court declared the Enforcement Act of 1870 unconstitutional.[23] That same year in U.S. v. Cruikshank[24] the Court said that the Fifteenth Amendment guaranteed not the right to vote (which the Court held came from the individual states), but the right not to be discriminated against in voting (which the Court held was a federal power). The schizophrenia of the ruling gave Southern states the vehicle they needed to disfranchise black citizens and roll back the gains of Reconstruction. As Northern occupation came to an end, white Southerners pushed to suppress two groups they considered dangerous—blacks and Populists.[25] When the weight of the federal actions discussed was coupled with state actions, the black vote was effectively crippled, and "By 1900, almost all southern states had revised their state constitutions to deny blacks the right to vote."[26]

Civil rights advocates anxiously awaited the Supreme Court's decision in Shelby County, Alabama v. Holder. Their angst was justified. The history of the black vote contains a series of setbacks and advances, which include Supreme Court decisions which have had the effect of hindering the voting climate for blacks, but several Supreme Court decisions have affirmed the sanctity of the ballot. In 1915, the Court declared grandfather clauses unconstitutional.[27] Then, in 1944, the white primary was declared unconstitutional.[28]

But soon after the Supreme Court case of Smith v. Allwright ruled white primaries unconstitutional, Alabama attempted to move to replace district voting with an at-large voter system. Then, in 1960, the Court

Sidebar 5.1

By 1890 many Southern states had instituted white primaries, which precluded non-white citizens from casting votes in primary elections. This inability to participate in the primary process meant that non-white voters could not effectively participate in selecting a candidate of their choice.

Amid Constitutional challenges, the U.S. Supreme Court upheld the white primary in the 1935 case of Grovey v. Townsend (295 U.S. 45); however, 9 years later, the Court declared the all-white primary unconstitutional.

declared racial gerrymandering[29] unconstitutional.[30] Finally, in 1966, a year after passage of the Voting Rights Act, poll taxes were declared unconstitutional.[31] It is, however, important to note that, until passage of the Voting Rights Act and for a time thereafter, intimidation still worked to dissuade many Southern blacks from voting as Jim Crow was "embedded in the region's structured race relations."[32] This history of judicial gains and legislative retreats reaffirms the merit of separation of powers, which acts as a constraint on abuses of power and/or abuses of the powerless.

The Voting Rights Act establishes substantial federal oversight in voting and contains both permanent and non-permanent provisions[33] that provide protection against both disenfranchisement and vote dilution. This chapter begins by outlining the provisions of the Voting Rights Act. Next, we examine the impacts—immediate, intermediate, and present-day—of the Act. After an analysis of the historical and present role of place in the African-American franchise, the chapter moves to a discussion of the contested nature of the franchise and the need for continuing safeguards for democracy, before ending with a brief discussion of Selma, today.

The Voting Rights Act of 1965

The Voting Rights Act protects against minority disfranchisement and minority vote dilution. It has already been stated that the Act contains both permanent and non-permanent, but renewable provisions. The latter provisions were drafted specifically for the purpose of addressing some place-based discriminatory patterns Congress observed, and while those temporary provisions are, by definition, not intended to be permanent, as long as there is a legislative determination that there is still a sufficient amount of voting discrimination such that the remedies Section 5 exacts are necessary to redress or deter such patterns, it is defensible that they remain. Section 2 is the primary permanent provision of the Act, and Section 5 is the primary temporary provision.

Section 2 of the Voting Rights Act (42 U.S C. §1973), as amended, states in the relevant part:

> (a) No voting qualification or prerequisite to voting or standard, practice, or procedure shall be imposed or applied by any State or political subdivision in a manner which results in a denial or abridgment of the right of any citizen of the United States to vote on account of race or color, or in contravention of the guarantees set forth in section 4(f)(2), as provided in subsection (b).
>
> (b) A violation of subsection (a) is established if, based on the totality of circumstances, it is shown that the political processes leading to nomination or election in the State or political subdivision are not equally open to participation by members of the class of citizens protected by subsection (a) in that its members have less opportunities than other members of the electorate to participate in the political process and to elect representatives of their choice.

Section 2 of the Voting Rights Act applies nationwide; Section 5 only applies to certain "covered jurisdictions."

Debo Adegbile, the NAACP Legal Defense Fund attorney who successfully argued the 2009 challenge to Section 5 of the Act and argued the most recent challenge,[34] terms Section 2 a "lesser remedy." Mr. Adegbile urges:

> Because the Court explored the idea that perhaps we don't need Section 5, and we can just go back to the case-by-case method under the other part of the Voting Rights Act, Section 2, which significantly puts the burden on voters in, for example, county commissions, school boards, towns, and parishes that the Department of Justice barely gets to, that the national civil rights groups don't get to as often as we would like to and that local lawyers on the ground don't always have adequate enough resources to bring these highly complex cases with multiple experts that need to testify to challenge after-the-fact. I want to emphasize this point, to challenge after-the-fact discrimination that is already having an impact in the community and then to try to set it aside after the votes are happening. After people who aren't entitled to be elected are serving as incumbents. It's a lesser remedy.[35]

While Section 2 remedies are available after an infraction, under Section 5 of the Voting Rights Act jurisdictions submit any voting alterations they wish to make to the federal authority to get approval for the changes prior to implementation through a process called "preclearance." Seemingly mundane things like the modification of a polling place as well as those many would consider more substantial, such as a move from electing to appointing judges and the annexation of a jurisdiction, require preclearance.[36] Jurisdictions submit their changes to the Department of Justice or a three-judge court in the District of Columbia for a determination regarding whether the requested change interferes with the ability of minority voters to participate in the political process. In this manner, Section 5 acts to both deter and block prohibited conduct.

The provisions of the Voting Rights Act—both temporary and permanent—are made possible by the grant of authority charged to Congress under the Fifteenth Amendment to the Constitution to impose legislation necessary to prevent discrimination in voting. The Act is both remedial and preventative. Section 5 has been termed the "strong medicine" of the Act, and it is a temporary provision. Currently, Section 5 covers nine states—Alabama, Alaska, Arizona, Georgia, Louisiana, Mississippi, South Carolina, Texas, and Virginia—and a number of township and county jurisdictions in other states are covered either in whole or in part.[37] The coverage formula for inclusion under the preclearance provisions of Section 5 is found in Section 4 of the Act, which the Supreme Court recently invalidated. The prerequisites under Section 4, paragraphs (a)–(c) of the Act, under which a state or jurisdiction would be subject to Section 5 preclearance, are paraphrased below. A state or jurisdiction is subject to the provisions of Section 4 of the Act if:

1) On November 1, 1964, it maintained a "test or device," which restricted individuals' opportunity to register and vote. Tests or devices include but are not limited to literacy tests and "vouching" systems.[38] This requirement is also satisfied if, "the Director of the Census determined that less than 50 percent of persons of voting age were registered to vote on November 1, 1964, or that less than 50 percent of persons of voting age voted in the presidential election of November 1964."[39]

2) A new prong was added to the coverage formula in 1970 and, under the 1970 provisions, locales that maintain a prohibited "test or device" as of November 1968 were included, as well as areas without the requisite (50 percent) voter registration statistics as of November 1968.

3) In 1975 provisions were added to include special protections for "language minority groups."[40] Voter registration records

from 1972 are used under this provision. Congress expanded
the term "test or device" to specifically include "the practice
of providing any election information, including ballots, only
in English in states or political subdivisions where members
of a single language minority constituted more than five
percent of the citizens of voting age."[41]

The Section 5 coverage formula uses statistics from 1964, 1968, and 1972, and any jurisdiction can be covered if it meets one of the above-stated criteria. An entire state can be included or certain jurisdictions within the state.

Critics lambast the fact that Section 5 coverage is triggered by the use of now decades-old data; however, proponents argue that while Section 5 has bail-in provisions, there are also bailout provisions. In order to bail out, a jurisdiction or state must file an action for declaratory judgment with the U.S. District Court for the District of Columbia and demonstrate a record of good behavior for a period of 10 consecutive years. In 1982 Congress revised the bailout provisions to indicate that successful bailout can only be granted upon evidence that the applicant has employed no discriminatory test or device for a period of 10 years and that all vestiges of discriminatory devices have been removed. Under the scheme, until bailout, any state or jurisdiction subject to Section 5 must get preclearance before it initiates any changes impacting voting rights. Federal court oversight in these matters has been helpful at protecting the minority franchise, especially by keeping such matters out of Southern state courts, which have historically failed to protect minority voters.

Immediate Impacts

The Act's influence was almost immediate. It suspended literacy tests and other voting impediments, and it authorized the appointment of federal registrars[42] in states and voting districts with a history of employing discriminatory practices to suppress the minority vote. In the event of discrimination, the Act authorized the Attorney General to send federal examiners to replace local registrars. Some 250,000 new black voters registered within just months of the passage of the Act; one testament to the immediate effectiveness of the Act is the fact that federal examiners registered one-third of all new black voters.[43]

While the Act resulted in a substantial rise in voter registration rates among the voting-age African-American population, a number of jurisdictions continued to employ voter dilution tactics. In a chapter on the impact of the Voting Rights Act on Alabama that appears in the book *Quiet Revolution in the South: The Impact of the Voting Rights Act 1965–1990*, Peyton McCrary et al. write:

> When the Voting Rights Act was adopted, most Alabama
> jurisdictions already used citywide or countywide elections
> designed, together with a "numbered-place" requirement, to
> dilute black voting strength. The state could best prevent black
> office holding without having to change its election laws (and thus
> be subject to the preclearance provision of section 5). Politicians
> in Alabama, as in the rest of the South, had long understood that
> at-large elections enable a white majority . . . to prevent minority
> representation altogether. Black office holding in Alabama was
> [therefore] achieved, by and large, only as a result of successful
> voting rights litigation challenging the use of at-large elections.[44]

But while voter dilution tactics were increasing, the rise in African-American voter registration rates was undeniable.

Some of the immediate impacts of the Act were shocking. For example, just 4 years after passage of the Act, the state of Mississippi led the nation in African-American turnout. While 74 percent of the eligible African-American voting-age population turned out to vote, it took another two decades before Mississippi elected its first African-American to Congress since Reconstruction.[45] The Supreme Court case of South Carolina v. Katzenbach[46] was one of the first challenges to the Voting Rights Act. In its majority opinion, the Supreme Court notes that the year before the Act, voter registration rates among the voting-age population of African-Americans in Louisiana, Mississippi, and Alabama, was "roughly 50 percentage points or more" below that of whites.[47] Registration rates among the black voting-age population in Alabama was approximately 19.4 percent; in Louisiana, it was 31.8 percent, and in Mississippi, it was only 6.4 percent; but after the Act, the gaps substantially narrowed.[48] However, increases in voter registration rates do not necessarily correspond to increases in voter turnout. Still, by 1975 there was considerable evidence that the effectiveness of the old Southern system of intimidation and violence was waning. According to a 1975 report published by the Commission on Civil Rights, even Southern states saw a decided increase in African-American voter turnout.[49]

Intermediate Impacts

Despite some leveling, decades after passage of the Act, black voter registration rates remained somewhat on a par with white registration rates. In part, this is attributable to increased registration numbers in Southern states, where a significant portion of America's African-American population still reside.[50] The table, compiled by Teaching Tolerance, illustrates these rates.

EXPANDING VOTING RIGHTS

Percentage of Registered Voters in Black Voting-Age Population 1960, 1971, 2008

One way to evaluate the success of the Voting Rights Act is to look at the percentages of eligible black voters who registered to vote before the Act passed and after.

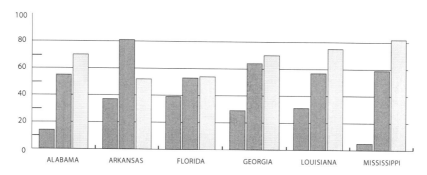

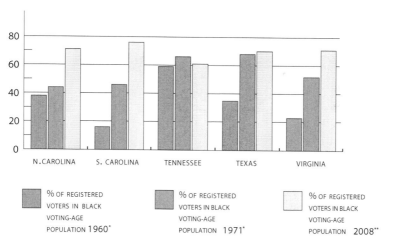

| | % OF REGISTERED VOTERS IN BLACK VOTING-AGE POPULATION 1960* | % OF REGISTERED VOTERS IN BLACK VOTING-AGE POPULATION 1971* | % OF REGISTERED VOTERS IN BLACK VOTING-AGE POPULATION 2008** |

*Source: Farragher, et. al. (2003). Out of Many: A History of the American People. (Upper Saddle River, NJ), p. 892.
**Source: Table 4b. Reported Voting and Registration of the Voting-Age Population, by Sex, Race and Hispanic Origin, for States: November 2008. Link through: www.census.gov/hhes/www/socdemo/voting/publications/p20/2008/tables.html

Figure 5.1 Percentage of registered voters in black voting–age population, 1960, 1971, 2008.

Teaching Tolerance is a project of the Southern Poverty Law Center, and it provides a number of resources, including classroom activities, to educators in order to facilitate student learning.[51] The figure above, Percentage of registered voters in the black voting-age population 1960, 1971, 2008, comes from its lesson plan titled "Expanding Voting Rights."

Looking at the Southern states—which include Alabama, Arkansas, Florida, Georgia, Louisiana, Mississippi, North Carolina, South Carolina, Tennessee, Texas, and Virginia—the table from 1960 (before passage of the Act) to 1971 (6 years after passage of the Act) reveals across-the-board increases in the percentage of the black voting-age population that registered. During that period, the most marked increases occurred in Alabama (to about 31 percent), Louisiana (to about 27 percent), and Mississippi (about 54 percent). From 1971 to 2008, some leveling occurs, but the impact of the Act is most apparent in the percent change from 1960 to 1971.

The Act had its successes, but challenges still remained. The election of black officials was the next hurdle in the voting rights struggle. From 1965 to 1985, Grofman and Handley note a marked increase in the number of blacks elected to office in Southern states; however, the authors caution that this increase is largely because the Act increased districts having a black majority,[52] and it does not indicate a substantial number of white voters voting for African-American candidates.[53] The authors note:

> In this article we examine the reasons for the growth in the number of black state legislators between the passage of the Voting Rights Act in 1965, when virtually no blacks held political office in the South, and 1985 (after the last round of redistricting). The argument is currently popular that the recent election of blacks to prominent political positions indicates the coming of a new era in southern politics—an era of increased willingness on the part of white voters to cast their ballots for black candidates. We demonstrate that this argument is misguided.[54]

Racial bloc voting still exists—among black and white Southerners—such that Grofman and Handley find that "districts that are at least 60% black are most likely to elect black legislators."[55] Their 1991 article found little evidence of a decrease in racially polarized voting in the American South.

In an effort to prevent prohibited voter disenfranchisement and voter dilution, and amid findings of continued discrimination, Congress reauthorized the non-permanent provisions of the Act in 1970, 1975, 1982, 1992, and 2006.[56] Findings of dilution were noted in each reauthorization attempt, and in 1982 the Congress found "a link between dilution and racially polarized voting." Continued findings of voter discrimination have focused more on vote dilution than the overt disenfranchisement that was historically the case. The old practice of vote dilution concentrated on gerrymandering, which was outlawed by the Supreme Court, but those old practices have given way to new means. The place-based patterns identified in this section make it easier to contemplate how new groups of minorities, especially Latinos (now the largest minority group in America) and other language-based minorities, might struggle for a place at the table in a modern South that has historically viewed its racial dynamic as black and white.

Present Import

Congress amassed a considerable record of continuing discrimination in voting prior to its most recent renewal of Section 5. In the face of this record, proponents of the Act should not be satisfied with short-term or intermediate gains. In *Requiem for a Nun*, noted Southern author, William Faulkner writes, "the past is not dead"; in fact, he continues, "it is not even past." Perhaps nowhere is this assertion truer than the American South with its living monuments to the dead all while assailing that the sins of the past are of no consequence to those living in the present.

The racial, ethnic, and economic composition of America is changing, and new groups of disenfranchised are rising. These new groups, too, deserve the protections the Act affords. Indeed, LDF Special Counsel Debo Adegbile believes that both Section 2 and Section 5 of the Act are still necessary. He states:

> So this is a dangerous question to explore this idea about whether case-by-case [under Section 2 of the Act] works when we know that history tells us that it hasn't, and we see that the record of discrimination says that what we needed is both Section 5 and Section 2 and other laws, and the Motor Voter Law, and the Help America Vote Act, and the Uniform and Overseas Voters Act, and six amendments to the Constitution, and perhaps some additional protections after the recent election to further protect voters. Democracy in America has been about gradual additions of people to the process. We started with democracy being for very few people, and then slowly gradually with a push from the people we have expanded participation. And so the idea that you would target the most effective thing to enfranchise people who were excluded and take down that protection is completely contrary to experience . . . [and] should give us some concern.[57]

The Voting Rights Act serves dual purposes. It acts as a remedy against past discrimination and a deterrent against future discrimination, and while minority voter participation rates have increased, what many perceive as attacks on voter access have risen. Legislative attempts at suppressing voter turnout are even more disconcerting when considering the findings of a consumer research social and demographic trends report released December 26, 2012, which states "unlike other minority groups whose increasing electoral muscle has been driven mainly by population growth, blacks' rising share of the vote in the past four presidential elections has been the result of rising turnout rates."[58] As a result, constraints on voter turnout could effectively act as a constraint on the black vote.

According to research tabulations of the Census Current Population Survey taken from the October 2012 monthly and November 2008 supplements, the racial and ethnic composition of the eligible electorate for 2012 and 2008, respectively broke down as follows: Whites comprised 71 percent of the eligible electorate in 2012 compared to 73 percent in 2008. Blacks comprised 12 percent of the eligible electorate in both 2012 and 2008. Hispanics comprised 11 percent of the eligible electorate in 2012 and 9 percent in 2008. Asians comprised 4 percent in 2012 compared to 3 percent in 2008, and those classifying as "other" comprised 2 percent of the eligible electorate in both 2012 and 2008. Exit poll rates for 2012 and 2008 show slightly higher percentages across the black and white categories and slightly decreased percentages across the Hispanic and Asian categories.[59] As the racial composition of the nation continues to change, new concerns about the continuing need for safeguards to protect the minority franchise are likely to grow, and many are likely to be geographically based.

Place Matters

Place is a primary consideration in electoral matters. It influences social attitudes, political affiliations, and is a consideration in redistricting matters. The salience of race is felt on multiple levels from the national, to regional, to state, and local matters, and it is evident in the intent and rationale for the Act. According to the Justice Department's website, "When Congress enacted the Voting Rights Act of 1965, it determined that racial discrimination in voting had been more prevalent in certain areas of the country." This section pays special attention to the significance of race in voting patterns and attitudes. It briefly assesses the role geography and history have played in recent challenges to Section 5 by covered states; it also examines place-based redistricting issues and restrictions, and it ends with a discussion of today's Alabama electorate.

Sidebar 5.2

Historian C. Vann Woodward discusses the roots of "Southern distinctiveness" in his work, *The Burden of Southern History*.

According to Woodward, both Northerners and Southerners were complicit in continuing the idea of "Southern distinctiveness." As the country tried to popularize the idea of "American exceptionalism," the American North used the South as a scapegoat—the source of all the moral failings of the country's past. Soon, Southerners began to revel in this "otherness," and painted the South as the source of virtue, purity, innocence, and traditionalism as contrasted with Northern aggression.

Most of the states covered by Section 5 are in the South, while only two of the covered states—Alaska and Arizona—are not. This is significant because sufficient regional differences in attitudes still persist in U.S. society. For example, voter registration rates for blacks vary by region, and at one point since passage of the Act, Southern blacks had a 13-point lower turnout rate than the Northwest.[60] Assessing racial attitudes in the 1990s, researchers Tuch and Martin note, "Southerners in general—and Deep South southerners in particular—are the least likely to endorse policies intended to ameliorate racial inequality."[61] Their 1997 article observed a persistent "Southern distinctiveness in voting."[62]

The fruits of this "Southern distinctiveness in voting" are evident at all levels—local, state, and national—but the impediments are particularly difficult to overcome at the national level. In the 2008 presidential election results, the pattern of Southern distinctiveness is especially salient in the Deep South.

President Obama's [2008] victory provides evidence of great progress, while also illustrating the ongoing salience of race in American democracy. Exit polls from the 2008 Presidential Election show that a record 95% of African-Americans, 67% of Latinos, and 62% of Asian Americans voted for President Obama nationally, but the President received the vote of only 43% of white voters. Whites were the only racial group that did not cast a majority of votes for President Obama. In addition, the results in Alabama, Mississippi, and Louisiana bring these national racially polarized results into even sharper focus . . . of the white voters in these three states, only 10% in Alabama, 11% in Mississippi and 14% in Louisiana pulled the lever for President Obama.[63]

The Joint Center for Political and Economic Activities attributes President Obama's lackluster performance among white voters, especially in the Southern states, to race.[64] Another report specifies that 2008 election data analysis shows that President Obama faced:

> [A] demonstrable challenge to winning voters in section 5-covered jurisdictions on the basis of his race—as well as ample other evidence that other candidates of color, particularly at the state and local levels, face even higher obstacles to winning elections.[65]

The long standing realization that race plays a role in voting patterns is part of the rationale for a race-conscious policy in matters that threaten to dilute minority voting strength. Yet, despite these racially polarized 2008 presidential election results, several commentators suggested that the election of President Obama meant that racial barriers in voting were over and that America was now a post-racial society.[66]

Claims that the election of America's first African-American president meant the country was now a "post-racial" society persisted. In 2006, soon after Congress' 25-year reauthorization of key provisions of the Voting Rights Act, including Section 5 (preclearance), the Municipal Utility District of Austin, Texas, brought suit. Texas, a covered jurisdiction under Section 5, challenged the constitutionality of the statute.[67] The U.S. District Court in the District of Columbia rejected the lawsuit. The municipal district requested review by the Supreme Court. The Supreme Court agreed to hear the case. Among others, Georgia Governor Sonny Perdue filed a brief in support of the plaintiff's (Texas) action.[68] Governor Perdue's state is also covered by Section 5 and, thereby, subject to preclearance requirements. In an amicus brief, Governor Purdue suggested that President Obama's recent election was "proof" that Georgia and other states should no longer be subject to Section 5.[69] Governor Perdue was not alone in his assertion. Part of the Municipal Utility District's argument, which sought to strike down Section 5 of the Voting Rights Act, was also that the election of President Obama proved America was living in a post-racial society, and so

At the 2006 Voting Rights Act Reauthorization signing ceremony held on the South Lawn of the White House, President George Bush said, "Today we renew a bill that helped bring a community on the margins into the life of American democracy. My administration will vigorously enforce the provisions of this law, and we will defend it in court." Soon after the signing, President Bush would be forced to do just that.

Section 5 was no longer necessary. The Supreme Court heard oral arguments on April 29, 2009—the one hundredth day of President Obama's presidency.

According to recent Census records, approximately 85 percent of Shelby County, Alabama, is white, and about 11 percent is black. In the state of Alabama 70 percent of the citizens are white, compared to 26.5 percent who self-classify as black.

The Texas challenge was unsuccessful, and the Court upheld Section 5, but other challenges would follow. The most recent challenge, Shelby County, Alabama v. Holder, was successful. The Court held the coverage formula used for subjecting jurisdictions to preclearance unconstitutional. Like the Municipal Utility District case, Shelby County asserted that Congress had exceeded its grasp and Section 5 should be invalidated. While Shelby County did not prevail on that claim, it was successful on the related claim that the coverage formula for Section 5 was unconstitutional.[70]

Redistricting

Protection for the franchise is about more than just being able to register to vote and/or cast a ballot; several 1960s cases establish the principle of "one person, one vote."[71] These cases predate the Voting Rights Act of 1965; however, through Section 2 of the Voting Rights Act, which prohibits minority vote dilution, the Voting Rights Act helps to enforce the principle of "one person, one vote." Results of the decennial Census are used to draw the lines that are used to determine political districts for the nation. These Census results are used to create districts of equal population size, and then create boundaries that determine electoral districts for each state. The same districts are used to determine the electoral districts for all levels of government: local, state, and federal representation. Unlike reapportionment, redistricting involves the drawing of boundaries.[72]

While federal data obtained from the Census is used, it is state bodies that are ultimately responsible for redrawing district lines (at the state level) and local and city and county governments at their respective levels. In the redistricting process, covered jurisdictions would be required to submit voting changes, including redistricting plans, to the Department of Justice for preclearance. Once again, changes that the Department of Justice or a three-judge Panel District Court determines as discriminatory would not be approved.[73]

Dilution of minority voting strength is not permitted. For this reason, race is an important consideration in redistricting; however, the 1993 Supreme Court ruling in Shaw v. Reno[74] limits consideration of the race to cases where race satisfies a "compelling state interest" in the redrawing of a district line. Here again, the Act is implicated, as adherence to the standards of the Voting Rights Act may satisfy such an interest. One of the traditional ways communities have tried to dilute minority-voting strength is through packing (compression of smaller minority districts into one). Another approach has been splitting or "cracking" minority districts, which splits up or dilutes minority voting strength.

Today's Alabama Electorate

In *Place and Politics: The Geographical Meditation of State and Society*, John Agnew argues that "place" is an ontological distinction readily applicable to the study of elections.[75] Alabama is known as the Heart of Dixie. The name suggests something about it that distinguishes it from other places, even places in the Deep South. Bordering places have influences from other regions, but to be in the "Heart of Dixie" suggests that the area remains somehow unpolluted by those influences that might corrupt border places. The state of Alabama comprises several distinct regions that include the Black Belt, among others. Still, Webster and Quinton suggest a "common social conditioning" present in Alabama counties.[76] But, even in the Heart of Dixie, "there are distinct geographies."[77]

While the Alabama electorate is still largely conservative, some shifts are notable. African-Americans represent 25 percent of the Alabama electorate, and although Latinos represent less than 4 percent, their numbers are growing, and their influence may be immediately felt on highly divisive issues. According to one study, minority group members are more likely to vote for "progressive initiatives"; while urban dwellers tend to be progressive, rural dwellers are not.[78] College students, too, tend to be more progressive in their attitudes, so as the population of Alabama goes through shifts (rural areas are losing population to urban areas and a growing creative class is forming around college campuses),[79] we may see these changes influencing voting patterns in the state, especially in urban areas and locations with high concentrations of college students.

Some, particularly traditionalists, may feel challenged by these changing demographics, but the composition of American society is changing, not just Alabama. The percentage of white share of the population has decreased with each subsequent generation. In fact, using the calculations from the March 2011 Community Population Survey for the civilian, non-institutional population, the Pew Research Center determined that while whites constituted 83 percent of those born between 1901 and 1927, among so called "Millennials" (those born from 1981 to 1993), whites comprise just 59 percent of the population. While Alabama did not go to

Obama, its changing electorate, including racial and ethnic minorities, the young, and women all turned out in record numbers to support the election of America's first African-American president. All these numbers are not yet available for the 2012 election, but early results indicate that this pattern remained consistent.

The Project of Democracy—Freedom is a Constant Struggle

While the focus of much of this book has been on the contraction of African-American voting rights, it is important to remember that throughout America's history the project of democracy has involved expansions of the voting rights of various categories of citizens. Because the original Constitution said very little about voting, matters were left to each state to decide. This realization makes it easier to understand how many Southern states cried foul when the federal government tried to "interfere" in voting, a matter that they perceived to be up to the individual states to decide.

Voting rights expansions did occur, and most of them occurred at the federal level. The first expansion involved the extension of voting rights to non-propertied white men. In the early days of the Republic, voting was limited. In fact, in most states, only white, male property owners could vote. Other states further limited voting to males who paid taxes or those who had some military service. The largely nominal grant of the franchise to African-Americans came through the Reconstruction Era Amendments. Women did not earn their suffrage until 1920 with the ratification of the Nineteenth Amendment. By the time of its ratification, the Women's Suffrage Movement had been going on for 80 years. A woman's right to vote was added to the United States Constitution only after a protracted battle. The expansion of voting rights protections for "racial and ethnic minorities" and "language minorities" has been addressed in detail, so it will not be restated here, but it represents important expansions to the project of democracy. Extension of the franchise to 18-year-olds came next, and it also occurred through a somewhat contested federal action. In its 1970 extension of the Voting Rights Act, Congress included a provision that lowered the national voting age from 21 years of age to 18. Again, states balked at a perceived challenge to their authority. Later, upheaval

Some of the reasons given why women should not have the right to vote included arguments that women who vote may not attend to their domestic duties and women were too irrational to make wise decisions.

about a court challenge[80] to Congress' ability to lower the voting age in non-federal elections resulted in the proposal and later ratification of a Constitutional amendment. The Twenty-sixth Amendment was adopted on July 1, 1971. This short examination of the expansion of voting rights reveals that such expansion has largely been accomplished through an increase in federal government involvement and oversight in such matters.

The presidential election of 2008 effectively closed the gap in voter turnout between blacks and whites. But a new set of restrictions aimed at influencing minority voting participation rates is rising. A number of proposed or enacted measures operate to block the road either at the registration stage, early voting station, or on Election Day itself. These include restrictions on registration drives (such as limiting when and where people can register), expanding eligibility requirements (such as proof of citizenship and durational residency requirements), increasing the disfranchisement of people with felony convictions, voter purges of the rolls,[81] reductions in early voting (including absentee ballots), and a barrage of restrictive photo identification laws.

The Contested Nature of Democracy

As stated earlier, the right to vote is a political right, not a civil right. Sometimes, you have to stand up for your rights. This section discusses recent threats to the protections granted in the Fifteenth Amendment and made manifest by the Voting Rights Act. Several cases will be examined. Each involves a Section 5-covered jurisdiction, and each illustrates the continuing need for Section 5 protections for the franchise.

The first case study involves college students at Prairie View A & M University. Prairie View A & M University is a historically black college located in the city of Prairie View in Waller County, Texas. In the 1970s, the Waller County Registrar intentionally acted to prevent most students at Prairie View A & M from registering to vote. The Registrar alleged that the students were not legal residents of the county and used this as the basis for the denial. A challenge was brought under Section 5 of the Act, and the case went to court. The Registrar was restrained from barring students to register to vote. Years later, in the 1990s, some Prairie View students

Political rights or liberties differ from civil rights. Civil rights include things such as the freedom to assemble. Political rights involve the abilities of citizens to participate in political activities, such as voting. Political rights can be both granted and protected by the government.

were indicted and charged with "illegal voting." The charges of illegal voting, which were later dropped, seemed to again be based on allegations that the students were not legal residents of the county. This extensive history provides the backdrop for a 2004 conflict.

In March 2004, two students from Prairie View announced that they were running for local office. A local District Attorney threatened to charge and prosecute the students if they voted in the election. The alleged charge would be "illegal voting." The local NAACP chapter sued the attorney. Unfortunately, that was not the end of the matter. Next, the Waller County Commissioners voted to significantly reduce the early voting polling hours at the polling location closest to campus. The act itself was heinous, but the fact that the students would be on spring break during the primary, and would therefore need to vote early, made the Board's actions even more odious. Despite being in a Section 5-covered jurisdiction, Waller County acted without submitting the change in polling place hours for required Section 5 preclearance. Finally, the County restored the early voting hours, but only after the NAACP filed suit—again. The Texas locale's attempts to thwart the students from voting appear to stem from dual concerns about race and age, and as both blocks of voters—minorities and students—tend to be more progressive, the aim of the attempts seems to be to take away the group's constitutionally given right to have a voice in politics.

The second case study occurred in Florida, another Section 5-covered jurisdiction. Decades after the Voting Rights Act's passage, the now famous 2000 presidential election operated to effectively disfranchise a group of voters, a large percentage of whom were minority voters. By 2000, the predicted shift in America's demographics was becoming evident. From 1962 to 2000 the African-American percentage of the voting age population increased from 9.2 percent to 11.9 percent. In the same election, Caucasians comprised 80.7 percent of the voting population, Latinos 5.4 percent, Asian-Americans 1.8 percent and other Americans 0.2 percent. According to the Census Bureau, 53.5 percent of the black voting-age population voted in the 2000 election as compared with 60.4 percent of the white voting-age population, and reverse migration trends resulted in a majority of America's African-American citizens, about 55 percent, residing in the South.[82]

In a throwback to the earlier Hayes–Tilden compromise, which resulted in the end of Reconstruction, the presidential election of 2000 pitted Republican George Bush against Democrat Al Gore. As the election results poured in, many newscasts ceded the election to Democrat, Al Gore. As the night continued, it became clear that the electoral votes for the state of Florida would decide the election. The controversy that resulted left the nation in limbo for in excess of a month. In the end, Florida's 25 electoral votes were awarded to Bush, and he won the election. Gore closed with 266 electoral votes; however the awarding of Florida's electoral votes to Gore instead of Bush would have changed the election results. If that controversy alone was not enough, Gore received more popular votes than Bush, and yet Bush still won the election.

The Commission on Civil Rights investigated, and its findings revealed some alarming patterns, which, if not in intent, in application, seemed to be race-based. There were numerous claims that blacks in Florida in the 2000 election were disenfranchised.[83] Voting irregularities in Florida included black college students being intimidated or turned away from the polls, irregular polling hours, confusing ballots, and outdated equipment.[84] According to Congressman John Lewis, these irregularities "demonstrate that African-Americans are not guaranteed the right to vote in this county" and that the situation in Florida was tantamount to denial of the right to have your vote count.[85]

The Commission on Civil Rights investigated the 2000 presidential election claims of disenfranchisement in Florida, and they identified several Election Day problems. A partial list of those problems follows. First, a law-enforcement checkpoint was set up in a black community, which impaired black voters from getting to the polls and resulted in numerous complaints. Second, along with the names of felons who were removed from the rolls, several non-felons had their names removed from the voting rolls. Third, there were numerous inadequate polling sites, including staffing problems. Fourth, polling places were moved without notice. Fifth, a number of precincts were given defective voting equipment. Finally, persons with disabilities had difficulty accessing numerous polling sites. Researchers discovered a "positive relationship between race and voter disenfranchisement."[86]

Prior to the matter being decided by the U.S. Supreme Court, the Florida Supreme Court ordered a recount of some 40,000 votes. In a 5 to 4 decision the U.S. Supreme Court overturned the Florida Supreme Court's ruling of the manual recount, and this made Bush the undisputed president. In its decision, the Supreme Court said the votes, "could not be accurately recounted and stop[ped] the recounting that had been ordered by the Florida Supreme Court."[87] While the Commission found no evidence of a conspiracy, the report did condemn Governor Jeb Bush and Florida Secretary of State Katherine Harris, who also served as George Bush's Florida leader for the election campaign, for failure to prevent the widescale Election Day problems.[88]

Criticism for the Florida Election Day problems continued to mount. Research found that African-American votes were more likely to be discounted than white votes in the 2000 presidential election, but Georgia Congressman and former civil rights leader, John Lewis, said that the 2000 election was more than about Republicans and Democrats, more than about Bush and Gore, more than about black and white. According to Lewis, the 2000 election was about "the right to vote."[89] Some positive results came from the incident. An Election Assistance Commission was formed in 2002. On October 29, 2002, Bush signed the bill authorizing the Commission. The Commission could supply funds needed to replace outdated voting equipment. Still, lingering questions about the disfranchisement of a large block of minority voters remain.

The above cases illustrate that the voting rights battle is far from finished. On the one hand, turnout in the 2008 presidential election was more diverse than the country had ever seen, but soon afterwards several states, including a number of Southern states, began to enact or, in the case of jurisdictions subject to preclearance under Section 5, tried to enact legislation that might have the impact of curtailing the minority vote. For example, the Department of Justice denied South Carolina's request for preclearance of a voter ID law. The DOJ found that minority voters were more likely than white voters to lack a photo ID that met the state standards. Alabama has imposed a photo ID requirement that is said to take effect in the 2014 statewide primary elections. Alabama's requirement is also subject to preclearance. Mississippi passed its voter ID law through a citizens' initiative. The citizens' initiative needs an implementing statute, and that statute was passed in the 2012 legislature. Mississippi's statute is also subject to preclearance from the Department of Justice. Voter identification laws disproportionately affect the ability of minorities to vote. In one Tennessee example, the restriction was so onerous as to deny a 96-year-old black woman the opportunity to vote because she could not supply an original copy of her marriage certificate.[90] The woman opined that voting was more difficult now than under Jim Crow.[91]

Like voter identification laws, restrictions on the voting rights of felons have a disproportionate impact on minorities. Michelle Alexander, author of *The New Jim Crow: Mass Incarceration in the Age of Colorblindness*, says,

> We use the criminal justice system to label people of color as "criminals" then engage in all the practices we left behind. Today it is perfectly legal to discriminate against criminals in nearly all the ways that it was once legal to discriminate against African-Americans.[92]

Fifty states regulate the voting rights of convicted felons; however, those regulations vary widely. A few states permit felons to vote while incarcerated (Maine and Vermont), but most states are far more restrictive. In Kentucky and Virginia a felon's voting rights can only be restored by application of the governor. Other states permit restoration of voting rights after completion of parole or supervised release. Some states restrict voting rights based on the type of crime committed, and others allow felons to resume their voting rights after they have been released from prison. In Alabama those felons convicted of certain types of violent crimes can never have their voting rights restored.[93]

Beyond Voter Registration

Since the grant of the franchise, black voter participation rates have been highly variable. Historical analyses on voter turnout rates conducted by the Social Science Data Analysis Network (SSDAN) reveal the following trends in black voter turnout rates:

> Historically, the percentage of black citizens who vote has tallied below the percentage of all citizens who vote. Since 1972, when the difference peaked at 10.9%, the gap has started to narrow. With a 1.8% decline, 1980 marked the first significant decrease in the percent difference, and 1984 followed with an even more substantial 4.6% reduction. Despite the gap widening again in 1988 and 1992, with the difference rising to 5.9% and 7.3% respectively, the difference again began to fall in 1996. In 2000, the percentage of all citizens who voted outweighed the percentage of black citizens who voted by only 1.2%. In 2008, and for the first time in a presidential election, black citizens voted at a higher rate than the greater population, outpacing all Americans by 2.6%.[94]

The SSDAN report suggests the "rise in voter turnout among black citizens in 2008 can most likely be attributed to the presence of a black Democratic presidential nominee."[95] The highest voter turnout rate recorded occurred in 1964[96]—the year prior to the Voting Rights Act—and it is likely that increased levels of black voter registration contributed to these numbers, especially as both political parties actively courted black voters. Beyerlein and Andrews explain:

> Black voter registration had been increasing at a steady pace since World War II and the Supreme Court's decision in Smith v. Allwright (1944). From a low level 3% in 1940, black registration in the South increased to 16.8% in 1950, 29.4% in 1960, and 43% in 1964—the year prior to the Voting Rights Act.[97]

This history establishes a clear point: even in an era when black voter registration rates were notoriously low, black voter turnout made a difference in elections. As a result, it is important to understand the factors that influence voter participation rates.

To be certain, research indicates that a number of factors—individual and structural— influence voter participation rates among blacks,[98] but social capital theory argues, "[political] participation emerges out of established social organization[s]—including formal organization[s] and informal social relationships."[99] Earlier chapters establish that during the 1960s formal and informal black networks grew exponentially. These "organizational attachments and personal relationships . . . [worked to] draw individuals into broader contacts and expose individuals to salient political ideas," which promoted heightened black political participation as early as 1960.[100] Both the organizations to which people belonged and their individual social networks influenced their pursuit of the ballot. Again, the quest was freedom, and the ballot became the symbol of freedom. It was discussed from church pulpits, on public transportation, and in various social settings. These "local movement centers" stirred the effort forward.[101] In this way, the idea diffused through black society acting as both a bond among members of the black community and a bridge connecting socially heterogeneous groups. Knowledge of the ballot and the potential power it wielded was communicated through social networks on an almost daily basis, but arguably that does not happen anymore. This raises the important question: Does social capital matter for voting patterns? This book argues that, then and now, social capital relationships can operate to foster heightened African-American political participation.

Simply put, social capital is the idea that networks have value. Sociologist James Coleman defines social capital by "its function"; therefore, it is "not a single entity, but a variety of different entities having two characteristics in common: they all consist of some aspect of social structure, and they facilitate certain actions of individuals who are within the structure."[102] Later researchers began to categorize social capital by types using labels such as external social capital and internal social capital, structural social capital and cognitive (i.e. cultural) social capital, or bonding social capital and bridging social capital. Fukuyama describes social capital as "the ability of people to work together for common purposes in groups and organizations," and it is accomplished through shared values and norms, which facilitate cooperation.[103] While the forms of social capital exist independently, they can reinforce each other.[104] For example, bonding forms of social capital occur between homogenous groups, and can facilitate a kind of "thick trust" between group members, while bridging social capital occurs across heterogeneous groups, which can facilitate a kind of "thin trust."

Use of the various categorizations of social capital can prove insightful in understanding varying levels of the political participation pre and post Voting Rights Act of 1965; however, national trends in voting patterns do not tell the whole story. Instead, a complete picture of how social capital influences political participation requires both micro and macro level analyses. For example, a 2012 Bi-Partisan Policy Center Report reveals some interesting trends in participation during the 2012 presidential election.[105] This report shows that voter participation still varies widely by state. In the 2012 presidential election, seven states had record low rates of voter participation turnout; these included Hawaii, Kansas, Montana, New York, Oklahoma, Utah and West Virginia.[106] Rates also vary by party affiliation. Among Democrats, Indiana, Oklahoma, Utah and West Virginia had record low turnout rates in the 2012 presidential election.[107] Republicans had record high turnout rates in Alabama and North Carolina; while in Hawaii, Republicans recorded record low turnout rates.[108]

Historically, structural inequalities have operated to constrain black voting patterns, but today both structural and individual level factors influence participation levels. Sometimes, the two—a history of black voter dilution tactics and a perception that the system operates to constrain minority voices—operate hand in hand and effectively become a self-fulfilling prophecy. While there have been concerted efforts that act as a restraint on some people or groups of people's right to vote, it is also true that in any given election, in any given part of the country, there are a number of eligible voters who fail to exercise the right granted to them by the Constitution. Sam Walker marched in Selma, and today he serves as a tour guide and historian with the National Voting Rights Museum and Institute in Selma. Mr. Walker has the opportunity to interact with museum visitors, sometimes from all over the world. On those occasions, he passes some of the Museum's standing exhibits, including a photo exhibit of the Selma to Montgomery March, the foot soldiers' exhibit,[109] and tributes to the Courageous Eight and Dallas County Voters League, and he is reminded of their sacrifices. For a while, Mr. Walker struggled to understand how some African-Americans failed to vote. Now, after some thought, he comes to the following conclusion:

> Well, everyone has their own interpretation. My explanation is that when the Voting Rights Act passed, and especially here in the South, people got the right to vote. People were excited about the opportunity. They thought that was really going to be the thing that changed everything. You know? They thought that it was going to bring them up. But after voting for thirty years and

you don't see no change in your conditions, you lose interest in that vehicle being a means of changing your condition. You know?[110]

In this millennium, little research has been done about the perception of restraint and how this acts to undermine political participation. This is an important area for future research.

Conclusion

We sit on the precipice of another critical moment in American society. The Voting Rights Act has benefitted Americans. It has ensured that composition of elected bodies is more representative of America, but while it has benefitted all Americans, the protections in place are especially aimed at minority groups including African-Americans, Native Americans, Latinos, and Asian-Americans, which include Pacific Islanders. The prevailing issue is whether or not the fact that some progress has been made means no additional safeguards are needed. In Congress' most recent reauthorization of provisions of the Voting Rights Act they determined that sufficient discrimination persists such as to warrant a 25-year extension. A rollback by the courts would substantially shift the nation's established system of checks and balances and could amount to widespread retreat from the protections established for the minority franchise.

As the demographics of America change, we grow closer to a time when there will be a white minority, and concerns about the role that race plays in contemporary American politics abound. Today, Selma still wrestles with the ghosts of its past and the promise of its future. In 2000, Selma elected its first black. That same year, a monument to Nathan Bedford Forrest was placed at the Smitherman building.[111] The Friends of Nathan Bedford Forrest and the United Daughters of the Confederacy paid for the monument. Petition was made to have the monument moved from the Smitherman Museum to a more prominent location in historic Selma—Confederate Circle in Old Live Oak Cemetery. Amid complaints from various groups and individuals, including civil rights groups, the 7-foot-tall monument was later moved there. Debate still continues. An April 13, 2013, article by Ashley Johnson titled "Options for Forrest Monument Unveiled to Council" appeared in *The Selma Times Journal*. According to the article, Selma City Council hopes to avoid a pending lawsuit scheduled in federal court in Mobile, Alabama, over the expansion of the Forrest monument.

Rogers' Diffusion of Innovations Theory explains how ideas spread among groups of people and help bring about cultural change in society.

This book illustrates how Diffusion of Innovations Theory can be used to understand the shift among important change agents in American society, which resulted in America's fulfillment of its 100-year-old promise to African-Americans guaranteed in the Fifteenth Amendment to the U.S. Constitution. But it is also a reminder that we are again at a critical moment in history. Throughout history, old ideas often masquerade as "new ideas." The Act addresses the dual problems of vote dilution and disenfranchisement. While disenfranchisement is largely a thing of the past, vote dilution appears to be the new game. In ways discussed earlier in this book, it has been established that the recent proliferation of voter identification laws and other legislation around the country has a disproportionate negative impact on minority voters' access to the polls. Put simply, this looks like voter dilution tactics and may amount to what the Supreme Court has called "pour[ing] old poison into new bottles."[112]

Recent efforts to constrain access to the ballot gained steam and national momentum after a record minority voter turnout in 2008, which resulted in the election of America's first African-American president. This "timing" heightens suspicions that such legislation amounts to backlash tactics such as those used throughout history to thwart black gains. Why does this book suggest that this is again a critical moment in history? Rogers' theory helps to explain that, too. According to Rogers, only 2.5 percent of the population, innovators, are necessary to adopt a new idea and begin the process of diffusing that idea throughout society. When innovators have access to important communication channels such as the media, the spread of ideas is even more plausible. As important policymakers, clergy, and political leaders continue to espouse the need to tighten access to the ballot as a means to protect against voter fraud, this idea gets carried through their social networks.

The import of social networks cannot be minimized. The black freedom struggle was sustained through social networks, and during the period under scrutiny here (post-Brown through to 1965), this is how the Movement moved. As social networks began to grow, the ideas they cultivated spread. Tuskegee faculty involved in the Movement communicated the idea with their students who took the ideas to their home communities and to Movement locations where they worked in the black freedom struggle and shared them there. The grassroots efforts of SNCC and CORE dispersed the ideas of the Movement locally (door-to-door, face-to-face), regionally, nationally, and globally. Decades prior to the arrival of SNCC in the Selma area, Amelia Boynton and her husband, Sam, went door-to-door to help people register to vote.[113] Later, members of the group the Boyntons helped organize, DCVL, would do the same. As momentum grew, DCVL would write and ask the Reverend Martin

Luther King Jr. and SCLC to come and join SNCC in their efforts in the area. Generations worked together, and a new group of leaders was born. The symbiotic nature of this cross-generational relationship is captured best by some language on the Veterans of Hope website stating that the "local community people adopted 'the children' of SNCC as their leaders and wards."

These expanding social networks served multiple purposes. They provided comfort, support, and even some protection for people in the Movement. In an interview with Bruce Hartford and Jean Wiley conducted for the Civil Rights Movement Veterans website, Ruby Sales supplies a strong and compelling example of the value of strong social networks to Movement efforts. During her time in Lowndes County, Sales stayed with the family of Clara Mall. Speaking about Mall, she says:

> Clara Mall played an incredible role in the Movement because her grandmother was involved with this white man that she had been involved with for years, and there was this kind of "hands off" policy to a degree for Clara. And so Clara was able to get away with things that most people in Lowndes County couldn't get away with. And the other thing is that she had lots of money compared to other people in Lowndes County, so she could give money to the Movement and buy gas and do all of that, and she was very committed to doing that.[114]

Social networks, especially perceived social networks, could also incite danger. As the Movement spread, workers noticed something: "White participation would incite local White people to violence."[115] This kind of visible challenge to the established Jim Crow Southern system of separation of the races incensed whites committed to maintaining the status quo. White response to the presence of Viola Liuzzo, Goodman and Schwerner, James Reeb, and Jonathan Daniels in Movement efforts was swift and virulent. In a visible way, the existence of these white martyrs for the Movement represented the beginning of cultural change in the larger white society. But the polar responses to their presence—the desire of some whites to kill them and the incensed outrage at their deaths espoused by other whites—was also a reminder of America's hypocrisy, in that the deaths of countless black men and women over the course of hundreds of years, some by violent lynchings for perceived infractions of the social order, did not generate such outrage.

Still, space was being transformed, and spatial boundaries that once existed were dissipating. Of course, these changes did not happen for everyone, and they did not happen quickly, especially in entrenched places like Lowndes County, Alabama; however, Ruby Sales argues that while nothing changed, everything changed. She states, "In a real way nothing really changed significantly in Lowndes County immediately. Except white people got meaner . . . [N]othing changes. Except black people change. Because they become more persistent. We become more persistent." The persistence that Ruby Sales outlines is exactly what is needed in the never-ending quest for freedom. Indeed, everything had changed. The precursor to the Black Panther organization was the LCFO, which was founded, in part, as a response to violence against civil rights workers in Lowndes County.[116] Formal resistance efforts in Bloody Lowndes County represented a radical change.

The recent effort to contract voting rights is a substantial blow, but it need not be a death sentence. Current conditions have improved, but to paraphrase a saying popular in the black church: "We as a nation (the Southern states included) ain't what we used to be, but we ain't what we ought to be either." Perhaps the gains of the last few decades lulled freedom fighters of the past into a sense of complacency and deadened new generations to the need to be ever vigilant. If that is the case, the Shelby County decision is an important wake-up call for both groups as well as all others interested in ensuring meaningful voting rights protection for all American citizens. The voting rights struggle did not begin with Shelby, nor will it end there. After all, freedom is a constant struggle.

Documents

Transcript of Fourteenth Amendment to the U.S. Constitution: Civil Rights (1868)

*T*he *Fourteenth Amendment to the U.S. Constitution is one of the Reconstruction Amendments. It is also one of the nation's most important social and political documents. After the Civil War, freedmen were problematic for the country. The Dred Scott v. Sanford (60 U.S. 393) decision handed down by the Supreme Court in 1857 established that even in free territory a slave was still the property his master and neither could be, nor was ever intended to be, a citizen of the U.S. The passage of the Fourteenth Amendment voided that decision.*

Congress adopted the Fourteenth Amendment on July 9, 1868. The document provides a definition of citizenship that clearly incorporates African-Americans, including those who were former slaves, and it affords all such "citizens" due process and equal protection under the law. As a social document, it marks a change in attitude (at least of some) and movement away from viewing African-Americans as chattel property to counting African-Americans as full citizens (not three-fifths). Further, the Amendment was an important political document during the Reconstruction Era in that it tied Southern representation in Congress to protection for the rights granted to African-American citizens under it.

AMENDMENT XIV

Section 1.

All persons born or naturalized in the United States, and subject to the jurisdiction thereof, are citizens of the United States and of the State wherein they reside. No State shall make or enforce any law which shall abridge the privileges or immunities of citizens of the United States; nor shall any State deprive any person of life, liberty, or property, without due process of law; nor deny to any person within its jurisdiction the equal protection of the laws.

Section 2.

Representatives shall be apportioned among the several States according to their respective numbers, counting the whole number of persons in each State, excluding Indians not taxed. But when the right to vote at any election for the choice of electors for President and Vice President of the United States, Representatives in Congress, the Executive and Judicial officers of a State, or the members of the Legislature thereof, is denied to any of the male inhabitants of such State, being twenty-one years of age, and citizens of the United States, or in any way abridged, except for participation in rebellion, or other crime, the basis of representation therein shall be reduced in the proportion which the number of such male citizens shall bear to the whole number of male citizens twenty-one years of age in such State.

Section 3.

No person shall be a Senator or Representative in Congress, or elector of President and Vice President, or hold any office, civil or military, under the United States, or under any State, who, having previously taken an oath, as a member of Congress, or as an officer of the United States, or as a member of any State legislature, or as an executive or judicial officer of any State, to support the Constitution of the United States, shall have engaged in insurrection or rebellion against the same, or given aid or comfort to the enemies thereof. But Congress may by a vote of two-thirds of each House, remove such disability.

Section 4.

The validity of the public debt of the United States, authorized by law, including debts incurred for payment of pensions and bounties for services in suppressing insurrection or rebellion, shall not be questioned. But neither the United States nor any State shall assume or pay any debt or obligation incurred in aid of insurrection or rebellion against the United States, or any claim for the loss or emancipation of any slave; but all such debts, obligations and claims shall be held illegal and void.

Section 5.

The Congress shall have the power to enforce, by appropriate legislation, the provisions of this article.

Source: U.S. National Archives & Records Administration, www.ourdocuments. gov/doc.php?doc=43&page=transcript.

DOCUMENT 2

Transcript of Fifteenth Amendment to the U.S. Constitution: Voting Rights (1870)

The Fifteenth Amendment granted suffrage to black men. Later, this protection was extended to black women, too. Congress passed the Amendment in February 1869; however, state ratification of the Amendment was a slow process.

Fortieth Congress of the United States of America;

At the third Session, Begun and held at the city of Washington, on Monday, the seventh day of December, one thousand eight hundred and sixty-eight.

A Resolution Proposing an amendment to the Constitution of the United States.

Resolved by the Senate and House of Representatives of the United States of America in Congress assembled, (two-thirds of both Houses concurring) that the following article be proposed to the legislature of the several States as an amendment to the Constitution of the United States which, when ratified by three-fourths of said legislatures shall be valid as part of the Constitution, namely:

Article XV.

Section 1.

The right of citizens of the United States to vote shall not be denied or abridged by the United States or by any State on account of race, color, or previous condition of servitude—

Section 2.

The Congress shall have the power to enforce this article by appropriate legislation.

Source: U.S. National Archives & Records Administration, www.ourdocuments. gov/doc.php?doc=44&page=transcript.

DOCUMENT 3

Transcript of Voting Rights Act (1965)

*T*he passage of the Voting Rights Act came almost 100 years after the grant of
suffrage in the Fifteenth Amendment. The 1965 Act includes "strong
medicine" in the form of Section 5 of the Voting Rights Act, which requires certain
covered jurisdictions to obtain preclearance before changing practicing impacting voting
rights laws. While initially adopted in 1965, Congress has extended the Act several
times.

*Section 2 of the Fifteenth Amendment grants Congress the power to create the Act.
Section 2 says, "Congress shall have power to enforce this article by appropriate
legislation."*

AN ACT To enforce the fifteenth amendment to the Constitution of the
United States, and for other purposes.
Be it enacted by the Senate and House of Representatives of the United
States of America in Congress assembled, That this Act shall be known as
the "Voting Rights Act of 1965."

SEC. 2.

No voting qualification or prerequisite to voting, or standard, practice, or
procedure shall be imposed or applied by any State or political subdivision
to deny or abridge the right of any citizen of the United States to vote
on account of race or color.

SEC. 3.

(a) Whenever the Attorney General institutes a proceeding under any
statute to enforce the guarantees of the fifteenth amendment in any State
or political subdivision the court shall authorize the appointment of Federal
examiners by the United States Civil Service Commission in accordance
with section 6 to serve for such period of time and for such political
subdivisions as the court shall determine is appropriate to enforce the
guarantees of the fifteenth amendment (1) as part of any interlocutory order
if the court determines that the appointment of such examiners is necessary
to enforce such guarantees or (2) as part of any final judgment if the court
finds that violations of the fifteenth amendment justifying equitable relief
have occurred in such State or subdivision: Provided, That the court need

not authorize the appointment of examiners if any incidents of denial or abridgement of the right to vote on account of race or color (1) have been few in number and have been promptly and effectively corrected by State or local action, (2) the continuing effect of such incidents has been eliminated, and (3) there is no reasonable probability of their recurrence in the future.

(b) If in a proceeding instituted by the Attorney General under any statute to enforce the guarantees of the fifteenth amendment in any State or political subdivision the court finds that a test or device has been used for the purpose or with the effect of denying or abridging the right of any citizen of the United States to vote on account of race or color, it shall suspend the use of tests and devices in such State or political subdivisions as the court shall determine is appropriate and for such period as it deems necessary.

(c) If in any proceeding instituted by the Attorney General under any statute to enforce the guarantees of the fifteenth amendment in any State or political subdivision the court finds that violations of the fifteenth amendment justifying equitable relief have occurred within the territory of such State or political subdivision, the court, in addition to such relief as it may grant, shall retain jurisdiction for such period as it may deem appropriate and during such period no voting qualification or prerequisite to voting, or standard, practice, or procedure with respect to voting different from that in force or effect at the time the proceeding was commenced shall be enforced unless and until the court finds that such qualification, prerequisite, standard, practice, or procedure does not have the purpose and will not have the effect of denying or abridging the right to vote on account of race or color: Provided, That such qualification, prerequisite, standard, practice, or procedure may be enforced if the qualification, prerequisite, standard, practice, or procedure has been submitted by the chief legal officer or other appropriate official of such State or subdivision to the Attorney General and the Attorney General has not interposed an objection within sixty days after such submission, except that neither the court's finding nor the Attorney General's failure to object shall bar a subsequent action to enjoin enforcement of such qualification, prerequisite, standard, practice, or procedure.

SEC. 4.

(a) To assure that the right of citizens of the United States to vote is not denied or abridged on account of race or color, no citizen shall be denied the right to vote in any Federal, State, or local election because of his failure to comply with any test or device in any State with respect to which the determinations have been made under subsection (b) or in any political subdivision with respect to which such determinations have been made as a separate unit, unless the United States District Court for the District of Columbia in an action for a declaratory judgment brought by such State or subdivision against the United States has determined that no such test or device has been used during the five years preceding the filing of the action for the purpose or with the effect of denying or abridging the right to vote on account of race or color: Provided, That no such declaratory judgment shall issue with respect to any plaintiff for a period of five years after the entry of a final judgment of any court of the United States, other than the denial of a declaratory judgment under this section, whether entered prior to or after the enactment of this Act, determining that denials or abridgments of the right to vote on account of race or color through the use of such tests or devices have occurred anywhere in the territory of such plaintiff. An action pursuant to this subsection shall be heard and determined by a court of three judges in accordance with the provisions of section 2284 of title 28 of the United States Code and any appeal shall lie to the Supreme Court. The court shall retain jurisdiction of any action pursuant to this subsection for five years after judgment and shall reopen the action upon motion of the Attorney General alleging that a test or device has been used for the purpose or with the effect of denying or abridging the right to vote on account of race or color.

If the Attorney General determines that he has no reason to believe that any such test or device has been used during the five years preceding the filing of the action for the purpose or with the effect of denying or abridging the right to vote on account of race or color, he shall consent to the entry of such judgment

(b) The provisions of subsection (a) shall apply in any State or in any political subdivision of a state which (1) the Attorney General determines maintained on November 1, 1964, any test or device, and with respect to which (2) the Director of the Census determines that less than 50 percentum of the persons of voting age residing therein were registered on November 1, 1964, or that less than 50 percentum of such persons voted in the presidential election of November 1964.

A determination or certification of the Attorney General or of the Director of the Census under this section or under section 6 or section 13 shall not be reviewable in any court and shall be effective upon publication in the Federal Register.

(c) The phrase "test or device" shall mean any requirement that a person as a prerequisite for voting or registration for voting (1) demonstrate the ability to read, write, understand, or interpret any matter, (2) demonstrate any educational achievement or his knowledge of any particular subject, (3) possess good moral character, or (4) prove his qualifications by the voucher of registered voters or members of any other class.

(d) For purposes of this section no State or political subdivision shall be determined to have engaged in the use of tests or devices for the purpose or with the effect of denying or abridging the right to vote on account of race or color if (1) incidents of such use have been few in number and have been promptly and effectively corrected by State or local action, (2) the continuing effect of such incidents has been eliminated, and (3) there is no reasonable probability of their recurrence in the future.

(e) (1) Congress hereby declares that to secure the rights under the fourteenth amendment of persons educated in American-flag schools in which the predominant classroom language was other than English, it is necessary to prohibit the States from conditioning the right to vote of such persons on ability to read, write, understand, or interpret any matter in the English language.

(2) No person who demonstrates that he has successfully completed the sixth primary grade in a public school in, or a private school accredited by, any State or territory, the District of Columbia, or the Commonwealth of Puerto Rico in which the predominant classroom language was other than English, shall be denied the right to vote in any Federal, State, or local election because of his inability to read, write, understand, or interpret any matter in the English language, except that, in States in which State law provides that a different level of education is presumptive of literacy, he shall demonstrate that he has successfully completed an equivalent level of education in a public school in, or a private school accredited by, any State or territory, the District of Columbia, or the Commonwealth of Puerto Rico in which the predominant classroom language was other than English.

SEC. 5.

Whenever a State or political subdivision with respect to which the prohibitions set forth in section 4(a) are in effect shall enact or seek to administer any voting qualification or prerequisite to voting, or standard, practice, or procedure with respect to voting different from that in force or effect on November 1, 1964, such State or subdivision may institute an action in the United States District Court for the District of Columbia for a declaratory judgment that such qualification, prerequisite, standard, practice, or procedure does not have the purpose and will not have the effect of denying or abridging the right to vote on account of race or color, and unless and until the court enters such judgment no person shall be denied the right to vote for failure to comply with such qualification, prerequisite, standard, practice, or procedure: Provided, That such qualification, prerequisite, standard, practice, or procedure may be enforced without such proceeding if the qualification, prerequisite, standard, practice, or procedure has been submitted by the chief legal officer or other appropriate official of such State or subdivision to the Attorney General and the Attorney General has not interposed an objection within sixty days after such submission, except that neither the Attorney General's failure to object nor a declaratory judgment entered under this section shall bar a subsequent action to enjoin enforcement of such qualification, prerequisite, standard, practice, or procedure. Any action under this section shall be heard and determined by a court of three judges in accordance with the provisions of section 2284 of title 28 of the United States Code and any appeal shall lie to the Supreme Court.

SEC. 6.

Whenever (a) a court has authorized the appointment of examiners pursuant to the provisions of section 3(a), or (b) unless a declaratory judgment has been rendered under section 4(a), the Attorney General certifies with respect to any political subdivision named in, or included within the scope of, determinations made under section 4(b) that (1) he has received complaints in writing from twenty or more residents of such political subdivision alleging that they have been denied the right to vote under color of law on account of race or color, and that he believes such complaints to be meritorious, or (2) that, in his judgment (considering, among other factors, whether the ratio of nonwhite persons to white persons registered to vote within such subdivision appears to him to be reasonably attributable to violations of the fifteenth amendment or whether substantial evidence exists that bona fide efforts are being made within such subdivision to comply with the fifteenth amendment), the appointment of examiners is otherwise necessary to enforce the guarantees of the fifteenth amendment, the Civil Service Commission shall appoint as many examiners for such subdivision as it may deem appropriate to prepare and maintain lists of persons eligible to vote in Federal, State, and local elections. Such examiners, hearing officers provided for in section 9(a), and other persons deemed necessary by the Commission to carry out the provisions and purposes of this Act shall be appointed, compensated, and separated without regard to the provisions of any statute administered by the Civil Service Commission, and service under this Act shall not be considered employment for the purposes of any statute administered by the Civil Service Commission, except the provisions of section 9 of the Act of August 2, 1939, as amended (5 U.S.C. 118i), prohibiting partisan political activity: Provided, That the Commission is authorized, after consulting the head of the appropriate department or agency, to designate suitable persons in the official service of the United States, with their consent, to serve in these positions. Examiners and hearing officers shall have the power to administer oaths.

SEC. 7.

(a) The examiners for each political subdivision shall, at such places as the Civil Service Commission shall by regulation designate, examine applicants concerning their qualifications for voting. An application to an examiner shall be in such form as the Commission may require and shall contain allegations that the applicant is not otherwise registered to vote.

(b) Any person whom the examiner finds, in accordance with instructions received under section 9(b), to have the qualifications prescribed by State law not inconsistent with the Constitution and laws of the United States shall promptly be placed on a list of eligible voters. A challenge to such listing may be made in accordance with section 9(a) and shall not be the basis for a prosecution under section 12 of this Act. The examiner shall certify and transmit such list, and any supplements as appropriate, at least once a month, to the offices of the appropriate election officials, with copies to the Attorney General and the attorney general of the State, and any such lists and supplements thereto transmitted during the month shall be available for public inspection on the last business day of the month and, in any event, not later than the forty-fifth day prior to any election. The appropriate State or local election official shall place such names on the official voting list. Any person whose name appears on the examiner's list shall be entitled and allowed to vote in the election district of his residence unless and until the appropriate election officials shall have been notified that such person has been removed from such list in accordance with subsection (d): Provided, That no person shall be entitled to vote in any election by virtue of this Act unless his name shall have been certified and transmitted on such a list to the offices of the appropriate election officials at least forty-five days prior to such election.

(c) The examiner shall issue to each person whose name appears on such a list a certificate evidencing his eligibility to vote.

(d) A person whose name appears on such a list shall be removed therefrom by an examiner if (1) such person has been successfully challenged in accordance with the procedure prescribed in section 9, or (2) he has been determined by an examiner to have lost his eligibility to vote under State law not inconsistent with the Constitution and the laws of the United States.

Sec. 8.

Whenever an examiner is serving under this Act in any political subdivision, the Civil Service Commission may assign, at the request of the Attorney General, one or more persons, who may be officers of the United States, (1) to enter and attend at any place for holding an election in such subdivision for the purpose of observing whether persons who are entitled to vote are being permitted to vote, and (2) to enter and attend at any place for tabulating the votes cast at any election held in such subdivision for the purpose of observing whether votes cast by persons entitled to vote are being properly tabulated. Such persons so assigned shall report to an examiner appointed for such political subdivision, to the Attorney General, and if the appointment of examiners has been authorized pursuant to section 3(a), to the court.

SEC. 9.

(a) Any challenge to a listing on an eligibility list prepared by an examiner shall be heard and determined by a hearing officer appointed by and responsible to the Civil Service Commission and under such rules as the Commission shall by regulation prescribe. Such challenge shall be entertained only if filed at such office within the State as the Civil Service Commission shall by regulation designate, and within ten days after the listing of the challenged person is made available for public inspection, and if supported by (1) the affidavits of at least two persons having personal knowledge of the facts constituting grounds for the challenge, and (2) a certification that a copy of the challenge and affidavits have been served by mail or in person upon the person challenged at his place of residence set out in the application. Such challenge shall be determined within fifteen days after it has been filed. A petition for review of the decision of the hearing officer may be filed in the United States court of appeals for the circuit in which the person challenged resides within fifteen days after service of such decision by mail on the person petitioning for review but no decision of a hearing officer shall be reversed unless clearly erroneous. Any person listed shall be entitled and allowed to vote pending final determination by the hearing officer and by the court.

(b) The times, places, procedures, and form for application and listing pursuant to this Act and removals from the eligibility lists shall be prescribed by regulations promulgated by the Civil Service Commission and the Commission shall, after consultation with the Attorney General, instruct examiners concerning applicable State law not inconsistent with the Constitution and laws of the United States with respect to (1) the qualifications required for listing, and (2) loss of eligibility to vote.

(c) Upon the request of the applicant or the challenger or on its own motion the Civil Service Commission shall have the power to require by subpoena the attendance and testimony of witnesses and the production of documentary evidence relating to any matter pending before it under the authority of this section. In case of contumacy or refusal to obey a subpoena, any district court of the United States or the United States court of any territory or possession, or the District Court of the United States for the District of Columbia, within the jurisdiction of which said person guilty of contumacy or refusal to obey is found or resides or is domiciled or transacts business, or has appointed an agent for receipt of service of process, upon application by the Attorney General of the United States shall have jurisdiction to issue to such person an order requiring such person to appear before the Commission or a hearing officer, there to produce pertinent, relevant, and nonprivileged documentary evidence if so ordered, or there to give testimony touching the matter under investigation, and any failure to obey such order of the court may be punished by said court as a contempt thereof.

SEC. 10.

(a) The Congress finds that the requirement of the payment of a poll tax as a precondition to voting (i) precludes persons of limited means from voting or imposes unreasonable financial hardship upon such persons as a precondition to their exercise of the franchise, (ii) does not bear a reasonable relationship to any legitimate State interest in the conduct of elections, and (iii) in some areas has the purpose or effect of denying persons the right to vote because of race or color. Upon the basis of these findings, Congress declares that the constitutional right of citizens to vote is denied or abridged in some areas by the requirement of the payment of a poll tax as a precondition to voting.

(b) In the exercise of the powers of Congress under section 5 of the fourteenth amendment and section 2 of the fifteenth amendment, the Attorney General is authorized and directed to institute forthwith in the name of the United States such actions, including actions against States or political subdivisions, for declaratory judgment or injunctive relief against the enforcement of any requirement of the payment of a poll tax as a precondition to voting, or substitute therefor enacted after November 1, 1964, as will be necessary to implement the declaration of subsection (a) and the purposes of this section.

(c) The district courts of the United States shall have jurisdiction of such actions which shall be heard and determined by a court of three judges in accordance with the provisions of section 2284 of title 28 of the United States Code and any appeal shall lie to the Supreme Court.

It shall be the duty of the judges designated to hear the case to assign the case for hearing at the earliest practicable date, to participate in the hearing and determination thereof, and to cause the case to be in every way expedited.

(d) During the pendency of such actions, and thereafter if the courts, notwithstanding this action by the Congress, should declare the requirement of the payment of a poll tax to be constitutional, no citizen of the United States who is a resident of a State or political subdivision with respect to which determinations have been made under subsection 4(b) and a declaratory judgment has not been entered under subsection 4(a), during the first year he becomes otherwise entitled to vote by reason of registration by State or local officials or listing by an examiner, shall be denied the right to vote for failure to pay a poll tax if he tenders payment of such tax for the current year to an examiner or to the appropriate State or local official at least forty-five days prior to election, whether or not such tender would be timely or adequate under State law. An examiner shall have authority to accept such payment from any person authorized by this Act to make an application for listing, and shall issue a receipt for such payment. The examiner shall transmit promptly any such poll tax payment to the office of the State or local official authorized to receive such payment under State law, together with the name and address of the applicant.

SEC. 11.

(a) No person acting under color of law shall fail or refuse to permit any person to vote who is entitled to vote under any provision of this Act or is otherwise qualified to vote, or willfully fail or refuse to tabulate, count, and report such person's vote.

(b) No person, whether acting under color of law or otherwise, shall intimidate, threaten, or coerce, or attempt to intimidate, threaten, or coerce any person for voting or attempting to vote, or intimidate, threaten, or coerce, or attempt to intimidate, threaten, or coerce any person for urging or aiding any person to vote or attempt to vote, or intimidate, threaten, or coerce any person for exercising any powers or duties under section 3(a), 6, 8, 9, 10, or 12(e).

(c) Whoever knowingly or willfully gives false information as to his name, address, or period of residence in the voting district for the purpose of establishing his eligibility to register or vote, or conspires with another individual for the purpose of encouraging his false registration to vote or illegal voting, or pays or offers to pay or accepts payment either for registration to vote or for voting shall be fined not more than $10,000 or imprisoned not more than five years, or both: Provided, however, That this provision shall be applicable only to general, special, or primary elections held solely or in part for the purpose of selecting or electing any candidate for the office of President, Vice President, presidential elector, Member of the United States Senate, Member of the United States House of Representatives, or Delegates or Commissioners from the territories or possessions, or Resident Commissioner of the Commonwealth of Puerto Rico.

(d) Whoever, in any matter within the jurisdiction of an examiner or hearing officer knowingly and willfully falsifies or conceals a material fact, or makes any false, fictitious, or fraudulent statements or representations, or makes or uses any false writing or document knowing the same to contain any false, fictitious, or fraudulent statement or entry, shall be fined not more than $10,000 or imprisoned not more than five years, or both.

SEC. 12.

(a) Whoever shall deprive or attempt to deprive any person of any right secured by section 2, 3, 4, 5, 7, or 10 or shall violate section 11(a) or (b), shall be fined not more than $5,000, or imprisoned not more than five years, or both.

(b) Whoever, within a year following an election in a political subdivision in which an examiner has been appointed (1) destroys, defaces, mutilates, or otherwise alters the marking of a paper ballot which has been cast in such election, or (2) alters any official record of voting in such election tabulated from a voting machine or otherwise, shall be fined not more than $5,000, or imprisoned not more than five years, or both

(c) Whoever conspires to violate the provisions of subsection (a) or (b) of this section, or interferes with any right secured by section 2, 3 4, 5, 7, 10, or 11(a) or (b) shall be fined not more than $5,000, or imprisoned not more than five years, or both.

(d) Whenever any person has engaged or there are reasonable grounds to believe that any person is about to engage in any act or practice prohibited by section 2, 3, 4, 5, 7, 10, 11, or subsection (b) of this section, the Attorney General may institute for the United States, or in the name of the United States, an action for preventive relief, including an application for a temporary or permanent injunction, restraining order, or other order, and including an order directed to the State and State or local election officials to require them (1) to permit persons listed under this Act to vote and (2) to count such votes.

(e) Whenever in any political subdivision in which there are examiners appointed pursuant to this Act any persons allege to such an examiner within forty-eight hours after the closing of the polls that notwithstanding (1) their listing under this Act or registration by an appropriate election official and (2) their eligibility to vote, they have not been permitted to vote in such election, the examiner shall forthwith notify the Attorney General if such allegations in his opinion appear to be well founded. Upon receipt of such notification, the Attorney General may forthwith file with the district court an application for an order providing for the marking, casting, and counting of the ballots of such persons and requiring the inclusion of their votes in the total vote before the results of such election shall be deemed final and any force or effect given thereto. The district court shall hear and determine such matters immediately after the filing of such application. The remedy provided in this subsection shall not preclude any remedy available under State or Federal law.

(f) The district courts of the United States shall have jurisdiction of proceedings instituted pursuant to this section and shall exercise the same without regard to whether a person asserting rights under the provisions of this Act shall have exhausted any administrative or other remedies that may be provided by law

SEC. 13.

Listing procedures shall be terminated in any political subdivision of any State (a) with respect to examiners appointed pursuant to clause (b) of section 6 whenever the Attorney General notifies the Civil Service Commission, or whenever the District Court for the District of Columbia determines in an action for declaratory judgment brought by any political subdivision with respect to which the Director of the Census has determined that more than 50 percentum of the nonwhite persons of voting age residing therein are registered to vote, (1) that all persons listed by an examiner for such subdivision have been placed on the appropriate voting registration roll, and (2) that there is no longer reasonable cause to believe that persons will be deprived of or denied the right to vote on account of race or color in such subdivision, and (b), with respect to examiners appointed pursuant to section 3(a), upon order of the authorizing court. A political subdivision may petition the Attorney General for the termination of listing procedures under clause (a) of this section, and may petition the Attorney General to request the Director of the Census to take such survey or census as may be appropriate for the making of the determination provided for in this section. The District Court for the District of Columbia shall have jurisdiction to require such survey or census to be made by the Director of the Census and it shall require him to do so if it deems the Attorney General's refusal to request such survey or census to be arbitrary or unreasonable.

SEC. 14.

(a) All cases of criminal contempt arising under the provisions of this Act shall be governed by section 151 of the Civil Rights Act of 1957 (42 U.S.C.1995).

(b) No court other than the District Court for the District of Columbia or a court of appeals in any proceeding under section 9 shall have jurisdiction to issue any declaratory judgment pursuant to section 4 or section 5 or any restraining order or temporary or permanent injunction against the execution or enforcement of any provision of this Act or any action of any Federal officer or employee pursuant hereto.

(c) (1) The terms "vote" or "voting" shall include all action necessary to make a vote effective in any primary, special, or general election, including, but not limited to, registration, listing pursuant to this Act, or other action required by law prerequisite to voting, casting a ballot, and having such ballot counted properly and included in the appropriate totals of votes cast with respect to candidates for public or party office and propositions for which votes are received in an election.

(2) The term "political subdivision" shall mean any county or parish, except that, where registration for voting is not conducted under the supervision of a county or parish, the term shall include any other subdivision of a State which conducts registration for voting.

(d) In any action for a declaratory judgment brought pursuant to section 4 or section 5 of this Act, subpoenas for witnesses who are required to attend the District Court for the District of Columbia may be served in any judicial district of the United States: Provided, That no writ of subpoena shall issue for witnesses without the District of Columbia at a greater distance than one hundred miles from the place of holding court without the permission of the District Court for the District of Columbia being first had upon proper application and cause shown.

SEC. 15.

Section 2004 of the Revised Statutes (42 U.S.C.1971), as amended by section 131 of the Civil Rights Act of 1957 (71 Stat. 637), and amended by section 601 of the Civil Rights Act of 1960 (74 Stat. 90), and as further amended by section 101 of the Civil Rights Act of 1964 (78 Stat. 241), is further amended as follows:

(a) Delete the word "Federal" wherever it appears in subsections (a) and (c);

(b) Repeal subsection (f) and designate the present subsections (g) and (h) as (f) and (g), respectively.

SEC. 16.

The Attorney General and the Secretary of Defense, jointly, shall make a full and complete study to determine whether, under the laws or practices of any State or States, there are preconditions to voting, which might tend to result in discrimination against citizens serving in the Armed Forces of the United States seeking to vote. Such officials shall, jointly, make a report to the Congress not later than June 30, 1966, containing the results of such study, together with a list of any States in which such preconditions exist, and shall include in such report such recommendations for legislation as they deem advisable to prevent discrimination in voting against citizens serving in the Armed Forces of the United States.

SEC. 17.

Nothing in this Act shall be construed to deny, impair, or otherwise adversely affect the right to vote of any person registered to vote under the law of any State or political subdivision.

SEC. 18.

There are hereby authorized to be appropriated such sums as are necessary to carry out the provisions of this Act

SEC 19.

If any provision of this Act or the application thereof to any person or circumstances is held invalid, the remainder of the Act and the application of the provision to other persons not similarly situated or to other circumstances shall not be affected thereby.

Approved August 6, 1965.

Source: U.S. National Archives & Records Administration, www.ourdocuments. gov/doc.php?doc=100&page=transcript.

DOCUMENT 4

The Four Freedoms Speech

*T*his speech constituted President Franklin Delano Roosevelt's 1941 State of
the Union address. It is significant because while war was underway in much
*of the world, America stood poised to make a decision about its involvement in the
conflict. In "The Four Freedoms," President Roosevelt clearly articulates why
Americans should care about this variance.*

*The specter of war threatened the deeply held American ideal of democracy.
In his address, President Roosevelt articulates several specific "freedoms," which
seem to go beyond the protections in the Bill of Rights, but these freedoms also
seemed intensely American. The "four freedoms" quickly resonated with U.S.
citizens and became deeply held American values worth fighting for—both at home
and abroad.*

*Ironically, after the world conflict was over, African-American citizens in the
US—many of whom fought in World War II and sought "double victory" at
home and abroad—came home to ill-treatment by the country. These citizens began
to talk about the hypocrisy of fighting for freedom abroad when they were not free
at home. Some began to frame their fight for equality in terms of the "four freedoms"
Roosevelt articulated.*

Annual Address to Congress, 1941

Mr. President, Mr. Speaker, Members of the Seventy-seventh Congress:

I address you, the Members of the Seventy-seventh Congress, at a
moment unprecedented in the history of the Union. I use the word
"unprecedented," because at no previous time has American security been
as seriously threatened from without as it is today.

Since the permanent formation of our Government under the
Constitution, in 1789, most of the periods of crisis in our history have related
to our domestic affairs. Fortunately, only one of these—the four-year War
Between the States—ever threatened our national unity. Today, thank God,
one hundred and thirty million Americans, in forty-eight States, have
forgotten points of the compass in our national unity.

It is true that prior to 1914 the United States often had been disturbed
by events in other Continents. We had even engaged in two wars with
European nations and in a number of undeclared wars in the West Indies,
in the Mediterranean and in the Pacific for the maintenance of American
rights and for the principles of peaceful commerce. But in no case had a
serious threat been raised against our national safety or our continued
independence.

What I seek to convey is the historic truth that the United States as a nation has at all times maintained clear, definite opposition, to any attempt to lock us in behind an ancient Chinese wall while the procession of civilization went past. Today, thinking of our children and of their children, we oppose enforced isolation for ourselves or for any other part of the Americas.

That determination of ours, extending over all these years, was proved, for example, during the quarter century of wars following the French Revolution.

While the Napoleonic struggles did threaten interests of the United States because of the French foothold in the West Indies and in Louisiana, and while we engaged in the War of 1812 to vindicate our right to peaceful trade, it is nevertheless clear that neither France nor Great Britain, nor any other nation, was aiming at domination of the whole world.

In like fashion from 1815 to 1914— ninety-nine years— no single war in Europe or in Asia constituted a real threat against our future or against the future of any other American nation.

Except in the Maximilian interlude in Mexico, no foreign power sought to establish itself in this Hemisphere; and the strength of the British fleet in the Atlantic has been a friendly strength. It is still a friendly strength.

Even when the World War broke out in 1914, it seemed to contain only small threat of danger to our own American future. But, as time went on, the American people began to visualize what the downfall of democratic nations might mean to our own democracy.

We need not overemphasize imperfections in the Peace of Versailles. We need not harp on failure of the democracies to deal with problems of world reconstruction. We should remember that the Peace of 1919 was far less unjust than the kind of "pacification" which began even before Munich, and which is being carried on under the new order of tyranny that seeks to spread over every continent today. The American people have unalterably set their faces against that tyranny.

Every realist knows that the democratic way of life is at this moment being directly assailed in every part of the world—assailed either by arms, or by secret spreading of poisonous propaganda by those who seek to destroy unity and promote discord in nations that are still at peace.

During sixteen long months this assault has blotted out the whole pattern of democratic life in an appalling number of independent nations, great and small. The assailants are still on the march, threatening other nations, great and small.

Therefore, as your President, performing my constitutional duty to "give to the Congress information of the state of the Union," I find it, unhappily, necessary to report that the future and the safety of our country and of our democracy are overwhelmingly involved in events far beyond our borders.

Armed defense of democratic existence is now being gallantly waged in four continents. If that defense fails, all the population and all the resources of Europe, Asia, Africa and Australasia will be dominated by the conquerors. Let us remember that the total of those populations and their resources in those four continents greatly exceeds the sum total of the population and the resources of the whole of the Western Hemisphere—many times over.

In times like these it is immature—and incidentally, untrue—for anybody to brag that an unprepared America, single-handed, and with one hand tied behind its back, can hold off the whole world.

No realistic American can expect from a dictator's peace international generosity, or return of true independence, or world disarmament, or freedom of expression, or freedom of religion—or even good business.

Such a peace would bring no security for us or for our neighbors. "Those, who would give up essential liberty to purchase a little temporary safety, deserve neither liberty nor safety."

As a nation, we may take pride in the fact that we are softhearted; but we cannot afford to be soft-headed.

We must always be wary of those who with sounding brass and a tinkling cymbal preach the "ism" of appeasement.

We must especially beware of that small group of selfish men who would clip the wings of the American eagle in order to feather their own nests.

I have recently pointed out how quickly the tempo of modern warfare could bring into our very midst the physical attack which we must eventually expect if the dictator nations win this war.

There is much loose talk of our immunity from immediate and direct invasion from across the seas. Obviously, as long as the British Navy retains its power, no such danger exists. Even if there were no British Navy, it is not probable that any enemy would be stupid enough to attack us by landing troops in the United States from across thousands of miles of ocean, until it had acquired strategic bases from which to operate.

But we learn much from the lessons of the past years in Europe—particularly the lesson of Norway, whose essential seaports were captured by treachery and surprise built up over a series of years.

The first phase of the invasion of this Hemisphere would not be the landing of regular troops. The necessary strategic points would be occupied by secret agents and their dupes—and great numbers of them are already here, and in Latin America.

As long as the aggressor nations maintain the offensive, they—not we —will choose the time and the place and the method of their attack.

That is why the future of all the American Republics is today in serious danger.

That is why this Annual Message to the Congress is unique in our history.

That is why every member of the Executive Branch of the Government and every member of the Congress faces great responsibility and great accountability.

The need of the moment is that our actions and our policy should be devoted primarily-almost exclusively—to meeting this foreign peril. For all our domestic problems are now a part of the great emergency.

Just as our national policy in internal affairs has been based upon a decent respect for the rights and the dignity of all our fellow men within our gates, so our national policy in foreign affairs has been based on a decent respect for the rights and dignity of all nations, large and small. And the justice of morality must and will win in the end.

Our national policy is this:

First, by an impressive expression of the public will and without regard to partisanship, we are committed to all-inclusive national defense.

Second, by an impressive expression of the public will and without regard to partisanship, we are committed to full support of all those resolute peoples, everywhere, who are resisting aggression and are thereby keeping war away from our Hemisphere. By this support, we express our determination that the democratic cause shall prevail; and we strengthen the defense and the security of our own nation.

Third, by an impressive expression of the public will and without regard to partisanship, we are committed to the proposition that principles of morality and considerations for our own security will never permit us to acquiesce in a peace dictated by aggressors and sponsored by appeasers. We know that enduring peace cannot be bought at the cost of other people's freedom.

In the recent national election there was no substantial difference between the two great parties in respect to that national policy. No issue was fought out on this line before the American electorate. Today it is abundantly evident that American citizens everywhere are demanding and supporting speedy and complete action in recognition of obvious danger.

Therefore, the immediate need is a swift and driving increase in our armament production.

Leaders of industry and labor have responded to our summons. Goals of speed have been set. In some cases these goals are being reached ahead of time; in some cases we are on schedule; in other cases there are slight but not serious delays; and in some cases—and I am sorry to say very important cases—we are all concerned by the slowness of the accomplishment of our plans.

The Army and Navy, however, have made substantial progress during the past year. Actual experience is improving and speeding up our methods of production with every passing day. And today's best is not good enough for tomorrow.

I am not satisfied with the progress thus far made. The men in charge of the program represent the best in training, in ability, and in patriotism. They are not satisfied with the progress thus far made. None of us will be satisfied until the job is done.

No matter whether the original goal was set too high or too low, our objective is quicker and better results. To give you two illustrations:

We are behind schedule in turning out finished airplanes; we are working day and night to solve the innumerable problems and to catch up.

We are ahead of schedule in building warships but we are working to get even further ahead of that schedule.

To change a whole nation from a basis of peacetime production of implements of peace to a basis of wartime production of implements of war is no small task. And the greatest difficulty comes at the beginning of the program, when new tools, new plant facilities, new assembly lines, and new ship ways must first be constructed before the actual materiel begins to flow steadily and speedily from them.

The Congress, of course, must rightly keep itself informed at all times of the progress of the program. However, there is certain information, as the Congress itself will readily recognize, which, in the interests of our own security and those of the nations that we are supporting, must of needs be kept in confidence.

New circumstances are constantly begetting new needs for our safety. I shall ask this Congress for greatly increased new appropriations and authorizations to carry on what we have begun.

I also ask this Congress for authority and for funds sufficient to manufacture additional munitions and war supplies of many kinds, to be turned over to those nations which are now in actual war with aggressor nations.

Our most useful and immediate role is to act as an arsenal for them as well as for ourselves. They do not need man power, but they do need billions of dollars worth of the weapons of defense.

The time is near when they will not be able to pay for them all in ready cash. We cannot, and we will not, tell them that they must surrender, merely because of present inability to pay for the weapons which we know they must have.

I do not recommend that we make them a loan of dollars with which to pay for these weapons—a loan to be repaid in dollars.

I recommend that we make it possible for those nations to continue to obtain war materials in the United States, fitting their orders into our own program. Nearly all their materiel would, if the time ever came, be useful for our own defense.

Taking counsel of expert military and naval authorities, considering what is best for our own security, we are free to decide how much should be kept here and how much should be sent abroad to our friends who by their determined and heroic resistance are giving us time in which to make ready our own defense.

For what we send abroad, we shall be repaid within a reasonable time following the close of hostilities, in similar materials, or, at our option, in other goods of many kinds, which they can produce and which we need.

Let us say to the democracies: "We Americans are vitally concerned in your defense of freedom. We are putting forth our energies, our resources and our organizing powers to give you the strength to regain and maintain a free world. We shall send you, in ever-increasing numbers, ships, planes, tanks, guns. This is our purpose and our pledge."

In fulfillment of this purpose we will not be intimidated by the threats of dictators that they will regard as a breach of international law or as an act of war our aid to the democracies which dare to resist their aggression. Such aid is not an act of war, even if a dictator should unilaterally proclaim it so to be.

When the dictators, if the dictators, are ready to make war upon us, they will not wait for an act of war on our part. They did not wait for Norway or Belgium or the Netherlands to commit an act of war.

Their only interest is in a new one-way international law, which lacks mutuality in its observance, and, therefore, becomes an instrument of oppression.

The happiness of future generations of Americans may well depend upon how effective and how immediate we can make our aid felt. No one can tell the exact character of the emergency situations that we may be called upon to meet. The Nation's hands must not be tied when the Nation's life is in danger.

We must all prepare to make the sacrifices that the emergency—almost as serious as war itself—demands. Whatever stands in the way of speed and efficiency in defense preparations must give way to the national need.

A free nation has the right to expect full cooperation from all groups. A free nation has the right to look to the leaders of business, of labor, and of agriculture to take the lead in stimulating effort, not among other groups but within their own groups.

The best way of dealing with the few slackers or trouble makers in our midst is, first, to shame them by patriotic example, and, if that fails, to use the sovereignty of Government to save Government.

As men do not live by bread alone, they do not fight by armaments alone. Those who man our defenses, and those behind them who build our defenses, must have the stamina and the courage which come from unshakable belief in the manner of life which they are defending. The mighty action that we are calling for cannot be based on a disregard of all things worth fighting for.

The Nation takes great satisfaction and much strength from the things which have been done to make its people conscious of their individual stake in the preservation of democratic life in America. Those things have toughened the fibre of our people, have renewed their faith and strengthened their devotion to the institutions we make ready to protect.

Certainly this is no time for any of us to stop thinking about the social and economic problems which are the root cause of the social revolution which is today a supreme factor in the world.

For there is nothing mysterious about the foundations of a healthy and strong democracy. The basic things expected by our people of their political and economic systems are simple. They are:

Equality of opportunity for youth and for others.

Jobs for those who can work.

Security for those who need it.

The ending of special privilege for the few.

The preservation of civil liberties for all.

The enjoyment of the fruits of scientific progress in a wider and constantly rising standard of living.

These are the simple, basic things that must never be lost sight of in the turmoil and unbelievable complexity of our modern world. The inner and abiding strength of our economic and political systems is dependent upon the degree to which they fulfill these expectations.

Many subjects connected with our social economy call for immediate improvement.

As examples:

We should bring more citizens under the coverage of old-age pensions and unemployment insurance.

We should widen the opportunities for adequate medical care.

We should plan a better system by which persons deserving or needing gainful employment may obtain it.

I have called for personal sacrifice. I am assured of the willingness of almost all Americans to respond to that call.

A part of the sacrifice means the payment of more money in taxes. In my Budget Message I shall recommend that a greater portion of this great defense program be paid for from taxation than we are paying today. No person should try, or be allowed, to get rich out of this program; and the principle of tax payments in accordance with ability to pay should be constantly before our eyes to guide our legislation.

If the Congress maintains these principles, the voters, putting patriotism ahead of pocketbooks, will give you their applause.

In the future days, which we seek to make secure, we look forward to a world founded upon four essential human freedoms.

The first is freedom of speech and expression—everywhere in the world.

The second is freedom of every person to worship God in his own way—everywhere in the world.

The third is freedom from want—which, translated into world terms, means economic understandings which will secure to every nation a healthy peacetime life for its inhabitants-everywhere in the world.

The fourth is freedom from fear—which, translated into world terms, means a world-wide reduction of armaments to such a point and in such a thorough fashion that no nation will be in a position to commit an act of physical aggression against any neighbor—anywhere in the world.

That is no vision of a distant millennium. It is a definite basis for a kind of world attainable in our own time and generation. That kind of world is the very antithesis of the so-called new order of tyranny which the dictators seek to create with the crash of a bomb.

To that new order we oppose the greater conception—the moral order. A good society is able to face schemes of world domination and foreign revolutions alike without fear.

Since the beginning of our American history, we have been engaged in change—in a perpetual peaceful revolution—a revolution which goes on steadily, quietly adjusting itself to changing conditions—without the concentration camp or the quick-lime in the ditch. The world order which we seek is the cooperation of free countries, working together in a friendly, civilized society.

This nation has placed its destiny in the hands and heads and hearts of its millions of free men and women; and its faith in freedom under the guidance of God. Freedom means the supremacy of human rights everywhere. Our support goes to those who struggle to gain those rights or keep them. Our strength is our unity of purpose. To that high concept there can be no end save victory.

Source: Franklin D. Roosevelt Presidential Library, www.fdrlibrary.marist.edu/pdfs/fftext.pdf.

DOCUMENT 5

The American Promise Speech

Time *magazine lists "The American Promise" as one of the ten greatest speeches. In this special address before Congress delivered on March 15, 1965, President Lyndon Baines Johnson denounces the violence in Selma, Alabama, and he pledges that the country will adopt meaningful voting rights legislation to protect the rights of African-American citizens. During his nationally televised address, President Johnson shocks the nation when he invokes the words of the Civil Rights Movement and says, "we shall overcome!"*

President Lyndon B. Johnson's Special Message to the Congress: The American Promise

March 15, 1965

[As delivered in person before a joint session at 9:02 p.m.]

Mr. Speaker, Mr. President, Members of the Congress:

I speak tonight for the dignity of man and the destiny of democracy.

I urge every member of both parties, Americans of all religions and of all colors, from every section of this country, to join me in that cause.

At times history and fate meet at a single time in a single place to shape a turning point in man's unending search for freedom. So it was at Lexington and Concord. So it was a century ago at Appomattox. So it was last week in Selma, Alabama.

There, long-suffering men and women peacefully protested the denial of their rights as Americans. Many were brutally assaulted. One good man, a man of God, was killed.

There is no cause for pride in what has happened in Selma. There is no cause for self-satisfaction in the long denial of equal rights of millions of Americans. But there is cause for hope and for faith in our democracy in what is happening here tonight.

For the cries of pain and the hymns and protests of oppressed people have summoned into convocation all the majesty of this great Government—the Government of the greatest Nation on earth.

Our mission is at once the oldest and the most basic of this country: to right wrong, to do justice, to serve man.

In our time we have come to live with moments of great crisis. Our lives have been marked with debate about great issues; issues of war and peace, issues of prosperity and depression. But rarely in any time does an issue lay bare the secret heart of America itself. Rarely are we met with a challenge, not to our growth or abundance, our welfare or our security, but rather to the values and the purposes and the meaning of our beloved Nation.

The issue of equal rights for American Negroes is such an issue. And should we defeat every enemy, should we double our wealth and conquer the stars, and still be unequal to this issue, then we will have failed as a people and as a nation.

For with a country as with a person, "What is a man profited, if he shall gain the whole world, and lose his own soul?"

There is no Negro problem. There is no Southern problem. There is no Northern problem. There is only an American problem. And we are met here tonight as Americans—not as Democrats or Republicans— we are met here as Americans to solve that problem.

This was the first nation in the history of the world to be founded with a purpose. The great phrases of that purpose still sound in every American heart, North and South: "All men are created equal"— "government by consent of the governed"—"give me liberty or give me death." Well, those are not just clever words, or those are not just empty theories. In their name Americans have fought and died for two centuries, and tonight around the world they stand there as guardians of our liberty, risking their lives.

Those words are a promise to every citizen that he shall share in the dignity of man. This dignity cannot be found in a man's possessions; it cannot be found in his power, or in his position. It really rests on his right to be treated as a man equal in opportunity to all others. It says that he shall share in freedom, he shall choose his leaders, educate his children, and provide for his family according to his ability and his merits as a human being.

To apply any other test—to deny a man his hopes because of his color or race, his religion or the place of his birth—is not only to do injustice, it is to deny America and to dishonor the dead who gave their lives for American freedom.

THE RIGHT TO VOTE

Our fathers believed that if this noble view of the rights of man was to flourish, it must be rooted in democracy. The most basic right of all was the right to choose your own leaders. The history of this country, in large measure, is the history of the expansion of that right to all of our people.

Many of the issues of civil rights are very complex and most difficult. But about this there can and should be no argument. Every American citizen must have an equal right to vote. There is no reason which can excuse the denial of that right. There is no duty which weighs more heavily on us than the duty we have to ensure that right.

Yet the harsh fact is that in many places in this country men and women are kept from voting simply because they are Negroes.

Every device of which human ingenuity is capable has been used to deny this right. The Negro citizen may go to register only to be told that the day is wrong, or the hour is late, or the official in charge is absent. And if he persists, and if he manages to present himself to the registrar, he may be disqualified because he did not spell out his middle name or because he abbreviated a word on the application.

And if he manages to fill out an application he is given a test. The registrar is the sole judge of whether he passes this test. He may be asked to recite the entire Constitution, or explain the most complex provisions of State law. And even a college degree cannot be used to prove that he can read and write.

For the fact is that the only way to pass these barriers is to show a white skin.

Experience has clearly shown that the existing process of law cannot overcome systematic and ingenious discrimination. No law that we now have on the books—and I have helped to put three of them there—can ensure the right to vote when local officials are determined to deny it.

In such a case our duty must be clear to all of us. The Constitution says that no person shall be kept from voting because of his race or his color. We have all sworn an oath before God to support and to defend that Constitution. We must now act in obedience to that oath.

GUARANTEEING THE RIGHT TO VOTE

Wednesday I will send to Congress a law designed to eliminate illegal barriers to the right to vote.

The broad principles of that bill will be in the hands of the Democratic and Republican leaders tomorrow. After they have reviewed it, it will come here formally as a bill. I am grateful for this opportunity to come here tonight at the invitation of the leadership to reason with my friends, to give them my views, and to visit with my former colleagues.

I have had prepared a more comprehensive analysis of the legislation which I had intended to transmit to the clerk tomorrow but which I will submit to the clerks tonight. But I want to really discuss with you now briefly the main proposals of this legislation,

This bill will strike down restrictions to voting in all elections—Federal, State, and local—which have been used to deny Negroes the right to vote.

This bill will establish a simple, uniform standard which cannot be used, however ingenious the effort, to flout our Constitution.

It will provide for citizens to be registered by officials of the United States Government if the State officials refuse to register them.

It will eliminate tedious, unnecessary lawsuits which delay the right to vote.

Finally, this legislation will ensure that properly registered individuals are not prohibited from voting.

I will welcome the suggestions from all of the Members of Congress— I have no doubt that I will get some—on ways and means to strengthen this law and to make it effective. But experience has plainly shown that this is the only path to carry out the command of the Constitution.

To those who seek to avoid action by their National Government in their own communities; who want to and who seek to maintain purely local control over elections, the answer is simple:

Open your polling places to all your people.

Allow men and women to register and vote whatever the color of their skin.

Extend the rights of citizenship to every citizen of this land.

THE NEED FOR ACTION

There is no constitutional issue here. The command of the Constitution is plain.

There is no moral issue. It is wrong—deadly wrong—to deny any of your fellow Americans the right to vote in this country.

There is no issue of States rights or national rights. There is only the struggle for human rights.

I have not the slightest doubt what will be your answer.

The last time a President sent a civil rights bill to the Congress it contained a provision to protect voting rights in Federal elections. That civil rights bill was passed after 8 long months of debate. And when that bill came to my desk from the Congress for my signature, the heart of the voting provision had been eliminated.

This time, on this issue, there must be no delay, no hesitation and no compromise with our purpose.

We cannot, we must not, refuse to protect the right of every American to vote in every election that he may desire to participate in. And we ought not and we cannot and we must not wait another 8 months before we get a bill. We have already waited a hundred years and more, and the time for waiting is gone.

So I ask you to join me in working long hours—nights and weekends, if necessary—to pass this bill. And I don't make that request lightly. For from the window where I sit with the problems of our country I recognize that outside this chamber is the outraged conscience of a nation, the grave concern of many nations, and the harsh judgment of history on our acts.

WE SHALL OVERCOME

But even if we pass this bill, the battle will not be over. What happened in Selma is part of a far larger movement which reaches into every section and State of America. It is the effort of American Negroes to secure for themselves the full blessings of American life.

Their cause must be our cause too. Because it is not just Negroes, but really it is all of us, who must overcome the crippling legacy of bigotry and injustice.

And we shall overcome.

As a man whose roots go deeply into Southern soil I know how agonizing racial feelings are. I know how difficult it is to reshape the attitudes and the structure of our society.

But a century has passed, more than a hundred years, since the Negro was freed. And he is not fully free tonight.

It was more than a hundred years ago that Abraham Lincoln, a great President of another party, signed the Emancipation Proclamation, but emancipation is a proclamation and not a fact.

A century has passed, more than a hundred years, since equality was promised. And yet the Negro is not equal.

A century has passed since the day of promise. And the promise is unkept.

The time of justice has now come. I tell you that I believe sincerely that no force can hold it back. It is right in the eyes of man and God that it should come. And when it does, I think that day will brighten the lives of every American.

For Negroes are not the only victims. How many white children have gone uneducated, how many white families have lived in stark poverty, how many white lives have been scarred by fear, because we have wasted our energy and our substance to maintain the barriers of hatred and terror?

So I say to all of you here, and to all in the Nation tonight, that those who appeal to you to hold on to the past do so at the cost of denying you your future.

This great, rich, restless country can offer opportunity and education and hope to all: black and white, North and South, sharecropper and city dweller. These are the enemies: poverty, ignorance, disease. They are the enemies and not our fellow man, not our neighbor. And these enemies too, poverty, disease and ignorance, we shall overcome.

AN AMERICAN PROBLEM

Now let none of us in any sections look with prideful righteousness on the troubles in another section, or on the problems of our neighbors. There is really no part of America where the promise of equality has been fully kept. In Buffalo as well as in Birmingham, in Philadelphia as well as in Selma, Americans are struggling for the fruits of freedom.

This is one Nation. What happens in Selma or in Cincinnati is a matter of legitimate concern to every American. But let each of us look within our own hearts and our own communities, and let each of us put our shoulder to the wheel to root out injustice wherever it exists.

As we meet here in this peaceful, historic chamber tonight, men from the South, some of whom were at Iwo Jima, men from the North who have carried Old Glory to far corners of the world and brought it back without a stain on it, men from the East and from the West, are all fighting together without regard to religion, or color, or region, in Viet-Nam. Men from every region fought for us across the world 20 years ago.

And in these common dangers and these common sacrifices the South made its contribution of honor and gallantry no less than any other region of the great Republic—and in some instances, a great many of them, more.

And I have not the slightest doubt that good men from everywhere in this country, from the Great Lakes to the Gulf of Mexico, from the Golden Gate to the harbors along the Atlantic, will rally together now in this cause to vindicate the freedom of all Americans. For all of us owe this duty; and I believe that all of us will respond to it.

Your President makes that request of every American.

PROGRESS THROUGH THE DEMOCRATIC PROCESS

The real hero of this struggle is the American Negro. His actions and protests, his courage to risk safety and even to risk his life, have awakened the conscience of this Nation. His demonstrations have been designed to call attention to injustice, designed to provoke change, designed to stir reform.

He has called upon us to make good the promise of America. And who among us can say that we would have made the same progress were it not for his persistent bravery, and his faith in American democracy.

For at the real heart of battle for equality is a deep-seated belief in the democratic process. Equality depends not on the force of arms or tear gas but upon the force of moral right; not on recourse to violence but on respect for law and order.

There have been many pressures upon your President and there will be others as the days come and go. But I pledge you tonight that we intend to fight this battle where it should be fought: in the courts, and in the Congress, and in the hearts of men.

We must preserve the right of free speech and the right of free assembly. But the right of free speech does not carry with it, as has been said, the right to holler fire in a crowded theater. We must preserve the right to free assembly, but free assembly does not carry with it the right to block public thoroughfares to traffic.

We do have a right to protest, and a right to march under conditions that do not infringe the constitutional rights of our neighbors. And I intend to protect all those rights as long as I am permitted to serve in this office.

We will guard against violence, knowing it strikes from our hands the very weapons which we seek—progress, obedience to law, and belief in American values.

In Selma as elsewhere we seek and pray for peace. We seek order. We seek unity. But we will not accept the peace of stifled rights, or the order imposed by fear, or the unity that stifles protest. For peace cannot be purchased at the cost of liberty.

In Selma tonight, as in every—and we had a good day there—as in every city, we are working for just and peaceful settlement. We must all remember that after this speech I am making tonight, after the police and the FBI and the Marshals have all gone, and after you have promptly passed this bill, the people of Selma and the other cities of the Nation must still live and work together. And when the attention of the Nation has gone elsewhere they must try to heal the wounds and to build a new community.

This cannot be easily done on a battleground of violence, as the history of the South itself shows. It is in recognition of this that men of both races have shown such an outstandingly impressive responsibility in recent days—last Tuesday, again today.

RIGHTS MUST BE OPPORTUNITIES

The bill that I am presenting to you will be known as a civil rights bill. But, in a larger sense, most of the program I am recommending is a civil rights program. Its object is to open the city of hope to all people of all races.

Because all Americans just must have the right to vote. And we are going to give them that right.

All Americans must have the privileges of citizenship regardless of race. And they are going to have those privileges of citizenship regardless of race.

But I would like to caution you and remind you that to exercise these privileges takes much more than just legal right. It requires a trained mind and a healthy body. It requires a decent home, and the chance to find a job, and the opportunity to escape from the clutches of poverty.

Of course, people cannot contribute to the Nation if they are never taught to read or write, if their bodies are stunted from hunger, if their sickness goes untended, if their life is spent in hopeless poverty just drawing a welfare check.

So we want to open the gates to opportunity. But we are also going to give all our people, black and white, the help that they need to walk through those gates.

THE PURPOSE OF THIS GOVERNMENT

My first job after college was as a teacher in Cotulla, Tex., in a small Mexican-American school. Few of them could speak English, and I couldn't speak much Spanish. My students were poor and they often came to class without breakfast, hungry. They knew even in their youth the pain of prejudice. They never seemed to know why people disliked them. But they knew it was so, because I saw it in their eyes. I often walked home late in the afternoon, after the classes were finished, wishing there was more that I could do. But all I knew was to teach them the little that I knew, hoping that it might help them against the hardships that lay ahead.

Somehow you never forget what poverty and hatred can do when you see its scars on the hopeful face of a young child.

I never thought then, in 1928, that I would be standing here in 1965. It never even occurred to me in my fondest dreams that I might have the chance to help the sons and daughters of those students and to help people like them all over this country.

But now I do have that chance—and I'll let you in on a secret—I mean to use it. And I hope that you will use it with me.

This is the richest and most powerful country which ever occupied the globe. The might of past empires is little compared to ours. But I do not want to be the President who built empires, or sought grandeur, or extended dominion.

I want to be the President who educated young children to the wonders of their world. I want to be the President who helped to feed the hungry and to prepare them to be taxpayers instead of taxeaters.

I want to be the President who helped the poor to find their own way and who protected the right of every citizen to vote in every election.

I want to be the President who helped to end hatred among his fellow men and who promoted love among the people of all races and all regions and all parties.

I want to be the President who helped to end war among the brothers of this earth.

And so at the request of your beloved Speaker and the Senator from Montana; the majority leader, the Senator from Illinois; the minority leader, Mr. McCulloch, and other Members of both parties, I came here tonight—not as President Roosevelt came down one time in person to veto a bonus bill, not as President Truman came down one time to urge the passage of a railroad bill—but I came down here to ask you to share this task with me and to share it with the people that we both work for. I want this to be the Congress, Republicans and Democrats alike, which did all these things for all these people.

Beyond this great chamber, out yonder in 50 States, are the people that we serve. Who can tell what deep and unspoken hopes are in their hearts tonight as they sit there and listen. We all can guess, from our own lives, how difficult they often find their own pursuit of happiness, how many problems each little family has. They look most of all to themselves for their futures. But I think that they also look to each of us.

Above the pyramid on the great seal of the United States it says—in Latin—"God has favored our undertaking."

God will not favor everything that we do. It is rather our duty to divine His will. But I cannot help believing that He truly understands and that He really favors the undertaking that we begin here tonight.

Note: The address was broadcast nationally.

Source: Public Papers of the Presidents of the United States: Lyndon B. Johnson, 1965. *Volume I, entry 107, pp. 281–287. Washington, D. C.: Government Printing Office, 1966. Available at: www.lbjlib.utexas.edu/johnson/ archives.hom/speeches.hom/650315.asp.*

DOCUMENT 6

The Selma Times-Journal article, "Civil Rights Leaders Will Seek Sanction of Federal Court for March"

This article appeared on the front page of The Selma Times-Journal *on March 8, 1965, the day after the events of Bloody Sunday. While the paper did run advertisements from the local White Citizens' Councils that included veiled threats and it published other advertisements purportedly showing Dr. Martin Luther King Jr. at a communist training session, unlike many Southern newspapers,* The Selma Times-Journal *tried to provide some balance in its reporting of the events. In* The Race Beat: The Press, *the* Civil Rights Struggle, *and the* Awakening of a Nation, *Roberts and Klibanoff write, "Selma had something most other venues of civil rights activity did not: a local newspaper that visiting reporters could depend on. The Selma Times-Journal saw the historic importance of the story and took its responsibility seriously, providing detailed accounts that reporters found reliable." (2006, p. 389).*

Civil Rights Leaders Will Seek Sanction
Of Court For March

An aid of Dr. Martin Luther King, Jr. said the civil rights leader will come to Selma today to address a mass meeting tonight and to lead a second attempt by Negroes to march Tuesday from Selma to the state capitol in Montgomery. "We can't turn back now," Rev. Andrew Young said after yesterday's melee. "We'll file some papers in federal court Monday and then try to march again Tuesday."

Fifty-six Negroes were sent to the hospital with an assortment of injuries Sunday after state troopers and sheriff's possemen used tear gas, night sticks and horses to disperse more than 600 Negro marchers who ignored orders to disperse.

No attempt was made to arrest the group in the violent confrontation at the east end of Pettus Bridge.

When they showed no inclination to obey Trooper Major John Cloud's order to disperse, an estimated 100 troopers and possemen wearing gas masks stormed into the marchers and shoved, gassed and beat them back onto the bridge.

Horseback riding possemen and troopers on foot drove the Negroes across the bridge and herded them back to Brown's Chapel in a rout punctuated by sporatic clubbing and jabbing.

A brief outbreak of missile throwing by Negroes at the state and county officers who drove the Negroes back to the church was followed by a mop-up operation which cleared the George Washington Carver Homes housing development of everyone on the streets.

Troopers left their cars and armed themselves with shotguns and automatic rifles and moved through the project with Sheriff Jim Clark and his posse ordering everyone indoors.

At the Jeff Davis-Sylvan Street intersection possemen again used their clubs and tear gas in a brief skirmish with Negroes who shouted taunts at them. Sheriff Clark said one of the Negroes displayed a knife and then ran into a house, necessitating the use of gas to evict him.

When all of the Negroes were driven back into the housing project, troopers and the sheriff's department stood back and permitted ambulances to haul away the injured. After they were cleared out, officers moved in to clear the sidewalks and lawns around the two-story apartment buildings.

As the heavily armed state and county officers took over the city police jurisdiction over the protests of Selma Public Safety Director Wilson Baker, the city law enforcement supervisor ordered his force to evacuate the area.

Moments earlier, in an exchange between Baker and Sheriff Clark, Baker told the sheriff that quiet had already been restored in the Negro community and he saw no need for any further show of force by troopers and the posse.

"I've already waited a month too damn long about moving in," the sheriff retorted.

About 30 minutes later, when the sheriff's force and the troopers pulled out, city police moved back into the area and resumed normal police work.

James Bevel, addressing a mass rally that followed the march, criticized President Johnson for "not fulfilling his promises."

"Johnson knows that Negroes cannot vote here," he said.

In Atlanta, King said that in the light of Sunday's "tragic event" that he has "no alternative but to recommend to my close associates and the Negro people of Alabama to continue in their determined attempt to walk to Montgomery . . ."

King had said earlier that he would lead Sunday's march and his failure to appear and take part in it prompted ridicule for the Negro leader from Mayor Joe Smitherman.

"It should be very evident to the Negro people by now that King and the other leaders who ask them to break the laws are always absent from the violence, as he was today," the mayor noted.

Baker, who disagreed sharply with the policing of yesterday's march attempt, planned Saturday night to submit his resignation as public safety director today to city council.

Mayor Smitherman, after privately making agreements with county and state officials with which Baker did not agree, ordered the public safety director to use city police in helping the troopers break up the march.

Baker, who maintained that the Negroes should be arrested instead of gassed and beaten, if they refused to disperse, said he would resign rather than carry out the mayor's orders.

But when some city council members learned of his plans they intervened, and an agreement was worked out whereby the mayor, except for establishing policy, would leave city law enforcement planning and supervision to Baker in the future.

After the Sunday meeting, it was also agreed that city police would not participate, unless they were called in by the state, in breaking up the Sunday march. Police had one car on the scene across the bridge to operate as liason in this connection.

State troopers and county forces agreed under the arrangement, it was reported, that once the Negroes were driven back across the bridge that city police would be in charge of the return of the marchers to the church.

When this reported agreement was violated and the troopers and posse pressed the Negroes across town and into the housing development, Baker ordered his men to temporarily pull back.

Baker said he wanted to halt the marchers as they left the city and arrest them at Broad street if they refused to return to the church, but the mayor asked him not to interfere in the state's plans to break up the march with gas and force.

Mayor Smitherman said later last night on a television show telephone interview that, as mayor of Selma, he "concurred" with the governor's actions in halting the march.

The marchers made their initial attempt to leave Brown's Chapel around 1:30 p.m. Sunday and were turned back by city police less than a block from the church. But it was immediately apparent that the temporary delay was for regrouping and that they would come out again.

When the marchers neared the bridge, traffic was halted at Water Avenue and at the King's Bend Road-Highway 80 intersection across the bridge.

Hundreds of spectators jammed all unrestricted parking space and overflowed onto the parking area of businesses in the Selmont area where the confrontation was to take place.

State troopers, their cars lined up alongside the highway from the traffic light to the foot of the bridge, stood waiting while possemen between the buildings awaited orders to mount their horses.

When the marchers were within about 100 yards of where Maj. Cloud, Sheriff Clark and a line of troopers blocked the highway, orders were given for the officers to put on their gas masks.

Newsmen were asked to assemble in front of the Lehman Pontiac building and were assigned several troopers for their protection "if you obey the ground rules."

Col. Al Lingo watched from an automobile parked nearby.

When the marchers were within about 75 feet of where the troopers blocked the highway, May. Cloud gave the order for them to halt and disperse.

He told them the march would not continue and for them to disperse and go to their homes or back to the church. When the Negroes failed to withdraw, Cloud ordered "troopers forward."

For a few seconds the troopers, holding their nightsticks at each end, attempted to push the crowd back. Then both troopers and the marchers started falling, and in the scramble the violence erupted.

The march was led by Hosea Williams of the SCLC and John Lewis, a chairman of the Student Nonviolent Coordinating Committee. Lewis suffered a possible skull fracture but Williams was not injured in the showdown with state troopers.

About 100 troopers stopped the march under direct orders from Wallace. Maj. John Cloud, speaking over a loudspeaker, told the marchers to disperse and return to the church.

When they did not obey him, the troopers stormed into the double column line.

This failed to force the marchers back across the Alabama River bridge over which they had just walked, so the troopers began throwing tear gas grenades.

Meanwhile three white men, including a militant segregationist who recently attacked King were arrested late Sunday on charges of assaulting an FBI agent.

Jimmy George Robinson, 26, a member of the National States Rights party previously convicted of striking King with his fist, also was charged by city police with a separate case of assault and battery against the FBI agent. Another also was accused of taking the agent's camera.

The agent, Daniel Doyle of Little Rock, said he was attacked and his camera taken while he and other FBI men observed the attempted march. Whether the men knew Doyle was a federal officer or whether they mistook him for a photographer was not established.

The others arrested were identified by special agent Earl Dallness of the Mobile FBI office as Thomas Randall Kendrick, 21, and Noel D. Cooper, also 21.

As the troopers moved in on the marchers the first time, a crowd of several hundred white persons which had gathered about 100 yards away broke into cheers.

The cheering grew louder and the crowd shouted encouragement as the troopers heaved the grenades.

Although the crowd was loud and hostile, it made no attempt to break through heavy police lines to attack the marchers.

As the grenades exploded, the Negroes, who had regrouped after the first charge, knelt by the side of the road to pray. But finally the gas routed them and they began running back across the long bridge that leads into downtown Selma.

Some stumbled over fellow marchers as they ran in panic and state troopers hit them with clubs. The group had marched about a mile from the Browns Chapel A.M.E. Church and they were chased by the posse all the way back to the church.

One downtown street was lined with cars in which Negroes sat watching events.

Members of the posse beat on the hoods of the automobiles with their nightsticks and pointed their clubs at the drivers, shouting, "Get the hell out of town! Go on, I mean it! We want all the Niggers off the streets!"

The Negroes all left without protest. Thirty minutes after the marchers' encounter with the troopers a Negro could not be seen walking the streets.

Source: Courtesy of The Selma Times-Journal.

Notes

1 Introduction

1 Lyndon B. Johnson, Special Message to Congress: The American Promise (1965), para. 4, Lyndon Baines Johnson Library at University of Texas, accessed October 13, 2012, www.lbjlib.utexas.edu/johnson/archives.hom/speeches.hom/650315.asp.
2 Jack Hurst, *Nathan Bedford Forrest: A Biography*, first edition (New York: Vintage, 1994), 4.
3 The role of the past is a source of constant debate in the American South, and the Civil War is a deeply engrained part of the Southern past. The Civil War is not only remembered in the South, it is romanticized. In fact, monuments to Confederate leaders are so pervasive in many Southern towns that it has been stated that it seems the South won the war. (Hurst, *Nathan Bedford Forrest*)
4 Official City website for Montgomery Alabama, www.montgomeral.gov. According to recent Census data, Montgomery is about 49.6 percent black and 47.7 percent white. The city seal seems to embrace both realities of its history while simultaneously embracing its two largest racial groups.
5 W.E.B. DuBois, *The Souls of Black Folk*, reprint edition (New York: Tribeca Books, 2013), 142–143. In the book DuBois observes that blacks were so singularly consumed with the abolition of slavery that when it came it seemed the "literal Coming of the Lord."
6 Elizabeth Bogwardt, *A New Deal for the World: America's Vision for Human Rights* (Cambridge, MA: Belknap Press, 2005).
7 John Hope Franklin and Alfred Moss, *From Slavery to Freedom: A History of Negro Americans*, illustrated, sixth edition (New York: Knopf, 1988).
8 Ibid.
9 DuBois, *The Souls of Black Folk*, 142.
10 David C. Hsung, "Freedom Songs in the Modern Civil Rights Movement," *OAH Magazine of History* 19:4 (July 2005): 23–26.
11 Bernice Johnson Reagon later became one of the founders of the Freedom Singers.
12 Pete Seeger and Bob Reiser, *Everybody Says Freedom: The History of the Civil Rights Movement in Songs and Pictures* (New York: W.W. Norton & Company, 1989), xi.

13 W.E.B Du Bois, "Returning Soldiers," *The Crisis* 18: (May 1919): 13.

14 Much of Europe was already embroiled in the conflict, but the United States was not involved.

15 Franklin Delano Roosevelt, "The Four Freedoms Speech," January 6, 1941, http://docs.fdrlibrary.marist.edu/od4frees.html.

16 Ibid.

17 Ella Baker "became known as the godmother of SNCC" (Seeger and Reiser, *Everybody Says Freedom*, xviii). Baker was deeply concerned about the next generation. She believed in them, and she believed in their ability to effect change.

18 Larry Isaac, "Movement of Movements: Culture Moves in the Long Civil Rights Struggle," *Social Forces* 87:1 (2008): 33–63, 38.

19 Ibid.

20 Doug McAdam, *Political Process and the Development of Black Insurgency 1930–1970*, second edition (Chicago: University of Chicago Press, 1999).

21 Myrlie Evers and Manning Marable, *The Autobiography of Medgar Evers: A Hero's Life and Legacy Revealed through His Writings, Letters, and Speeches* (New York: Basic Civitas Books, 2006), 154.

22 U.S. Constitution, amend. 15, sec. 1

23 Bill Perlman, in discussion with the author, December 19, 2012.

24 Everett M. Rogers, *Diffusion of Innovations*, fifth edition (New York: Free Press, 2003), 34.

25 David Garrow, *Protest at Selma: Martin Luther King, Jr., and the Voting Rights Act of 1965* (New Haven: Yale University Press, 1980).

26 Charles E. Fager, *Selma, 1965: The March that Changed the South* (New York: Scribner, 1974).

27 Wally Vaughn and Hattie Campbell Davis, Eds., *The Selma Campaign 1963–1965: The Decisive Battle of the Civil Rights Movement* (Dover, MA: The Majority Press, Inc., 2006).

28 Mary Stanton, *From Selma to Sorrow: The Life and Death of Viola Liuzzo* (Athens: University of Georgia Press, 2000).

29 Charles Eagles, *Outside Agitator: Jon Daniels and the Civil Rights Movement in Alabama* (Tuscaloosa: University of Alabama Press, 2000).

30 John J. Green, "Community Development as Social Movement: A Contribution Models of Practice." *Community Development* 39:1 (2008): 50–62.

31 Alexander Keyssar, *The Right to Vote: The Contested History of Democracy in the United States,* revised edition (Philadelphia, PA: Basic Books, 2009).

32 Historical sociology sees history as something that is: 1) knowable; 2) produced in a space–time context; and 3) subject to interpretation (Charles Tilly, "Historical Sociology," in *Current Perspectives in Social Theory*, Eds. Scott G. McNall and Gary N. Howe, Vol. I. (Greenwich, CT: JAI Press, 1980); Charles Tilly, "Three Visions of History and Theory," *History and Theory* 46: 2 (2007): 299–307). In this manner it differs from: 1) traditional/positivist historical approaches, which tend to be more reductionist in nature; 2) those historical research approaches that seek history without historicism (John M. Hobson and George Lawson, "What is History in International Relations?" *Millennium: Journal of International Studies* 37:2 (2008): 421); and 3) historical approaches that reject theory in favor of sweeping, grand narratives (Hobson and Lawson, "What is History", 423–427).

33 Anthony Giddens, *The Constitution of Society: Outline of the Theory of Structuration* (Berkeley: University of California Press, 1984).

34 John M. Hobson et al., "Historical Sociology," in *The International Studies Encyclopedia*, Ed. Robert A. Denmark (UK: Wiley–Blackwell/International Studies Association, 2010), 11–13.

35 Rogers, *Diffusion of Innovations*.

36 Ibid., 12.

37 Green, "Community Development."

38 Many social science theories ignore the element of time; however, Rogers, a professor of rural sociology, makes time a central element of the theory. As such, this theory is uniquely adaptable to a socio-historical examination of the voting rights struggle. The acceptance of the new idea is a process, which, if adopted, occurs over time.

39 Wayne A. Santoro, "The Civil Rights Movement and the Right to Vote: Black Protest, Segregationist Violence and the Audience," *Social Forces* 86:4 (June 2008): 1340–1414

40 Raymond Boudon, The *Uses of Structuralism* (Ann Arbor, MI: Heinemann, 1971), 48.

41 Giddens, *The Constitution of Society*, 25–26.

42 Edward A. Tiryakian, "Emile Durkheim and Social Change," in *The Blackwell Encyclopedia of Sociology*, Ed. George Ritzer (Hoboken: Blackwell, 2007), 126–164.

43 Yi-Fu Tuan and Steven Hoelscher, *Space and Place: The Perspective of Experience* (Minneapolis: University of Minnesota Press, 2001).

44 James Slevin, "Time–Space," in *Blackwell Encylopedia of Sociology*, Ed. George Ritzer (2007) doi:10.1111/b.9781405124331.2007.x.

45 Giddens, *The Constitution of Society*.

46 Jacquelyn Dowd Hall, "The Long Civil Rights Movement and the Political Uses of the Past," *The Journal of American History* 91:4 (March 2005): 1233–1263.

47 Eric Foner, "1866: The Birth of Civil Rights," Gilder Lehrman, accessed November 11, 2012, www.gilderlehrman.org/multimedia#3339.

48 Rogers, *Diffusion of Innovations*, 37.

49 Ibid.

50 Northwest Austin Municipal Utility District No. 1 v. Holder. 557 U.S. 193 (2009).

51 Amy Davidson, "In Voting Rights Scalia Sees a 'Racial Entitlement'," *New Yorker*, February 28, 2013, www.newyorker.com/online/blogs/closeread/2013/02/in-voting-rights-scalia-sees-a-racial-entitlement.html.

During oral arguments for Shelby County, Alabama v. Holder, a case brought by Shelby County, Alabama, which challenges the constitutionality of Section 5 of the Voting Rights Act, a *New Yorker* article quotes Justice Anton Scalia as saying:

This last enactment [of Section 5], not a single vote in the Senate against it. And the House is pretty much the same. . . . I think it is attributable, very likely attributable, to a phenomenon that is called perpetuation of racial entitlement. It's been written about. Whenever a society adopts racial entitlements, it is very difficult to get out of them through the normal political processes.

52 Mississippi Public Broadcasting Report, "Activists Rally for Civil Rights and Section 5," May 1, 2013, http://mpbonline.org/News/article/miss._activists_rally_ for_ civil_ rights _and_ section_5.

53   Ibid.

54   C. Wright Mills, *The Sociological Imagination* (New York: Oxford University Press, 1959).

55   C. Vann Woodward, with a foreword by William E. Leuchtenburg, *The Burden of Southern History*, updated third edition (Baton Rouge: Louisiana State University Press, 2008).

56   Ibid.

57   Ibid., 27–28.

58   Donald E. Pease, *The New American Exceptionalism* (Minneapolis: University of Minnesota Press, 2009), 10.

American exceptionalism first emerged in the 1920s. This concept hinted at the moral superiority of the U.S. and opined that while the United States was a nation with a relatively short history, it was, nevertheless, a country based upon a common creed which made it quantitatively and qualitatively different from other countries.

59   Seymour Martin Lipset, *American Exceptionalism: A Two Edged Sword* (New York: W.W. Norton & Company, 1997).

60   Lipset, *American Exceptionalism*, 268.

61   Woodward, *Burden*, 259–260.

62   Woodward, *Burden*.

63   The Pew Research Center for the People & The Press "Civil War at 150: Still Relevant, Still Divisive."April 8, 2011, www.people-press.org/files/legacy-pdf/04-08-11%20Civil%20War%20Release.pdf.

64   Ibid.

65   Nicholas A. Valentino and David O. Sears, "Old Times There are Not Forgotten: Race and Partisan Realignment in the Contemporary South." *American Journal of Political Science* 49:3 (2005): 672–688, 685.

66   See South Carolina v. Katzenbach 383 U.S. 301 (1966). In this case the Supreme Court effectively called the temporary provisions of the Act an extraordinary measure appropriate for extraordinary times and states, "exceptional conditions can justify legislative measures not otherwise appropriate." Ibid., at 334.

67   See Shelby County, Alabama v. Eric Holder, Jr., No. 12–96, slip op. (U.S. Supreme Ct., June 25, 2013).

68   Katzenbach was the first challenge to the newly implemented Congressional Act. In it, the court upheld the Act stating that while it was "[an] uncommon exercise of congressional power," the same could be justified on the basis of "exceptional conditions." See South Carolina v. Katzenbach 383 U.S, at 334.

69   Shelby County, slip op.

70   See Amy Davidson, "In Voting Rights, Scalia Sees a 'Racial Entitlement,'" *New Yorker*, February 28, 2013, accessed March 1, 2013; Jess Bravin, "Scalia Calls Voting Act a 'Racial Preferment,'" *Wall Street Journal online*, April 16, 2013, accessed April 16, 2013, http://m.us.wsj.com/articles/a/SBI00014241278873243458045784270232436676262?mg+reno64-wsj.

71   Section 5 proponents categorically rejected the categorization while those in favor of some overhaul to Section 5 embraced the label. Here, again, an appreciation of history and the deeply held American creed is instructive as, throughout history, American exceptionalism expressly rejects the idea of entitlements.

72 CNN Newsroom, "Court Guts Voting Rights Act." Aired June 25, 2013–14:00 ET.

73 Ibid.

74 According to journalist Alan Liptak, the 5 to 4 vote split largely "along ideological lines." Chief Justice Roberts wrote the majority opinion, which was joined by Antonin Scalia, Anthony M. Kennedy, Clarence Thomas, and Samuel A. Alito, Jr. Justice Thomas joined the majority opinion but also wrote a concurring opinion stating he would find Section 5 of the Act unconstitutional and strike it down. Justices Ruth Bader Ginsburg, Steven G Breyer, Sonia Sotomayor, and Elena Kagan dissented. Republican presidents appointed all justices on the majority opinion; while Democratic presidents appointed all of the justices joining in the dissent. See Alan Liptak, "Supreme Court Invalidated Part of Voting Rights Act." *New York Times*, June 25, 2013.

75 Shelby County, slip op. at 4.

76 557 U.S. 193.

77 Shelby County v. Alabama, quoting Katzenbach at 330.

78 Shelby County, slip op. at 3.

79 Shelby County, Alabama v. Eric Holder, Jr., No. 12–96, slip op. at 24 (U.S. Supreme Ct., June 25, 2013)(Ginsburg, Breyer, Sotomayor & Kagan, JJ., dissenting).

80 Liptak, "Supreme Court Invalidated."

81 See Jackie Calmes et al., "On Voting Case, Reaction From 'Deeply Disappointed' to 'It's about Time.'" *The New York Times*, Politics Section. June 25, 2013.

82 Shelby County v. Holder, Dissent, 24–25.

83 Steve Suitts, "Voting Rights, the Supreme Court, and the Persistence of Southern History." *Southern Spaces*, accessed 24 June, 2013, http://southernspaces. org/2013?voting-rights-supreme-court-and-persistence-southern-history (June 4, 2013).

84 By this I mean to acknowledge the continuing significance of race and history in this analysis, not to suggest that either the South or white Americans must be put on a pedestal of eternal shame for past ills.

85 William Faulkner, *Requiem for a Nun* (New York: Vintage Books, 1950).

86 James Loewen, *Lies My Teacher Told Me: Everything Your American History Textbook Got Wrong* (New York: Simon & Schuster, 2007).

87 Ibid., 2.

88 Debate continues to center around the impact of redistricting on voting rights. However, since the passage of the Act, new groups of disenfranchised have emerged.

89 Kenneth Andrews, *Freedom Is a Constant Struggle: The Mississippi Civil Rights Movement and Its Legacy*, first edition (Chicago: University of Chicago Press, 2004), preface.

90 Emilye Crosby, "'Doesn't Everybody Want to Grow Up to be Ella Baker?': Teaching Movement History," in *Civil Rights History from the Ground Up: Local Struggles, a National Movement*, Ed. Emilye Crosby, (Athens: University of Georgia Press, 2011), 448–476, 469.

91 Bernice Johnson Reagon, Sweet Honey in the Rock, *Ella's Song* (Flying Fish label, 1983).

2   One Moment in Time

1   J.L. Chestnut Jr. and Julia Cass, *Black in Selma* (New York: Farrar, Straus and Giroux, 1990), 184.

2   Allen M. Tullos, "The Black Belt," *Southern Spaces,* April 19, 2004, www.southernspaces.org/2004/black-belt.

3   Elizabeth Partridge, *Marching for Freedom: Walk Together Children and Don't You Grow Weary,* first edition (New York:Viking Juvenile, 2009).

4   Charles S. Bullock III and Mark J. Rozell, *The Oxford Handbook of Southern Politics* (New York: Oxford University Press, 2012), 265.

5   Hardeep Phull, *Story Behind the Protest Song: A Reference Guide to the 50 Songs That Changed the 20th century,* first edition (Westport, CT: Greenwood Publishing Group, 2008); Taylor Branch, *At Canaan's Edge: America in the King Years, 1965–1968* (New York: Simon & Schuster, Inc., 2007), 80.

6   Ruby Sales interview conducted by Blackside, Inc. on December 12, 1988, for Washington University Libraries, Film and Media Archive, Henry Hampton Collection "*Eyes on the Prize II: America at the Crossroads 1965 to 1985,*" Washington University Digital Gateway. Text available http://digital.wustl.edu/e/eii/eiiweb/sal5427.0903.142rubysales.html.

7   In Rogers' theory, the rate of adoption of an innovation is normally distributed and resembles a bell curve. See Figure 2.2.

8   Seventeen counties are included in Alabama's Black Belt, and a number of them— Dallas, Lowndes, Marengo, and Montgomery—were hotbeds during the Civil Rights Movement.

9   Ronald C. Wimberly and Libby V. Morris, *The Southern Black Belt: A National Perspective* (Lexington, KY: TVA Rural Studies, 1997).

10   U.S. Census Bureau, 2010 Census, accessed via www.al.com/census/index.ssf.

11   Gene Roberts and Hank Klibanoff, *The Race Beat: The Press, the Civil Rights Struggle, and the Awakening of a Nation* (New York: Vintage, 2007), 375.

12   Branch, *At Canaan's Edge,* 6.

13   City of Selma website, Retrieved October 17, 2012. http://selma-al.gov/.

14   Stokely Carmichael, *Ready for Revolution: The Life and Struggles of Stokely Carmichael (Kwame Ture)* (New York: Scribner, 2003), 442–443.

15   Samuel Walker, interview by author, audio recording, Selma, AL, July 11, 2012.

16   Charles E. Cobb Jr., *On the Road to Freedom: A Guided Tour of the Civil Rights Movement* (Chapel Hill, NC: Algonquin Books, 2008), 226.

17   Branch, *At Canaan's Edge*; Hasan K. Jeffries, *Bloody Lowndes: Civil Rights and Black Power in Alabama's Black Belt* (New York: New York University Press, 2009).

18   Branch, *At Canaan's Edge,* 6.

19   Ibid.

20   Everett Rogers, *Diffusion of Innovations,* fifth edition (New York: Free Press, 2001), 169

21   Ibid., 221.

22   Ibid., 37.

23   Tullos, "The Black Belt."

24   "The State of the South 1872," *The Nation: A Weekly Journal* 14 (New York: E.L. Godkin & Co. Publishers, 1872), 197–198.

25   On January 1, 1863, President Abraham Lincoln issued the Emancipation Proclamation, freeing all slaves held within any state or territory at rebellion with the United States, but the Emancipation Proclamation relied on the president's war powers, and it did not cover slaves held in Northern states or in Southern territories not in rebellion with the United States. Permanent emancipation of all slaves would require a Congressional Act. Further, any changes to the U.S. Constitution would require the ratification (i.e., adoption) by at least two–thirds of the states. The first months of the year 1865 were monumental. On January 31, 1865, Congress passed the Thirteenth Amendment, which prohibits slavery, and sent it to the states for ratification. On March 4, 1865, President Lincoln took his second oath of office. On April 9, 1865, General Robert E. Lee, commander of the Confederate Army of Northern Virginia, surrendered at Appomattox Courthouse, and on April 14, 1865, President Lincoln was assassinated.

26   The Thirteenth, Fourteenth, and Fifteenth Amendments to the United States Constitution are popularly known as the Reconstruction Era Amendments. The Thirteenth Amendment eliminated slavery. Ratification of the Thirteenth Amendment by the states did not occur until December 6, 1865. The Fourteenth Amendment (ratified July 9, 1868) establishes that all those born in the United States are U.S. citizens, and guarantees due process to all. The last of the Reconstruction Era amendments—the Fifteenth Amendment (ratified February 3, 1870)—grants the right to vote and states that this right cannot be denied on the basis of race; however, the grant of the vote did not enforce or protect the right.

27   Eric Foner, *Reconstruction: America's Unfinished Revolution, 1863–1877* (New York: Harper Perennial Modern Classics, 2002).

28   Ibid.

29   Ibid.

30   Ibid.

31   In a Gilder Lehrman video series, historian Eric Foner argues that the birth of Civil Rights occurred in 1866, when Congress passed the Civil Rights Act of 1866, which established principles of equality of laws. Neither the 1866 Act nor its more famous later relative, the Civil Rights Act of 1964, guarantees the right to vote. Foner argues that in many ways the 1866 Act is stronger and affords more protections than the Civil Rights Act of 1964 (The Gilder Lehrman Institute of American History, "1866: The Birth of Civil Rights," accessed November 11, 2012, www.gilderlehrman.org/multimedia#3339.

32   Nicholas Lemann, *Redemption: The Last Battle of the Civil War* (New York: Farrar, Straus and Giroux, 2007); Leon F. Litwack, *Been in the Storm So Long: The Aftermath of Slavery*, first edition (New York: Vintage, 1980).

33   Black Codes emerged in the Southern states soon after the abolition of slavery. The Codes limited the civil rights and civil liberties of blacks; they also criminalized vagrancy and imposed punishment (including confinement and being forced to work on prison farms) for loitering. Jim Crow laws emerged largely after Reconstruction and sought to maintain a separate social system between blacks and whites.

34   David J. Garrow, *Protest at Selma: Martin Luther King, Jr., and the Voting Rights Act of 1965* (New Haven, CT: Yale University Press, 1980); Jeffries, *Bloody Lowndes*; Brian K. Landsberg, *Enforcing Civil Rights: Race Discrimination and the Department*

of Justice (Studies in Government and Public Policy) (Lawrence: University Press of Kansas, 1997).

35   Jeffries, *Bloody Lowndes*, 13. Lowndes County was known by another name—Bloody Lowndes. This name came from the county's long reputation for controlling and curtailing the political and social movements of African-Americans, which included a long history of violent mob lynchings of African-American men dating back to the late 1880s (Ibid., 17–19).

36   Ibid.

37   Ibid, 57. This attention to Lowndes County is especially relevant because in order to march from Selma to Montgomery, the protestors would have to go through Bloody Lowndes County.

38   Isabel Wilkerson, *The Warmth of Other Suns: The Epic Story of America's Great Migration*, reprint edition (New York: Vintage, 2011).

39   Annie Pearl Avery, interview by author, audio recording, Selma, AL, July 11, 2012.

40   See National Park Service website, retrieved January 10, 2013, www.nps.gov/nr/ twhp/wwwlps/lessons/133semo/133facts1.htm.

41   National Park Service, *Selma to Montgomery* pamphlet.

42   Carmichael, *Ready for Revolution*; James Forman, *The Making of Black Revolutionaries*, illustrated edition (Seattle: University of Washington Press, 1997); John Lewis and Michael D'Orso, *Walking with the Wind: A Memoir of the Movement* (San Diego, CA: Harvest, 1999).

43   A July 9, 1964 order by Circuit Judge James Hare banned all marches and mass meetings and forbade the assembly of three or more African-Americans. The order specifically named some four-dozen individuals and fifteen organizations, and it threatened the very existence of the movement. See Wally Vaughn and Hattie Campbell Davis, Eds., *The Selma Campaign 1963–1965: The Decisive Battle of the Civil Rights Movement* (Dover, MA: The Majority Press, Inc., 2006). Judge Hare's injunction rendered DCVL's emblazoned request even more courageous.

44   Branch, *At Canaan's Edge*; and Landsberg, *Enforcing Civil Rights*, which states that, while legislation was under discussion, it had not been passed, and the promises of the Fifteenth Amendment, the most basic element of free government, went largely unfulfilled. Poll taxes had already been declared a violation of the Fourteenth Amendment and literacy tests outlawed, but all these measures depended upon enforcement by Southern courts.

45   Landsberg, *Enforcing Civil Rights*.

46   Branch, *At Canaan's Edge*; Juan Williams, *Eyes on the Prize: America's Civil Rights Years, 1954–1965* (New York: Viking Penguin, Inc., 1987).

47   Landsberg, *Enforcing Civil Rights*.

48   Ibid., 39–43.

49   Ibid.

50   Selma officials often tried to decry Sheriff Clark's acts and paint him as a lone wolf, but in a public statement Reverend Martin Luther King Jr. made clear that this strategy was ineffective. During one exchange, Sheriff Clark made the media turn off their cameras and then struck SCLC executive staff member C.T. Vivian across the face so hard that it knocked Vivian down the stairs and caused Vivian's mouth to bleed, and Clark to suffer a linear fracture on one of his fingers. In the media, newly elected Selma mayor, Joe Smitherman, and his newly appointed public safety

official, Wilson Baker, tried to lay blame for the incident solely on Clark. That tactic might have been successful except that Martin Luther King Jr. publicly stated, "I'm here to tell you that the businessmen, the mayor of this city, and everybody in the white power structure of this city must take responsibility for everything that Jim Clark does in this community" (Williams, J., *Eyes on the Prize*, 265).

51   Ibid.

52   Charles Spigner, "Jimmy Lee Jackson," *Encyclopedia of Alabama*, accessed January 13, 2013, www.encyclopediaofalabama.org/face/Article.jsp?id=h-2011.

53   Many people in the movement were connected to Marion. Coretta Scott King grew up about 12 miles from Marion, the county seat. Andrew Young's wife, Jean, grew up in Marion. Andrew Young was a student pastor there.

54   Townsend Davis, *Weary Feet, Rested Souls: A Guided History of the Civil Rights Movement* (New York: W.W. Norton & Company, 1998), 121–123.

55   Williams, J., *Eyes on the Prize*, 264–265.

56   Vaughn and Davis, *The Selma Campaign*.

57   Spigner, "Jimmy Lee Jackson."

58   Pete Seeger and Bob Reiser. *Everybody Says Freedom: A History of the Civil Rights Movement in Songs and Pictures* (New York: W.W. Norton & Company, 1989).

59   Williams, J., *Eyes on the Prize*, 265.

60   In various sources Jackson's first name is sometimes spelled Jimmy and sometimes Jimmie. Throughout this book, Jackson's name will be spelled Jimmie, unless the quoted or referenced source spells it otherwise.

61   Interview with Richard Valeriani, conducted by Blackside, Inc. on December 10, 1985, for *Eyes on the Prize: America's Civil Rights Years (1954–1965)*, Washington University Libraries, Film and Media Archive, Henry Hampton Collection. http://digital.wustl.edu/e/eop/eopweb/val0015.0857.101richardvaleriani.html.

62   Spigner, "Jimmy Lee Jackson."

63   Williams, J., *Eyes on the Prize*, 265.

64   Spigner, "Jimmy Lee Jackson."

65   Some of the major news outlets carried the story of Jimmie Lee Jackson, including a February 27, 1965 article by Roy Reed called "Wounded Negro dies in Alabama," which appeared in *New York Times*. In the article, Jackson, who made a statement prior to succumbing to his wounds, is quoted as saying he was "clubbed down" by police. Roy Reed, "Wounded Negro dies in Alabama," *The New York Times* (New York), February 27, 1965.

66   Williams, J., *Eyes on the Prize*, 267.

67   Ibid.

68   In the biblical story of Esther, her uncle Mordecai, a Jew, compelled his niece, Esther, the wife of the king, to go in to the king and plead for the lives of the Jewish people scheduled for execution. (Esther, *Holy Bible* (Grand Rapids, MI: Zondervan, 1984), Chapters 2–4.)

69   Seeger and Reiser, *Everybody Says Freedom*, 191.

70   Many members of SNCC were openly critical of the March. SNCC's people were "on the ground" in Dallas and Perry counties. At the time, SCLC had no permanent people in the area. SNCC was concerned that if SCLC followed its usual course (come into an area, march, and then leave), SNCC and the people of Perry and Dallas counties would be left to pick up the pieces.

71 However, it should be noted that on Bloody Sunday few people had provisions for a 3-day journey.

72 Branch, *At Canaan's Edge*.

73 SNCC elected not to participate in the march that would later become known as Bloody Sunday; however, Ruby Nell Sales indicates that SNCC presence was still strong. In a personal interview with the author she states, "SNCC [members] could participate [if they wanted]. John Lewis wanted to participate. But what most people did was to shadowbox. We were too much in the movement to totally be out of an action like that."

74 Branch, *At Canaan's Edge*, 44.

75 David Garrow, *Bearing the Cross: Martin Luther King, Jr., and the Southern Christian Leadership Conference* (New York: William Morrow Paperbacks, 2004).

76 Dara N. Byrne, *The Unfinished Agenda of the Selma-Montgomery Voting Rights March* (Hoboken, NJ: John Wiley & Sons, 2005), 31.

77 Williams, J., *Eyes on the Prize*, 269.

78 Lewis and D'Orso, *Walking with the Wind*, 340.

79 Ibid.

80 Ibid.

81 In some works, Joanne Bland is identified as Joanne Blackmon.

82 Joanne Bland Interview OH 009.1, "Journey to Selma 2002," Oral History Project, University of Wisconsin, June 8, 2002.

83 Lewis and D'Orso, *Walking with the Wind*, 338.

84 Garrow, *Bearing the Cross*, 398.

85 Alston Fitts III, "Bloody Sunday,"*Encyclopedia of Alabama*, accessed July 11, 2012, www.encyclopediaofalabama.org/face/Article.jsp?id=h-1876.

86 Ibid. Fitts records that 40 separate canisters of tear gas, 12 smoke cans, and 8 cans of nausea gas were deployed on the March protestors.

87 Fitts, "Bloody Sunday;"; Fager, *Selma, 1965*.

88 Charles Fager, *Selma, 1965: The March that Changed the South* (New York: Scribner, 1974).

89 Bland, "Journey to Selma"interview.

90 Claude Sitton, national editor of *The New York Times*, had a rule that anywhere King went in the South, he was to be covered. Sitton knew the potential for violence or demonstration that King generated, and he vowed that *The New York Times* would be there to cover it. Since Brown, some 10 years earlier, only one Northern newspaper had continuously covered the Civil Rights Movement. That paper was *The New York Times*. Now the *Los Angeles Times* was entering the fold. Additionally, because of threatened legal actions against *The New York Times*, the paper had limited its presence in the South, particularly Alabama, for fear that they would be served while there. Soon, major newspapers across the country and broadcast media began to regularly cover King and the Movement (Roberts and Klibanoff, *The Race Beat*).

91 Fager, *Selma, 1965*, 94: Roberts and Klibanoff, *The Race Beat*, 386.

92 Annie Pearl Avery, interview by author, audio recording, Selma, AL, July 11, 2012.

93 Richard Valeriani, Blackside interview, December 10, 1985.

94 Rogers, *Diffusion of Innovations*, 19.

95 Williams, J., *Eyes on the Prize*, 273.

96 Jayasri Majumdar Hart. Hartfilms. *Sisters of Selma* DVD produced in cooperation with Alabama Public Broadcasting Corporation, 2007.

97 Fager, *Selma, 1965*; Williams, J., *Eyes on the Prize*; Taylor Branch, *Parting the Waters: America in the King Years 1954–1963* (New York: Simon & Schuster, Inc., 1988) and Hart, *Sisters of Selma*. Hart provides a detailed examination of Catholic sisters from all over the United States who requested permission to come to Selma to fight for the rights of African-American citizens. Individuals and organizations from across the nation came, but the sisters were a very visible assembly. In their accounts, many credit Vatican II as their compulsion to respond. One sister stated, "[it was] a call for sisters to get out of their habits and go where the need was." In the film, one Catholic priest, Father Doyle, says, "It's time for the [Catholic] church to be visible." Those from the Midwest were the first to respond. Other orders included the Sisters of St. Joseph of Carondelet, the Sisters of Loretto, and the Sisters of Charity of the Blessed Virgin Mary. A number of Sisters of St. Joseph of Rochester, New York, were already missioned in Selma, Alabama and served under Father Oulett at St. Elizabeth's Parish, but, without question, Sister Antona Ebo, a black Franciscan Sister of Mary from St. Louis, was the sister who garnered the most attention. Ironically, despite the sisters' ardent commitment to march for equal treatment and voting rights for blacks, the Cardinal of St. Louis insisted the sisters be segregated.

98 At a March 6, 1965 meeting at SNCC headquarters in Atlanta which was held prior to the original march, the group decided to continue its grassroots efforts in Alabama and Mississippi and not to play a pivotal role in the march; however, because of SNCC's long commitment in the area and relationships with people in the community, SNCC members who so desired were granted permission to participate (Forman, *The Making of Black Revolutionaries*).

99 Byrne, *The Unfinished Agenda*, 32.

100 Williams, J., *Eyes on the Prize*, 274.

101 U.S. Highway 80 is an east–west highway, which is the most direct route from Selma to Montgomery.

102 In fact, after Bloody Sunday, Bland states, "[Our] parents wanted to get shotguns and kill white people for hurting [their] children, but it also made our parents join the movement." ("Journey to Selma" interview, 2002.)

103 Stokely Carmichael commented, "I'm not saying we shouldn't pay tribute to Rev. Reeb; what I'm saying is that if we're going to pay tribute to one, we should also pay tribute to the other [meaning Jimmie Lee Jackson] . . . And I think we have to analyze why [Johnson] sent flowers to Mrs. Reeb, and not to Mrs. Jackson" (quoted in Julian Bond's speech at Campaign for America's Future, Take Back America Conference, June 2, 2004, Washington, DC, retrieved October 2012, www.ourfuture.org/docUploads/tba2004-wed_bond.doc.)

104 "About Ella Baker," Ella Baker School website, retrieved May 1, 2013, www. ellabakerschool.net/resources/about-ella-baker/ella-bakers-life.

105 Johnson, "The American Promise" speech.

106 Williams, J., *Eyes on the Prize*, 283.

107 National Park Service, *Selma to Montgomery* pamphlet.

108 Harper Lee, *To Kill a Mockingbird*, 50th Anniversary edition (New York: HarperCollins, 2010 [1960]), 364–365.

109   Mary Stanton, *From Selma to Sorrow: The Life and Death of Viola Liuzzo* (Athens: University of Georgia Press, 2000); Taylor Branch, *At Canaan's Edge*, 153.

110   "Says Alabama Marches Were 'Sex Orgies,'" *The Gettysburg Times*, April 1, 1965, p. 2, column 5; See Stanton, *From Selma to Sorrow*, 144.

111   Stanton, *From Selma to Sorrow*, 147.

112   Although Selma had been the site of much bloodshed associated with the marches, Bloody Lowndes was the backdrop for two later deaths associated with the Selma campaign: those of Viola Liuzzo and Jonathan Daniels.

113   National Park Service, *Stars for Freedom* pamphlet.

114   National Park Service, *Stars for Freedom* pamphlet.

115   Seeger and Reiser, *Everybody Says Freedom*.

116   Bland, "Journey to Selma" interview.

117   Charles Fager, *Selma, 1965*.

118   Rogers, *Diffusion of Innovations*, 342.

119   Rogers outlines five adopter categories. Recognition of these adopter categories, and especially how the diffusion of ideological innovation works, may aid in both understanding and explaining the continuing pervasiveness of racism, an ill that American society popularly likes to envision it has eradicated (*Diffusion of Innovations*, 37).

120   Stanton, *From Selma to Sorrow*, 51.

121   Ibid.

122   Following her death, Viola Liuzzo was vilified in the media. These attacks were deliberate attempts to discredit both Mrs. Liuzzo and the movement. See Stanton, *From Selma to Sorrow*, 222.

123   Roberts and Klibanoff, *The Race Beat*, 382.

124   Ibid.

125   Rogers, *Diffusion of Innovations*, 191.

126   Branch, *Parting the Waters*, 302.

127   Charles Eagles, *Outside Agitator: Jon Daniels and the Civil Rights Movement in Alabama* (Tuscaloosa: University of Alabama Press, 2000).

128   Lewis and D'Orso, *Walking with the Wind*, 347.

129   See Rogers, *Diffusion of Innovations*, 15–16 for this discussion. While Rogers' theory is generally adaptable to the adoption of new forms of technology, it can also be used to predict the likelihood that new ideas will take root. Rogers admits that not all innovations get adopted. Five qualities help to predict the viability of social change. Those five qualities are: 1) Relative advantage (this quality asks if this idea is better than the superseding one); 2) Compatibility with existing values and practices (this quality asks to what extent the innovation is in accord with existing norms and values); 3) Simplicity and ease of use (this quality asks if the idea is too complicated to be understood); 4) Trialability (this quality asks if the new idea can be safely tested and the results observed without great harm); and 5) Observability (this quality) asks if the results are readily observable.

130   Rogers, *Diffusion of Innovations*, 92.

3   Portrait of a Nation

1   Paul Kellstedt, *The Mass Media and the Dynamics of America's Racial Attitudes* (New York: Cambridge University Press, 2003), 2.

2   The surveys Kellstedt relied on were reprinted in Hadley Cantril with Mildred Strunk, *Public Opinion, 1935–1946* (Princeton: Princeton University Press, 1951).

3   Kellstedt, *The Mass Media.*

4   Gene Roberts and Hank Klibanoff, *The Race Beat: The Press, the Civil Rights Struggle, and the Awakening of a Nation* (New York: Vintage, 2007), 195.

5   Kay Mills, *This Little Light of Mine: The Life of Fannie Lou Hamer* (Lexington: University of Kentucky Press, 2007).

6   Doug McAdam, *Political Process and the Development of Black Insurgency, 1930–1970*, second edition (Chicago: University of Chicago Press, 1999), 11.

7   Everett Rogers, *Diffusion of Innovations*, fifth edition (New York: Free Press, 2001).

8   The Supreme Court heard oral arguments in the case of Shelby County, Alabama v. Holder on February 27, 2013. This action, brought by an Alabama municipality, sought to declare Section 5 of the Voting Rights Act unconstitutional, representing a retreat from the social innovation under examination.

9   Rogers, *Diffusion of Innovations*, 23.

10   Ibid, 318.

11   Ibid, 20.

12   Roberts and Klibanoff, *The Race Beat.*

13   Ibid.

14   In his 1959 Pulitzer Prize address, Southern journalist, Ralph McGill, states, "one of the curses of newspapering was, and is, the 'cult of objectivity.'" McGill continues, "Objectivity, of course, was a formula invented for escaping from the recklessly slanted news of the good old days. Print both sides, we said, and let the people make up their minds. But we overdid it." (Ralph McGill, 1959 Pulitzer Prize address. See Calvin Logue, *Ralph McGill Speaks*, 140–148).

15   James C. Cobb, *Away Down South: A History of Southern Identity* (New York: Oxford University Press, Inc., 2007), 26. Cobb notes there was a "long standing sense of the South as not simply a distinct subset of American society, but a world and a way of life not only apart but behind." He says that, in the 1700s, the South emerged as a distinctive place, and language and religion became deep markers of these differences; by the time of the Civil War, segregation became not only an element of the Southern way of life, but its essence. In the face of assaults on their "way of life", white Southerners began to see their destiny in regional terms, not national terms.

16   Increasingly during this time those in the black freedom struggle, especially the members of SNCC, began to link their freedom struggle with the African freedom struggle.

17   The Civil Rights Division had an initial staff of twelve. This group was charged with investigating and dismantling racial discrimination in the broad area of voting (Brian Landsberg, *Enforcing Civil Rights: Race Discrimination and the Department of Justice* (Lawrence: University Press of Kansas, 1997).

18   Department of Justice, "Introduction to Federal Voting Rights Laws," www.justice. gov/crt/about/vot/intro/intro_a.php.

19   Nicholas Lemann, *Redemption: The Last Battle of the Civil War* (New York: Farrar, Straus and Giroux, 2007); Eric Foner, *A Short History of Reconstruction*, first edition (New York: Harper Perennial, 1990).

20 Jennifer Ritterhouse, *Growing up Jim Crow: How Black and White Southern Children Learned Race* (Chapel Hill: University of North Carolina Press, 2006); Roberts and Klibanoff, *The Race Beat*, 38)

21 Isabel Wilkerson, *The Warmth of Other Suns: The Epic Story of America's Great Migration*, reprint edition (New York: Vintage, 2011).

22 The phrase "Any place that is North and West, And not South" is a line from the Langston Hughes poem, *One Way Ticket*. In Hughes, Langston, *The Collected Poems of Langston Hughes* (Vintage Edition), edited by Arnold Rampersad. (Vintage; 1st Vintage classics edition, 1994), 361.

23 Mills, *This Little Light*, xix.

24 "One Day it Will Be Monday" was published April 9, 1953—almost a full year before the Supreme Court rendered its decision. McGill writes, "Days come and go, and Monday is among them, and one of these Mondays the Supreme Court of the United States is going to hand down a ruling which may, although it is considered by some unlikely, outlaw the South's dual school system, wholly or in part." (quoted in Roberts and Klibanoff, *The Race Beat*, 48).

25 McGill's actual views on race relations were more moderate, and over the course of his long career there were times when his views might fairly be classed as conservative.

26 Roberts and Klibanoff, *The Race Beat*, 164.

27 Ibid.

28 Ibid., 348.

29 Eric J. Sundquist, *King's Dream: The Legacy of Martin Luther King, Jr.'s I Have a Dream Speech* (New Haven, CT: Yale University Press, 2009), 90.

30 The 13-month boycott lasted from early December 1955 to late December 1956.

31 Taylor Branch, *At Canaan's Edge: America in the King Years, 1965–1968* (New York: Simon & Schuster, Inc., 2007).

32 Ibid, 417–426. The plan was to bring the Freedom Rides to an end in Alabama with attacks in Anniston and Birmingham.

33 Ibid.

34 Larry Isaac, "Movement of Movements: Culture Moves in the Long Civil Rights Struggle," *Social Forces* 87:1 (2008): 33–63. doi: 10.1353/sof.0.0086, 45.

35 Annie Pearl Avery, interview by author, audio recording, Selma, AL, July 11, 2012.

36 Ibid.

37 E. Franklin Frazier and C. Eric Lincoln, *The Negro Church in America/The Black Church Since Frazier* (New York: Schocken, 1974).

38 Malcolm X started the Los Angeles mosque, and he and the Honorable Elijah Mohammad disagreed on how to respond to the incident; this disagreement deepened a growing rift between the two (Claude Andrew Clegg III, *An Original Man: The Life and Times of Elijah Muhammad* (New York: St. Martin's Griffin, 1998), 170; Manning Marable, *Malcolm X: A Life of Reinvention* (New York: Viking Penguin, Inc., 2011).

39 Rick Bowers, *Spies of Mississippi: The True Story of the Spy Network that Tried to Destroy the Civil Rights Movement* (Washington, DC: National Geographic Children's Books, 2010); Williams, J., *Eyes on the Prize: America's Civil Rights Years, 1954–1965* (New York: Viking Penguin, Inc., 1987).

40 Taylor Branch, *Parting the Waters: America in the King Years 1954–1963* (New York: Simon & Schuster, Inc., 1988), 825.

41 Five days after President Johnson signed the Voting Rights Act into law, riots broke out in Watts. Those burning Watts linked their struggle to that of blacks some 3,000 miles away: "Young people in Watts were throwing rocks and Molotov cocktails, crying 'this is for Selma' or 'this is for Birmingham'" (Ibid., 352).

42 Janet L. Abu-Lughod, *Race, Space, and the Riots in Chicago, New York, and Los Angeles* (New York: Oxford University Press, 2007).

43 Ibid.

44 Juan Williams, *Eyes on the Prize: America's Civil Rights Years, 1954–1965* (New York: Viking Penguin, Inc., 1987).

45 Pete Seeger and Bob Reiser, *Everybody Says Freedom: A History of the Civil Rights Movement in Songs and Pictures* (New York: W.W. Norton & Company, 1989), 183.

46 The 1957 Act survives despite Strom Thurmond's 24-hour and 18-minute filibuster from the Senate floor, which is still the longest recorded filibuster in Senate history (*Branch, At Canaan's Edge*).

47 Ibid.

48 Ibid.

49 Ibid.

50 Williams, *Eyes on the Prize*

51 James Forman, *The Making of Black Revolutionaries*, illustrated edition (Seattle: University of Washington Press, 1997), Forman quoting Toure.

52 Carson Clayborne. *In Struggle: SNCC and the Black Awakening of the 1960s*, (Cambridge, MA: Harvard University Press, 1981), 134.

53 Forman, *The Making of Black Revolutionaries*.

54 Ibid, 406.

55 David J Garrow, *Bearing the Cross: Martin Luther King, Jr., and the Southern Christian Leadership Conference* (New York: William Morrow Paperbacks, 2004), 224. Throughout the 1960s, SNCC identified strongly with the African freedom struggle. According to Clayborne Carson's book, *In Struggle: SNCC and the Black Awakening of the 1960s*, (Cambridge: Harvard University Press, 1981), during a 1964 trip to Africa, some members of SNCC met briefly with Malcolm X. The former leader in the Nation of Islam had recently formed the Organization of Afro-American Unity (OAU), and he wanted to cultivate a relationship with SNCC. Prior to his death, Malcolm X said that the most significant event of 1964 was "the successful linking together of our problem with the African problem" (135).

56 Lucy enrolled on February 3, 1956; she was suspended 3 days later.

57 David Garrow, *Protest at Selma: Martin Luther King, Jr., and the Voting Rights Act of 1965* (New Haven, CT: Yale University Press, 1980); Hasan K. Jeffries, *Bloody Lowndes: Civil Rights and Black Power in Alabama's Black Belt* (New York: NYU Press, 2009).

58 Dara Byrne, *The Unfinished Agenda of the Selma-Montgomery Voting Rights March* (Hoboken, NJ: John Wiley & Sons, 2005), 29. The Twenty-fourth Amendment, which eliminates poll taxes in federal elections, is ratified on January 23, 1964.

59 Branch, *At Canaan's Edge*.

60 The Tenth Amendment affords states sovereign immunity to govern themselves in matters not specifically reserved to the federal government or denied to the

states by the Constitution. A part of the original Bill of Rights, this Amendment alleviates some of the tension between the federal government and the states created by Federalism.

61 In subsequent years, the Supreme Court ruled that interposition is not a valid doctrine and that the power to declare a federal law invalid rests squarely with the federal government, not the states.

62 On August 28, 1963, at the March on Washington, Martin Luther King Jr. stood in front of the Lincoln Memorial and delivered his famous "I Have a Dream" speech. In the text of the speech, King referenced the doctrines of interposition and nullification. King said, "I have a dream that one day, down in Alabama, with its vicious racists, with his governor having his lips dripping with the words of interposition and nullification; one day right there in Alabama, little black boys and black girls will be able to join hands with little white boys and white girls as sisters and brothers. I have a dream today."

63 Seth Cagin and Philip Dray, *We are Not Afraid: The Story of Goodman, Schwerner, and Chaney, and the Civil Rights Campaign for Mississippi* (New York: Bantam Books, 1988), 2.

64 Taylor Branch, *Pillar of Fire: America in the King Years 1963–65* (New York: Simon & Schuster, Inc., 1999).

65 Branch, *Parting the Waters*.

66 Fannie Lou Hamer was incarcerated for her voter registration efforts, and she was forced to pull down her undergarments, hike her dress, and bear innumerable strikes with a leather strap at the hands of two jail trustees (Bruce Watson, *Freedom Summer: The Savage Season of 1964 That Made Mississippi Burn and Made America a Democracy* (New York: Penguin Books, 2011); Bowers, *Spies of Mississippi*. One "jail trustee" charged with beating her reported that he was only permitted to stop striking her after her flesh was torn apart and she lay across the table bleeding (Bowers, *Spies of Mississippi*, 57).

67 Williams, J., *Eyes on the Prize*, 242.

68 Ibid. Hamer's testimony was so effective that, as it was being televised, President Johnson called an impromptu press conference and had it preempted; however, Hamer's testimony was televised uninterrupted later that evening. See http://americanradioworks.publicradio.org/features/sayitplain/flhamer.html

69 Forman, The *Making of Black Revolutionaries*.

70 McAdam, *Political Process*, 192.

71 Ibid.

72 Ibid,168.

73 Forman, The *Making of Black Revolutionaries*, 374.

74 Over 6,000 mourners attended Medgar Evers' public funeral event, but because people "considered them [SNCC] too rowdy" the group was relegated to the back of the funeral procession line, which effectively meant they would not be able to gain admittance to the service" (Seeger and Reiser, Everybody Says Freedom, 146).

75 Marshall Frady, *Wallace: The Classic Portrait of Alabama Governor George Wallace* (New York: Random House, 1996); Dan Carter, *The Politics of Rage: George Wallace, the Origins of the New Conservatism and the Transformation of American Politics* (Baton Rouge: Louisiana State University Press, 1996).

76 Ibid.

77   Daniel McCabe and Paul Stekler. *George Wallace: Settin' the Woods on Fire*, Ed. Daniel McCabe and Paul Stekler (Alexandria, VA: PBS Home Video, 2000), quote attributed to George Wallace.

78   Ibid.; Frady, *Wallace*; Carter, *The Politics of Rage*.

79   Carter, *The Politics of Rage*, 11.

80   Forman, *The Making of Black Revolutionaries*, 347.

81   Jim Clark, *The Economist*, June 14, 2007. www.economist.com/node/9333348.

82   Carter, *The Politics of Rage*.

83   See www.crmvet.org/tim/timhis65.htm.

84   McAdam, *Political Process*.

85   Neil R. McMillen, *The Citizens' Council: Organized Resistance to the Second Reconstruction, 1954–64* (Champaign: University of Illinois Press, 1994).

86   Forman, *The Making of Black Revolutionaries*.

87   Ibid, 345.

88   Williams, J., *Eyes on the Prize*, 39.

89   Williams, J., *Eyes on the Prize*; Michael Vinson Williams, *Medgar Evers: Mississippi Martyr* (Fayetteville: University of Arkansas Press, 2011), 182.

90   Williams, J., *Eyes on the Prize*; Branch, *Parting the Waters*.

91   Williams, J., *Eyes on the Prize*.

92   Williams, M. *Medgar Evers*.

93   Gilder Lehrman Institute, "Abraham Lincoln Second Inaugural Address," www.scribd.com/doc/69061125/The-Inaugural-address-of-President-Abraham-Lincoln-delivered-at-the-National-Capitol-March-4-1865#fullscreen.

94   John Dittmer, *Local People: The Struggle for Civil Rights in Mississippi* (Urbana: University of Illinois Press, 1995).

95   Prior to food stamps, the Department of Agriculture ran a federal surplus commodity food program, which provided actual food to state, local, and private welfare groups, and those groups would disseminate the food to those in need.

96   Dittmer, *Local People*, 144.

97   Ibid.

98   Ibid., 145.

99   Change agents like Harry Belafonte, Sidney Poitier, and comedian Dick Gregory got involved in both fundraising and food delivery, but the local community helped organize the distribution efforts.

100   Dittmer, *Local People*, 146.

101   Garrow, *Bearing the Cross*

102   Dittmer, *Local People*.

103   Forman, The *Making of Black Revolutionaries*, 347.

104   Forman, The *Making of Black Revolutionaries*.

105   Ibid.

106   Ibid., 348.

107   Ibid., 349.

108   Howard Zinn, "Registration in Alabama," *New Republic* 149 (October 26, 1963): 11–12.

109   Despite this, demonstrations occurred almost daily.

110   Zinn, "Registration in Alabama."

111   Seeger and Reiser, *EverybodySays Freedom*, 171.

112 Howard Zinn, "Alabama: Freedom Day in Selma (from SNCC: The New Abolitionists)," in *The Zinn Reader: Writings on Disobedience and Democracy*, first edition (New York: Seven Stories Press, 1997), 75–90.

113 Garrow, *Protest at Selma*, 32.

114 Ibid.

115 Seeger and Reiser, *Everybody Says Freedom*, 185.

116 Forman, *The Making of Black Revolutionaries*, 354.

117 Forman, *The Making of Black Revolutionaries*; Garrow, *Protest at Selma*.

118 Contentions existed among many of the civil rights groups, including a long rivalry between SNCC and SCLC (Garrow, *Protest at Selma*, 254).

119 Increasingly, those on the front lines of the Movement in places like Mississippi began to question the utility of non-violence. SNCC addressed the issue of "armed self defense" in the spring of 1964 (Forman, *The Making of Black Revolutionaries*). Forman believed "nonviolence was just one step in the development of black people." Belinda Robnett, "We Don't Agree: Collective Identity Justification Work in Social Movement Organizations," *Research in Social Movements, Conflicts, and Change* 26 (2005): 380–388, 225), argues that despite its stance on nonviolence, Forman, Moses, and others could continue to align themselves with SNCC due to a shared collective identity. On one occasion, SNCC Greenwood, Mississippi field director Bob Moses maintained guns in the office, and Stokely Carmichael was dispatched to remove them (Forman, *The Making of Black Revolutionaries*). By the October 1964 SNCC board meeting, Forman says it was clear that the organization, which began in 1960, was at a crossroads. The founding members of SNCC had been largely black, middle class, and urban. By Freedom Summer, the ranks of both rural, poor blacks and college-educated whites swelled. SNCC's focus on public accommodations, and its voting rights agenda especially, appealed to poor blacks in the rural South. The public tension focused on the role and presence of "college educated" whites, and this tension ultimately resulted in the expulsion of whites from the group; however, there is support for the conclusion that race was used largely as a proxy for the mounting class-based tensions in the group.

120 It should be noted that King's hesitation to earlier commit to the Alabama Project does not mean he was absent from the state. Coretta Scott King was born and raised in nearby Marion, Alabama.

121 Garrow, *Protest at Selma*.

4   Everyday People

1 Everett Rogers, *Diffusion of Innovations*, fifth edition (New York: Free Press, 2001), 205.

2 Charles Tilly, "Historical Sociology," in *Current Perspectives in Social Theory* eds. Scott G. McNall and Gary N. Howe. Vol. I. (Greenwich, CT: JAI Press, 1980), 306.

3 Rogers, Diffusion of Innovations, 93.

4 Veterans of the Civil Rights Movement website, "Oral History Interview with Ruby Nell Sales" Interviewed by Jean Wiley and Bruce Hartford, September 2005 www.cvet.org/nars/ruby sale.htm.

5   Albert Bandura, Social Learning Theory (Englewood Cliffs, NJ: Prentice Hall, 1977).

6   Ruby Sales. Interview by Jean Wiley and Bruce Hartford. "Growing up in the black church." Veterans of the Civil Rights Movement, Oral History Project. September 2005 www.veteransofhope.org/veterans/ruby-sales.

7   In The Souls of Black Folk, African-American sociologist William Edward Burghart DuBois describes this "double consciousness" as the process of being both invisible and at the same time imminently noticeable by difference and marked as inferior. DuBois writes, "one ever feels his two-ness, an American, a Negro; two souls, two thoughts, two unreconciled strivings; two warring ideals in one dark body, whose dogged strength alone keeps it from being torn asunder." (3)

8   Ruby Sales. Interview for Oral History Project with the Civil Rights Memorial Veterans website. www.crmvet.org/nars/rubysale.htm.

9   Ruby Sales, interview conducted by Blackside, Inc. on December 12, 1988, for Film and Media Archive, Henry Hampton Collection. "Eyes on the Prize II: America at the Crossroads 1965 to 1985." Washington University Libraries, Film and Media Archive, Henry Hampton Collection. 1988.

10 Ruby Nell Sales, Veterans of the Civil Rights Movement interview (supra note 4).

11 Ibid.

12 Ibid.

13 Donnie Summerlin, "Samuel Younge Jr," Encyclopedia of Alabama, September 2, 2008 www.encyclopediaofalabama.org/face/Article.jsp?id+h-1669.

14 Ibid.

15 Clayborne Carson. In Struggle: SNCC and the Black Awakening of the 1960s (Cambridge, MA: Harvard University Press, 1981).

16 Ibid., 188.

17 James Forman, Sammy Younge Jr.: The First Black College Student to Die in the Black Liberation Movement (New York: Grove Press, 1968).

18 Veterans of the Civil Rights Movement, "Oral History Interview Ruby Nell Sales."

19 Ibid. The quotes used in this chapter for Ruby Nell Sales are taken from various sources: Oral history interviews, including Veterans of the Civil Rights Movement September 2005 interview with Jean Wiley and Bruce Hartford; Eyes on the Prize II interview with Blackslide on December 12, 1988; and the Veterans of Hope interview as well as Bloody Lowndes: Civil Rights and Black Power in Alabama's Black Belt by Hasan Jeffries.

20 Joanne Bland, Interview OH 009.1, "Journey to Selma 2002." Oral History Project. University of Wisconsin. June 8, 2002.

21 Lee Formwalt, University of Madison-Wisconsin 2002 Oral History Project "Journey to Selma".

22 Bill Perlman, interview by author via telephone, audio recording, December 19, 2012.

23 Ibid.

24 Ibid.

25 Annie Pearl Avery, interview by author, audio recording, Selma, AL, July 11, 2012.

26 Ibid.

27   Robert P. Moses and Charles Cobb, *Radical Equations: Civil Rights from Mississippi to the Algebra Project* (Boston: Beacon Press, 2002), 4.

28   Ibid.

29   Ibid., 32.

30   Sam Walker, interview by author, audio recording, Selma, AL, July 11, 2012.

31   Ibid.

32   Frederick D, Reese, interview by author, audio recording, Selma, AL, February 9, 2013.

33   Ibid.

34   While many communities contain people from a similar economic class, stark residential segregation patterns meant that many African-Americans of various class standings were compelled to live in the same neighborhood.

35   Frederick D, Reese, interview by author, audio recording, Selma, AL, February 9, 2013.

36   Frederick D. Reese interview, National Voting Rights Museum and Institute Archives, NVRMI 2004-0007.

37   Tuskegee Institute (now known as Tuskegee University) is a historically black college located in Tuskegee, Alabama, which is 87 miles from Selma.

38   In 1895, Booker T. Washington, who later authored *Up From Slavery: An Autobiography*, delivered his Atlanta Compromise Speech in front of a largely white audience at Cotton States and International Exposition in Atlanta. In his address, Booker T. Washington assures his listeners that "uppity" blacks (such as those seeking to agitate for voting rights) would not be a concern and instead blacks would be content to accept segregation and labor with their hands. In exchange, blacks would be provided basic vocational education, such as that provided at Tuskegee Institute during its early years (Louis R. Harlan, Booker T. Washington, Vol. II: *The Wizard Of Tuskegee, 1901–1915* (New York: Oxford University Press, 1986); Louis R. Harlan, "A Black Leader in the Age of Jim Crow," in *The Racial Politics of Booker T. Washington*, eds. Donald Cunnigen et al., Research in Race and Ethnic Relations, Vol. XIII (Bingley, UK: Emerald Group Publishing, 2006)).

39   Charles Gomillion was a sociology professor at Tuskegee Institute and President of the Tuskegee Civic Association, which campaigned for African-American voting rights as early as the 1930s and continued to do so for decades (Martin Luther King Jr., *Stride Toward Freedom: The Montgomery Story*, illustrated, reprint edition (Boston: Beacon Press, 2010), 178). Gomillion's challenge to the way voting lines were drawn resulted in a Supreme Court case.

40   Gomillion v. Lightfoot, 364 U.S. 339 (1960).

41   Sam Walker, interview by author, audio recording, Selma, AL, July 11, 2012.

42   Annie Pearl Avery, interview by author, audio recording, Selma, AL, July 11, 2012.

43   Ibid.

44   Ibid.

45   Ibid.

46 · Willy Vaughn and Hattie Campbell Davis, eds., *The Selma Campaign 1963–1965: The Decisive Battle of the Civil Rights Movement* (Dover: The Majority Press, Inc. 2006).

47   Sam Walker, interview by author, audio recording, Selma, AL, July 11, 2012.

48   Bill Perlman, interview by author via telephone, audio recording, December 19, 2012.

49   Ibid.

50   Frederick D. Reese, interview by author, audio recording, Selma, AL, February 9, 2013.

51   After the March on Washington, Jack Gould, the influential television critic for *The New York Times*, wrote, "the gentle entrance and exit of so much petitioning humanity was an editorial in movement" (Gene Roberts and Hank Klibanoff, *The Race Beat: The Press, the Civil Rights Struggle, and the Awakening of a Nation* (New York: Vintage, 2007), 346). Images of demonstrators civilly and peacefully protesting for the right to vote, especially in the face of Southern brutality such as that often demonstrated by people like Bull Connor and Jim Clark, became important tools for persuading people observing the conflict in the media that change was needed.

52   Frederick D. Reese, interview by author, audio recording, Selma, AL, February 9, 2013.

53   Cynthia Griggs Fleming, *In the Shadow of Selma: The Continuing Struggle for Civil Rights in the Rural South* (Lanham: Rowman & Littlefield Publishers, 2004), 143.

54   Fleming, *In the Shadow of Selma*.

55   Ibid., 145.

56   Ibid.

57   Ibid.

58   Rebecca Woodham, "Lowndes County Freedom Organization," *Encyclopedia of Alabama*, accessed September 24, 2008, para 1. www.encyclopediaofalabama.org/face/Article.jsp?id=h-1781

59   Hasan K. Jeffries, *Bloody Lowndes: Civil Rights and Black Power in Alabama's Black Belt* (New York: New York University Press, 2009).

60   Ibid.

61   Ibid.

62   Jeffries, *Bloody Lowndes*.

63   Paul Felix Lazarsfeld et al., *The People's Choice: How the Voter Makes Up His Mind in a Presidential Campaign* (New York, Columbia University Press, 1944), 151ff.

64   Laura Anderson, "James Reeb," *Encyclopedia of Alabama*, March 2009 www.encyclopediaofalabama.org/face/Article.jsp?id+h-2054.

65   Charles Eagles, *Outside Agitator: Jon Daniels and the Civil Rights Movement in Alabama* (Tuscaloosa: University of Alabama Press, 2000).

66   Rebecca Woodham, "Jonathan Myrick Daniels." *Encyclopedia of Alabama*, accessed September 24, 2008.

67   Ibid.

68   Forman, *Sammy Younge*.

69   Faith S. Holsaert et al., eds., *Hands on the Freedom Plow: Personal Accounts by Women in SNCC* (Urbana: University of Illinois Press, 2010), 481–482.

70   Ibid., 481.

71   Ibid.

72   Ibid., 149.

73   Vouching was one of many impediments Alabama used to curtail the black vote.

74 Invisible Giants of the Voting Rights Movement Coming into View, "Mrs. Annie Cooper's Living History, Arrested by Jim Clark, Selma, Alabama," March 1, 1996, OH 118, NVRMI 2004-0021.

75 Mary Stanton, *From Selma to Sorrow: The Life and Death of Viola Liuzzo* (Athens: University of Georgia Press, 2000).

76 Ibid.

77 Ibid., 138.

78 Ibid., 136.

79 Ibid.

80 Holsaert, *Hands on the Freedom Plow.*

5   Aftermath

1 Alexander Keyssar, *The Right to Vote, The Contested History of Democracy in the United States* (New York: Basic Books, 2000), 323.

2 Associated Press, Washington, "Reagan Signs 'Crown Jewel' of Rights," The Desert News, June 29, 1982.

3 Debo Adegbile, comments, "U.S. Supreme Court Hearing on the Constitutionality of the Voting Rights Act," NAACP Legal Defense and Educational Fund, Inc. Sponsored Sessions, 2013 Jubilee Bridge Crossing Celebration. March 2, 2013.

4 "Protecting Minority Voters: The Voting Rights Act at Work 1982–2005," National Commission on the Voting Rights Act, (Lawyer's Committee for Civil Rights under Law, 2006), 2. www.lawyerscommittee.org/admin/voting_rights/documents/files/0023.pdf

5 Ibid, 11, quoting Howell Raines, *My Soul is Rest: Movement Day in the Deep South Remembered* (New York: Putnam, 1977), 337.

6 Everett Rogers, *Diffusion of Innovations*, fifth edition (New York: Free Press, 2001), 265.

7 Ibid., 343.

8 Johnson, Lyndon B., Special Message to Congress: The American Promise (1965), Lyndon Baines Johnson Library at University of Texas, Published Papers, accessed October 13, 2012, www.lbjlib.utexas.edu/johnson/archives.hom/speeches.hom/650315.asp.

9 A cloture vote is a Senate procedure aimed to bring debate on a bill to a quick end. It is a means often employed to overcome a filibuster—such as the one South Carolina Senator, Strom Thurmond, employed in opposition to the Civil Rights Act of 1957—and it allows Senate to vote to impose time limits on the consideration of a bill.

10 Steven F. Lawson, *In Pursuit of Power: Southern Blacks and Electoral Politics, 1965 to 1982* (New York: Columbia University Press, 1985), 4.

11 It should again be noted that "the change in attitudes" referenced does not mean the entire nation adopted the idea. Instead, it refers to the shift among trusted opinion leaders, like President Johnson and various members of Congress, which helped trigger bigger changes in the rate of adoption among various adopter groups.

12 C. Vann Woodward, *The Strange Career of Jim Crow*, commemorative edition (New York: Oxford University Press, 2001). Woodward termed the growing civil unrest

that emerged among African-Americans in the post-World War II era, the "Second Reconstruction."

13 John Hope Franklin and Alfred Moss. *From Slavery to Freedom: A History of Negro Americans*, illustrated, sixth edition (New York: Knopf, 1988), 220.

14 Ibid.

15 Dewey M. Clayton, "A Funny Thing Happened on the Way to the Voting Precinct: A Brief History of Disenfranchisement in America," *Black Scholar* 34: 3 (2004): 42–53.

16 Derrick Bell, *Faces at the Bottom of the Well: The Permanence of Racism* (New York: Basic Books, 1992), 98n.

17 Clayton, "A Funny Thing Happened."

18 Congress' aim was for the Commission to comprise seven Democrats, seven Republicans, and one Independent, but that was not the case.

19 Derrick Bell, *Race, Racism and American Law* (New York: Aspen Publishers, 2000); Bell, *Faces at the Bottom of the Well*, 98n; Clayton, "A Funny Thing Happened."

20 Bell, *Race, Racism, and American Law*, 52.

21 Franklin and Moss, *From Slavery to Freedom*, 230.

22 U.S. v. Reese, 92 U.S. 214 (1876).

23 Between 1870 and 1871 Congress passed a series of enforcement acts designed to provide black equal protection under the law by protecting the right to vote, be on a jury, and receive due process. The later Civil Rights Act of 1875 is also sometimes referred to as the Enforcement Act. In 1883, the Supreme Court declared this act, which prohibited the exclusion of blacks from juries as unconstitutional.

24 U.S. v. Cruikshank, 92 U.S. 542 (1876).

25 J. Peck, "Constitution fails its roots, prof says: Wayne Flynt traces past of state document," *Huntsville Times* (Huntsville, AL), 2, www.al.com/search/index.ssf?/base/news/1098954973277921.xml?huntsvilletimes?nlocal.

26 Clayton, "A Funny thing Happened," 44.

27 Guinn v. United States, 238 U.S. 347 (1915).

28 Smith v. Allwright, 321 U.S. 649 (1944).

29 Racial gerrymandering is the intentional drawing of districts and boundaries for prohibited racially discriminatory purposes.

30 Gomillion v. Lightfoot, 36 U.S. 339 (1960).

31 Harper v. Virginia State Board of Election, 383 U.S. 663 (1966).

32 Gerald R. Webster and Nicholas Quinton. "The Electoral Geographies of Two Segregationist ('Jim Crow') Referenda in Alabama." *Political Geography* 29 (2010): 370.

33 Section 2 to the Act is a permanent provision; Section 5 and various parts of Sections 6–9 and 13, however, are not permanent and must be renewed by Congress. An additional section, Section 203, was added in 1975. That section also requires the voters in certain jurisdictions to be afforded language assistance.

34 The most recent challenge, Shelby County v. Holder, is discussed later in this chapter.

35 Debo Adegbile, comments, "U.S. Supreme Court Hearing on the Constitutionality of the Voting Rights Act," NAACP Legal Defense and Educational Fund, Inc. Sponsored Sessions, 2013 Jubilee Bridge Crossing Celebration, March 2, 2013.

36 However, jurisdictions do have the right to appeal.

37 "Section 5 Covered Jurisdictions," The U.S. Department of Justice, Civil Rights Division Homepage, www.justice.gov/crt/about/vot/sec_5/covered.php.

38 Vouching was a process that required a voter applicant to have a voter "vouch" for their good character as a condition of registration. Registered voters could only vouch for a limited number of applicants, and because few black voters were registered, this system acted to preclude minorities from the voter registration rolls.

39 "Section 4 of the Voting Rights Act," The U.S. Department of Justice, Civil Rights Division, www.justice.gov/crt/about/vot/misc/sec_4.php.

40 American Indian, Asian American, Alaskan Natives, and those of "Spanish heritage" were each defined as "language minorities."

41 "Section 4 of the Voting Rights Act," The U.S. Department of Justice website www.justice.gov/crt/about/vot/misc/sec_4.php.

42 "Sections 6–9 and 13 of the Act enable the Attorney General to certify jurisdictions for examiner/observer coverage."

43 "Voting Rights Act (1965)," www.ourdocuments.gov/doc.php?flash=true&doc=100.

44 Peyton McCrary et al., "Alabama," in Davidson and Groffman, *Quiet Revolution in the South: The Impact of the Voting Rights Act, 1965–1990.* op. cit., 39.

45 Frank Parker, *Black Votes Count: Political Empowerment in Mississippi After 1965*, first edition (Chapel Hill: The University of North Carolina Press, 1990).

46 Katzenbach, the Attorney General of the United States, was the person President Johnson instructed to draft tough voting rights legislation.

47 South Carolina v. Katzenbach, 383 U.S. 301 (1966) at 313.

48 Ibid.

49 U.S. Commission on Civil Rights report, "The Voting Rights Act: Ten Years Later" (January 1975), 329, 337, 345–346.

50 Some of this pattern is attributable to reverse migration trends in place since the late 1960s where significant numbers of African-Americans are returning to the South.

51 See www.teachingtolerance.org. The website for the organization describes itself as "a place for educators to find thought-provoking news conversation and support for those who care about diversity, equal opportunity and respect for differences in schools."

52 In order to avoid diluting minority-voting strength, which is prohibited under Section 2 of the Voting Rights Act, states are permitted (and sometimes required) to create majority/minority voting districts during redistricting, especially when there has been substantial minority growth since the last Census. Redistricting is discussed later in the chapter.

53 Bernard Grofman and Lisa Handley, "The Impact of the Voting Rights Act on Black Representation in Southern State Legislatures," *Legislative Studies Quarterly* 16:1 (February 1991): 111–128.

54 Ibid., 111.

55 Ibid.

56 "The History of Federal Voting Laws: The Voting Rights Act of 1965," The U.S. Department of Justice, Civil Rights Division Homepage, www.justice.gov/crt/about/vot/intro/intro_b.php.

57   Debo Adegbile, comments, "U.S. Supreme Court Hearing on the Constitutionality of the Voting Rights Act," NAACP Legal Defense and Educational Fund, Inc. Sponsored Sessions, 2013 Jubilee Bridge Crossing Celebration, March 2, 2013.

58   Paul Taylor, "The Growing Electoral Clout of Blacks is Driven by Turnout, Not Demographics," *Pew Research Social and Demographic Trends Report*, Pew Research Center, Washington DC, December 26, 2012, available at www.pewsocialtrends. org/2012/12/26/the-growing-electoral-clout-of-blacks-is-driven-by-turnout-not-demographics/.

59   According to the Pew Center report, "[in] 2012 blacks and whites both appear to have cast a slightly higher share of votes (72% and 13%, respectively) then their share of eligible voters (71% and 12%), while Hispanics and Asians cast a lower share of votes (10% and 3%) send their share of eligible voters (11% and 4%)." www.pewsocialtrends.org/2012/12/26/the-growing-electoral-clout-of-blacks-is-driven-by-turnout-not-demographics/.

60   Ronald W. Waters, *Black Presidential Politics in America: A Strategic Choice* (New York: State University of New York (SUNY) Press, 1988), 38.

61   Steven A. Tuch and Jack K. Martin, eds., "Regional Differences in Whites' Racial Policy Attitudes," in *Racial Attitudes in the 1990s: Continuity and Change* (Westport, CT: Praeger Publishers, 1997), 165–176.

62   Ibid., 173.

63   "Post-Racial America? Not Yet: Why the Fight for Voting Rights Continues After the Election of President Barack Obama," a report by the Political Participation Group, NAACP Legal Defense and Educational Fund, Inc., 2009, 3.

64   David A. Bositis, "Blacks and the 2008 Elections: A Preliminary Analysis," *Focus Magazine* (December, 2009), 13, available at: http://jointcenter.org/index.php/content/download/2338/15387/file/post%20election.pdf).

65   "Post-Racial America," 6.

66   "Post-Racial America," 4.

67   Rather than seek bailout (which requires a 10-year clean record of no discriminatory behavior), Texas sought to invalidate the preclearance portion of the Act.

68   President Obama lost Georgia. In fact, he garnered the support of only 23 percent of white voters in the state.

69   Jim Galloway, "Perdue Joins Texas and Voting Rights Case," *Atlanta Journal Constitution*, March 19, 2009, 3B.

70   It should be noted that, "At the time the Act was first considered by Congress, it was noted by Atty. Gen. Nicholas Katzenbach that the coverage formula was not perfect, as it would allow some jurisdictions guilty of discrimination to evade coverage." U.S. Commission on Civil Rights, op. cit, 6–7.

71   Reynolds v. Sims, 377 U.S. 533 (1964); Wesberry v. Sanders, 376 U.S. 1 (1964); Baker v. Carr, 369 U.S. 186 (1962).

72   Reapportionment is the process whereby the seats in the House of Representatives are allocated to each state based on their population size, determined by the Census.

73   Section 2 of the Act makes it clear that voting practices with "discriminatory effects," that is, those that offer minorities "less opportunity than other members of the electorate to participate in the political process and to elect representatives

of their choice," are prohibited. The same section acts as a prohibition against redistricting plans adopted with a discriminatory purpose.

74 Shaw v. Reno, 509 U.S. 630 (1993).

75 John Agnew, *Place and Politics: The Geographical Meditation of State and Society* (London: Allen and Unwin, 1987).

76 Gerald R. Webster and Nicholas Quinton, "The Electoral Geographies of Two Segregationist ('Jim Crow') Referenda in Alabama," *Political Geography* 29: (2010): 370–380.

77 Ibid.

78 Ibid.

79 Webster and Quinton, "The Electoral Geographies," 370–380.

80 Oregon v. Mitchell, 400 U.S. 112 (1970).

81 A voter purge in Florida which erroneously flagged and purged 12,000 voters from the roles was found to be flawed. Over 70 percent of those voters were African-American or Latinos. See Wendy Weiser and Margaret Chen, Brennan Center for Justice, "Recent Voter Incidents", 2 (2008), available at http://brennan./3cdn.net/e827230204c5668706_p0m6b54k.pdf.

82 *The Black Population: 2000* (Washington, DC: U.S. Census Bureau, 2001), 3, available at www.census.gov/prod/2001pubs/c2kbr01-5.pdf.

83 Clayton, "A Funny Thing Happened."

84 Ibid.

85 John Lewis, "Not All Votes Count." *The New York Times*, Opinion, December 2, 2000, www.nytimes.com/2000/12/02/opinion/02JLEW.html.

86 Revathi Hines, "The Silent Voices: 2000 Presidential Election and the Minority Vote in Florida," *Western Journal of Black Studies* 26:2 (Summer 2002): 71–75.

87 Hanes Walton, Jr., and Robert Smith, *American Politics and the African-American Quest for Universal Freedom* (New York: Longman, Inc., 2003), 163.

88 The Commission approved the report by a vote of 6 to 2; the two dissenters were the lone Republican members of the Commission.

89 John Lewis, "We march today to be counted," *Newsweek* 136:24 (2000): 38.

90 "Shame! 96-Year-Old Woman: Voting Now More Difficult Than During Jim Crow" *NewsOne*, October 10, 2011, available at http://newsone.com/1575525/voting-now-more-difficult-than-during-jim-crow/.

91 Ibid.

92 Michelle Alexander, *The New Jim Crow: Mass Incarceration in the Age of Colorblindness* (New York: New Press, 2010), 2.

93 NAACP Legal Defense and Educational Fund, "Defending Democracy: Confronting Modern Barriers to Voting Rights in America." (Baltimore: NAACP, 2011). (Appendix 4, Felon Disenfranchisement at Different Stages of Incarceration/Post-Incarceration by State, 50) www.naacpldf.org/files/publications/Defending%20Democracy%2012-5-11.pdf.

94 Social Science Data Analysis Network (SSDAN) Report, "Trends in Voter Turnout," accessed May 6, 2013, www.ssdan.net/sites/default/files/briefs/vtbrief.pdf.

95 Ibid.

96 Ibid. The SSDAN report states, "Overall, however, the percentage of Americans who take to the polls has decreased by 11.1% from the 1964 high 69.3%."

97   Kraig Beyerlein and Kenneth T. Andrews, "Black Voting During the Civil Rights Movement: A Micro-Level Analysis, *Social Forces* 87:1 (September 2008): 65–93, 68.

98   Structural inequalities against blacks have lessened (which is not to suggest that such inequalities do not still exist; only that compared to the caste system that operated previously, conditions have improved); however, spatial inequality still exists. Urban dwellers are less likely to be disenfranchised than those who live in rural areas, and recent impediments such as voter ID laws and the curtailment of early voting enacted in a number of jurisdictions across the nation disproportionately impact those of lower social-class standing.

99   Beyerlein and Andrews, "Black Voting During the Civil Rights Movement,"67.

100   Ibid., 85.

101   This term is taken from Aldon Morris, *The Origins of the Civil Rights Movement* (New York: Free Press, 1984).

102   James S. Coleman, *Foundations of Social Theory* (Cambridge, MA. Harvard University Press, 1990), 302.

103   Francis Fukuyama, *Trust: The Social Virtues and the Creation of Prosperity* (London: Hamish Hamilton, 1995), 10.

104   Norman Uphoff and C. M. Wijayaratna, "Demonstrated Benefits from Social Capital: The Productivity of Farmer Organizations in Gal Oya, Sri Lanka," *World Development* 28 (2000): 1875–1890.

105   Bi-Partisan Policy Center, "2012 Election Turnout Dips Below 2008 and 2004 Levels: Number Of Eligible Voters Increases By Eight Million, Five Million Fewer Votes Cast." Washington, DC, November 8, 2012, accessed May 6, 2013. http:// bipartisanpolicy.org/sites/default/files/2012%20Voter%20Turnout%20Report.pdf.

106   Ibid.

107   Ibid.

108   Ibid.

109   The foot soldiers exhibit recognizes the contributions made by many ordinary people.

110   Sam Walker, interview by author, audio recording, Selma, AL, July 11, 2012.

111   The building now serves as a museum, but during the Civil War it operated as a Confederate hospital.

112   Reno v. Bossier Parish School Board, 528 U.S. 329, 366 (2000) (Souter, J. Concurring in part, dissenting in part.)

113   Amelia Boynton Robinson, interview *Eyes on the Prize: America in the Civil Rights Years* December 6, 1985, Washington University Digital Gateway http:// digital.wustl.edu/cgi/t/text/text-idx?c=eop;cc=eop;q1=selma;rgn=main;view= text;idno=rob0015.0101.089;hi=0.

114   Veterans of Civil Rights Movement, Ruby Sales interview.

115   Ibid.

116   Larry Isaac, "Movement of Movements: Culture Moves in the Long Civil Rights Struggle," *Social Forces* 87:1 (2008): 46.

Bibliography

Abu-Lughod, Janet L. *Race, Space, and Riots in Chicago, New York, and Los Angeles.* New York: Oxford University Press, 2007.

Achebe, Chinua. *Things Fall Apart.* London: William Heinemann Ltd., 1958.

Adegbile, Debo. "*U.S. Supreme Court Hearing on the Constitutionality of the Voting Rights Act.*" Comments at NAACP Legal Defense and Educational Fund, Inc. Sponsored Sessions, 2013 Jubilee Bridge Crossing Celebration, March 2, 2013.

Agnew, John. *Place and Politics: The Geographical Meditation of State and Society.* London: Allen and Unwin, 1987.

Alexander, Michelle. *The New Jim Crow: Mass Incarceration in the Age of Colorblindness.* New York: New Press, 2010.

Alston III, Fitts. "Bloody Sunday." *Encyclopedia of Alabama.* Accessed July 11, 2012. www.encyclopediaofalabama.org/face/Article.jsp?id=h-1876.

Anderson, Laura. "James Reeb." *Encyclopedia of Alabama.* Accessed March 16, 2009. www.encyclopediaofalabama.org/face/Article.jsp?id+h-2054.

Andrews, Kenneth. *Freedom is a Constant Struggle: The Mississippi Civil Rights Movement and its Legacy.* First edition. Chicago: University of Chicago Press, 2004.

Ansolabehere, Stephen, Nathaniel Persily, and Charles Stewart III. "Race, Region, and Vote Choice in the 2008 Election: Implications for the Future of the Voting Rights Act." *Harvard Law Review* 123:6 (2010): 1385–1436.

Associated Press, Washington. "Reagan Signs 'Crown Jewel' of Rights." *The Desert News,* June 29, 1982.

Associated Press, Washington. "Says Alabama Marches Were 'Sex Orgies.'" *The Gettysburg Times,* April 1, 1965.

Avery, Annie Pearl. Interview by author, audio recording. Selma, AL, July 11, 2012.

Bageant, Joe. *Deer Hunting with Jesus: Dispatches from America's Class War.* New York: Crown Publishers, 2007.

Baker v. Carr, 369 U. S. 186 (1962).

Bandura, Albert. *Social Learning Theory.* Englewood Cliffs, NJ: Prentice Hall, 1977.

Bell, Derrick A. *Faces at the Bottom of the Well: The Permanence of Racism.* New York: Basic Books, 1992.

Bell, Derrick A. *Race, Racism and American Law.* New York: Aspen Publishers, 2000.

Beyerlein, Kraig, and Kenneth T. Andrews. "Black Voting During the Civil Rights Movement: A Micro-Level Analysis." *Social Forces* 87:1 (September 2008): 65–93.

Bhabha, Homi K. *The Location of Culture.* New York: Routledge Classics, 2004.

Bi-Partisan Policy Center. "2012 Election Turnout Dips Below 2008 and 2004 Levels: Number Of Eligible Voters Increases By Eight Million, Five Million Fewer Votes Cast." Washington, DC, November 8, 2012. Accessed May 6, 2013. http://bipartisanpolicy.org/sites/default/files/2012%20Voter%20Turnout%20Report.pdf.

Bland, Joanne. Interview OH 009.1, "Journey to Selma 2002." Oral History Project, University of Wisconsin, June 8, 2002.

Bogwardt, Elizabeth. *A New Deal for the World: America's Vision for Human Rights.* Cambridge, MA: Belknap Press, 2005.

Bond, Julian. Speech at Campaign for America's Future, Take Back America Conference, June 2, 2004, Washington, DC. Accessed October 23, 2012. www.ourfuture.org/docUploads/tba2004-wed_bond.doc.

Bositis, David A. "Blacks and the 2008 Elections: A Preliminary Analysis." *Focus magazine,* December 2009. Available at: http://jointcenter.org/index.php/content/download/2338/15387/file/post%20election.pdf.

Boudon, Raymond. *The Uses of Structuralism.* Ann Arbor, MI: Heinemann, 1971.

Bowers, Rick. *Spies of Mississippi: The True Story of the Spy Network that Tried to Destroy the Civil Rights Movement.* Washington, DC: National Geographic Children's Books, 2010.

Branch, Taylor. *Parting the Waters: America in the King Years, 1954–1963.* New York: Simon & Schuster, Inc., 1988.

Branch, Taylor. *Pillar of Fire: America in the King Years, 1963–65.* New York: Simon & Schuster, Inc., 1999.

Branch, Taylor. *At Canaan's Edge: America in the King Years, 1965–1968.* New York: Simon & Schuster, Inc., 2007.

Bravin, Jess. "Scalia Calls Voting Act a 'Racial Preferment'." *The Wall Street Journal Online,* April 16, 2013. Available at http://m.us.wsj.com/articles/a/SBI0001424127887324345804578427023243667626?mg+reno64-wsj.

Bullock III, Charles S., and Mark J. Rozell. *The Oxford Handbook of Southern Politics.* New York: Oxford University Press, 2012.

Byrne, Dara. *The Unfinished Agenda of the Selma-Montgomery Voting Rights March.* Hoboken, NJ: John Wiley & Sons, 2005.

Cagin, Seth, and Philip Dray. *We Are Not Afraid: The Story of Goodman, Schwerner, and Chaney, and the Civil Rights Campaign for Mississippi.* New York: Bantam Books, 1988.

Calmes, Jackie, Robbie Brown, and Campbell Robertson. "On Voting Case, Reaction From 'Deeply Disappointed' to 'It's about Time.'" *The New York Times,* June 25, 2013, Politics Section. www.nytimes.com/2013/06/26/us/politics/on-voting-case-reaction-from-deeply-disappointed-to-its-about-time.html?_r=0.

Cantril, Hadley with Mildred Strunk. *Public Opinion, 1935–1946.* Princeton, NJ: Princeton University Press, 1951.

Carmichael, Stokely. *Ready for Revolution: The Life and Struggles of Stokely Carmichael (Kwame Ture)*. New York: Scribner, 2003.

Carson, Clayborne. *In Struggle: SNCC and the Black Awakening of the 1960s*. Cambridge, MA: Harvard University Press, 1981.

Carson, Clayborne. Introduction to *Stride Toward Freedom: The Montgomery Story*, by Martin Luther King, Jr. Illustrated, reprint edition. Boston: Beacon Press, 2010.

Carter, Dan T. *The Politics of Rage: George Wallace, the Origins of the New Conservatism and the Transformation of American Politics*. Baton Rouge: Louisiana State University Press, 1996.

Chesnut Jr., J.L., and Julia Cass. *Black in Selma*. New York: Farrar, Straus and Giroux, 1990.

Clayton, Dewey M. "A Funny Thing Happened on the Way to the Voting Precinct: A Brief History of Disenfranchisement in America." *Black Scholar* 34:3 (2004): 42–53.

Clegg III, Claude Andrew. *An Original Man: The Life and Times of Elijah Muhammad*. New York: St. Martin's Griffin, 1998.

Clowse, Barbara Barksdale. *Ralph McGill: A Biography*. Macon, GA: Mercer University Press, 1998.

CNN Newsroom. "Court Guts Voting Rights Act." Aired June 25, 2013-14:00 ET. Transcript available at http://edition.cnn.com/TRANSCRIPTS/1306/25/cnr.09.html.

Cobb Jr., Charles E. *On the Road to Freedom: A Guided Tour of the Civil Rights Movement*. Chapel Hill, NC: Algonquin Books, 2008.

Cobb, James C. *Away Down South: A History of Southern Identity*. New York: Oxford University Press, 2007.

Cobbs, Elizabeth H., and Petric J. Smith. *Long Time Coming: An Insider's Story of the Birmingham Church Bombing that Rocked the World*. Birmingham, AL: Crane Hill, 1994.

Coleman, James S. *Foundations of Social Theory*. Cambridge, MA: Harvard University Press, 1990.

Cooke, Sam. "A Change is Gonna Come" on *Ain't That Good News*, RCA, 1963.

Cooper, Annie. "Invisible Giants of the Voting Rights Movement Coming into View, 'Mrs. Annie Cooper's Living History, Arrested by Jim Clark, Selma, Alabama.'" OH 118, NVRMI 2004–0021. March 1, 1996.

Crosby, Emilye. "'Doesn't Everybody Want to Grow Up to be Ella Baker?': Teaching Movement History." *Civil Rights History from the Ground Up: Local Struggles, a National Movement*. Edited by Emilye Crosby, 448–476. Athens: University of Georgia Press, 2011.

Davidson, Amy. "In Voting Rights Scalia Sees, 'Racial Entitlement'." *New Yorker*, February 28, 2013. www.newyorker.com/online/blogs/closeread/2013/02/in-voting-rights-scalia-sees-a-racial-entitlement.html.

Davidson, Chandler. *Minority Vote Dilution*. Washington, DC: Howard University Press, 1984.

Davidson, Chandler. *Quiet Revolution in the South: The Impact of the Voting Rights Act, 1965–1990*. Princeton, NJ: Princeton University Press, 1994.

Davis, Townsend. *Weary Feet, Rested Souls: A Guided History of the Civil Rights Movement*. New York: W.W. Norton & Company, 1998.

Department of Justice. "Introduction to Federal Voting Rights Laws." www.justice. gov/crt/about/vot/intro/intro_a.php.

Dittmer, John. *Local People: The Struggle for Civil Rights in Mississippi*. First edition. Champaign: University of Illinois Press, 1995.

DuBois, W.E.B. *The Souls of Black Folk*. Reprint edition. New York: Tribeca Books, 2013.

DuBois, W.E.B. "Returning Soldiers." *The Crisis*, 18, (May 1919).

Eagles, Charles. *Outside Agitator: Jon Daniels and the Civil Rights Movement in Alabama*. Tuscaloosa: University of Alabama Press, 2000.

Ella Baker School website. "About Ella Baker." Accessed May 1, 2013. www. ellabakerschool.net/resources/about-ella-baker/ella-bakers-life

Evers, Myrlie and Manning Marable. *The Autobiography of Medgar Evers: A Hero's Life and Legacy Revealed through His Writings, Letters, and Speeches*. New York: Basic Civitas Books, 2006.

Fager, Charles E. *Selma, 1965: The March that Changed the South*. New York: Scribner, 1974.

Fanon, Frantz. *Black Skin, White Masks* [Peau noire, masques blancs]. Translated by Richard Philcox. Revised edition. New York: Grove Press, 2008.

Faulkner, William. *Requiem for a Nun*. New York: Vintage Books, 1950.

Finley, Keith M. *Delaying the Dream: Southern Senators and the Fight Against Civil Rights, 1938–1965*. Baton Rouge: Louisiana State University Press, 2008.

Fleming, Cynthia Griggs. *In the Shadow of Selma: The Continuing Struggle for Civil Rights in the Rural South*. Lanham, MD: Rowman & Littlefield Publishers, 2004.

Foner, Eric. *A Short History of Reconstruction*. First edition. New York: Harper Perennial, 1990.

Foner, Eric. *Reconstruction: America's Unfinished Revolution, 1863–1877*. New York: Harper Perennial Modern Classics, 2002.

Foner, Eric. "1866: The Birth of Civil Rights." The Gilder Lehrman Institute of American History. Accessed November 11, 2012. www.gilderlehrman.org/ multimedia#3339.

Foner, Eric. "The Reconstruction Amendments: Official Documents as Social History." The Gilder Lehrman Institute of American History. Accessed December 5, 2012. www.gilderlehrman.org/history-by-era/reconstruction/essays/ reconstruction-amendments-official-documents-social-history.

Forman, James. *Sammy Younge, Jr.: The First Black College Student to Die in the Black Liberation Movement*. New York: Grove Press, 1968.

Forman, James. *The Making of Black Revolutionaries*. Illustrated edition. Seattle: University of Washington Press, 1997.

Formwalt, Lee. "Journey to Selma." University of Madison-Wisconsin, Oral History Project, 2000.

Frady, Marshall. *Wallace: The Classic Portrait of Alabama Governor George Wallace*. New York: Random House, 1996.

Frank, Thomas. *What's the Matter with Kansas?: How Conservatives Won the Heart of America*. New York: Henry Holt and Company, LLC., 2004.

Franklin, John Hope, and Alfred Moss. *From Slavery to Freedom: A History of Negro Americans*. Illustrated, sixth edition. New York: Knopf, 1988.

Frazier, E. Franklin, and C. Eric Lincoln. *The Negro Church in America/The Black Church Since Frazier*. New York: Schocken, 1974.

Fukuyama, Francis. *Trust: The Social Virtues and the Creation of Prosperity*. London: Hamish Hamilton, 1995.

Gaillard, Frye. *Cradle of Freedom: Alabama and the Movement that Changed America*. Tuscaloosa: University of Alabama Press, 2004.

Galloway, Jim. "Perdue Joins Texas and Voting Rights Case." *Atlanta Journal Constitution*. Atlanta, GA, March 19, 2009.

Garrow, David J. *Protest at Selma: Martin Luther King, Jr., and the Voting Rights Act of 1965*. New Haven, CT: Yale University Press, 1980.

Garrow, David J. *Bearing the Cross: Martin Luther King, Jr., and the Southern Christian Leadership Conference*. New York: William Morrow Paperbacks, 2004.

Giddens, Anthony. *The Constitution of Society: Outline of the Theory of Structuration*. Berkeley: University of California Press, 1984.

Gilder Lehrman Institute of American History. "Abraham Lincoln Second Inaugural Address." www.scribd.com/doc/69061125/The-Inaugural-address-of-President-Abraham-Lincoln-delivered-at-the-National-Capitol-March-4-1865#fullscreen.

Gilder Lehrman Institute of American History. "1866: The Birth of Civil Rights." www.gilderlehrman.org/multimedia#3339.

Gomillion v. Lightfoot, 364 U.S. 339 (1960).

Green, John J. "Community Development as Social Movement: A Contribution to Models of Practice." *Community Development* 39:1 (2008): 50–62.

Grofman, Bernard and Lisa Handley. "The Impact of the Voting Rights Act On Black Representation in Southern State Legislatures." *Legislative Studies Quarterly*, 16:1 (February 1991): 111–128.

Guinn v. United States, 238 U.S. 347 (1915).

Hall, Jacquelyn Dowd. "The Long Civil Rights Movement and the Political Uses of the Past." *The Journal of American History* 91:4 (March 2005): 1233–1263.

Hamblin, Robert L., Jerry L. L. Miller, and D. E. Saxton. "Modeling use Diffusion." *Social Forces* 57:3 (March 1979): 799–811. http://search.ebscohost.com.umiss.lib.olemiss.edu/login.aspx?direct=true&db=sih&AN=5279778&site=ehost-live&scope=site.

Hamer, Fannie Lou. Testimony. http://americanradioworks.publicradio.org/features/sayitplain/flhamer.html.

Hamlin, Christopher M. *Behind the Stained Glass: A History of Sixteenth Street Baptist Church*. Birmingham, AL: Crane Hill, 1998.

Hanes Walton Jr., and Robert Smith. *American Politics and the African-American Quest for Universal Freedom*. New York: Longman, Inc., 2003.

Harlan, Louis R. *Booker T. Washington: Volume II, The Wizard Of Tuskegee, 1901–1915*. New York: Oxford University Press, 1986.

Harlan, Louis R. "A Black Leader in the Age of Jim Crow." In *The Racial Politics of Booker T. Washington*, edited by Donald Cunnigen, Rutledge M. Dennis and Myrtle Gonza Glascoe. Research in Race and Ethnic Relations, Volume 13. Bingley, UK: Emerald Group Publishing, 2006.

Harper v. Virginia State Board of Election, 383 U.S. 663 (1966).

Hart, Jayasri Majumdar. Hartfilms. *Sisters of Selma* in cooperation with Alabama Public Broadcasting Corporation, 2007.

Hines, Revathi. "The Silent Voices: 2000 Presidential Election and the Minority Vote in Florida." *Western Journal of Black Studies*, 26:2 (2002): 71–75.

Hobson, John M., and George Lawson. "What is History in International Relations?" *Millennium: Journal of International Studies* 37:2 (2008): 415–435.

Hobson, John M., George Lawson, and Justin Rosenberg. "Historical Sociology." In *The International Studies Encyclopedia*, edited by Robert A. Denemark. Chichester, UK: Wiley-Blackwell/International Studies Association, 2010

Holsaert, Faith S., Martha Prescod, Norman Noonan, Judy Richardson, Betty Garman Robinson, Jean Smith Young, and Dorothy M. Zellner, Eds. *Hands on the Freedom Plow: Personal Accounts by Women in SNCC*. Urbana: University of Illinois Press, 2010.

Holy Bible. Book of Esther. Grand Rapids, MI: Zondervan, 1984.

Hsung, David C. "Freedom Songs in the Modern Civil Rights Movement." *OAH Magazine of History* 19:4 (July 2005): 23–26.

Hurst, Jack. *Nathan Bedford Forrest: A Biography*. First edition. New York: Vintage, 1994.

Ifill, Sherrilyn. *On the Courthouse Lawn: Confronting the Legacy of Lynching in the Twenty-First Century*. Boston: Beacon Press, 2007.

Isaac, Larry. "Movement of Movements: Culture Moves in the Long Civil Rights Struggle." *Social Forces* 87: (2008): 33–63.

Jeffries, Hasan K. *Bloody Lowndes: Civil Rights and Black Power in Alabama's Black Belt*. New York: New York University Press, 2009.

Johnson, Ashley. "Options for Forrest Monument Unveiled to Council." *The Selma Times Journal*, April 13, 2013. Available at www.selmatimesjournal.com/2013/04/13/options-for-forrest-monument-unveiled-to-council.

Johnson, Lyndon B. "Special Message to Congress: The American Promise (1965)." Lyndon Baines Johnson Library at University of Texas. Accessed October 13, 2012. www.lbjlib.utexas.edu/johnson/archives.hom/speeches.hom/650315.asp.

Kellstedt, Paul. *The Mass Media and the Dynamics of America's Racial Attitudes*. New York: Cambridge University Press, 2003.

Keyssar, Alexander. *The Right to Vote: The Contested History of Democracy in the United States*. Revised edition. Philadelphia, PA: Basic Books, 2009.

King Jr., Martin Luther. *Stride Toward Freedom: The Montgomery Story*. Illustrated, reprint edition. Boston: Beacon Press, 2010.

Landsberg, Brian K. *Enforcing Civil Rights: Race Discrimination and the Department of Justice (Studies in Government and Public Policy)*. Lawrence: University Press of Kansas, 1997.

Landsberg, Brian K. *Free at Last to Vote: The Alabama Origins of the 1965 Voting Rights Act*. Lawrence: University Press of Kansas, 2007.

Lawson, Steven F. *Black Ballots: Voting Rights in the South, 1944–1969*. New York: Columbia University Press, 1976.

Lawyer's Committee for Civil Rights under Law. "Protecting Minority Voters: The Voting Rights Act at Work 1982–2005." *National Commission on the Voting Rights Act*. 2006. www.lawyerscommittee.org/admin/voting_rights/documents/files/0023.pdf.

Lazarsfeld, Paul Felix, Bernard Berelson, and Hazel Gaudet. *The People's Choice: How the Voter Makes up His Mind in a Presidential Campaign*. New York: Columbia University Press, 1944.

Lee, Harper. *To Kill a Mockingbird*. 50th Anniversary Edition. New York: HarperCollins, 2010 [1960].

Lemann, Nicholas. *Redemption: The Last Battle of the Civil War*. New York: Farrar, Straus and Giroux, 2007.

Lewis, John. "Not All Votes Count." *The New York Times*. Opinion, December 2, 2000. www.nytimes.com/2000/12/02/opinion/02JLEW.html.

Lewis, John, and Michael D'Orso. *Walking with the Wind: A Memoir of the Movement*. San Diego, CA: Harvest, 1999.

Litwack, Leon F. *Been in the Storm So Long: The Aftermath of Slavery*. First edition. New York: Vintage, 1980.

Lipset, Seymour Martin. *American Exceptionalism: A Two Edged Sword*. New York: W.W. Norton & Company, 1997.

Liptak, Alan. "Supreme Court Invalidated Part of Voting Rights Act." *The New York Times*, June 25, 2013. Available at www.nytimes.com/2013/06/26/us/supreme-court-ruling.html?pagewanted=all.

Loewen, James. *Lies My Teacher Told Me: Everything Your American History Textbook Got Wrong*. New York: Simon & Schuster. 2007.

Logue, Calvin M. Ed. *Ralph McGill Speaks*. Volume 2. Durham, NC: Moore Publishing, 1969.

The Lowndes County Freedom Organization. Videocassette. Directed by Dwight Cammeron. Tuscaloosa: The University of Alabama Center for Public Television and Radio, 1995.

McAdam, Doug. *Freedom Summer*. New York: Oxford University Press, 1988.

McAdam, Doug. *Political Process and the Development of Black Insurgency 1930–1970*. Second edition. Chicago: University of Chicago Press, 1999.

McCabe, Daniel, and Paul Stekler. *George Wallace: Settin' the Woods on Fire*, edited by Daniel McCabe and Paul Stekler. Alexandria, VA: PBS Home Video, 2000.

McCrary, Peyton, Jerome A. Gray, Edward Still, and Huey L. Perry. "Alabama." In Chandler Davisdon *Quiet Revolution in the South: The Impact of the Voting Rights Act, 1965–1990*. Princeton, NJ: Princeton University Press, 1994.

McGill, Ralph. "One Day it Will Be Monday." *The Atlanta Constitution*, April 9, 1953.

McGill, Ralph. *The South and the Southerner*. Athens: University of Georgia Press, 1992.

McMillen, Neil R. *The Citizens' Council: Organized Resistance to the Second Reconstruction, 1954–64*. Champaign: University of Illinois Press, 1994.

Marable, Manning. *Malcolm X: A Life of Reinvention*. New York: Viking Penguin, Inc., 2011.

Martin, Harold. *Ralph McGill, Reporter*. Boston: Little, Brown, 1973.

Mills, C. Wright. *The Sociological Imagination*. New York: Oxford University Press, 1959.

Mills, Kay. *This Little Light of Mine: The Life of Fannie Lou Hamer*. Lexington: University of Kentucky Press, 2007.

Mississippi Public Broadcasting Report, "Activists Rally for Civil Rights and Section 5," May 1, 2013 http://mpbonline.org/News/article/miss._activists_rally_for_civil_rights_and_section_5.

Morris, Aldon. *The Origins of the Civil Rights Movement*. New York: Free Press, 1984.

Moses, Robert P., and Charles Cobb. *Radical Equations: Civil Rights from Mississippi to the Algebra Project*. Boston: Beacon Press, 2002.

NAACP Legal Defence and Educational Fund. "Post-Racial America? Not Yet: Why the Fight for Voting Rights Continues After the Election of President Barack Obama." A report by the Political Participation Group of the NAACP. Baltimore: NAACP, 2009.

NAACP Legal Defence and Educational Fund. "Defending Democracy: Confronting Modern Barriers to Voting Rights in America." Baltimore: NAACP, 2011. www.naacpldf.org/files/publications/Defending%20Democracy%2012-5-11.pdf.

National Park Service. *Selma to Montgomery* pamphlet. Retrieved January 10, 2013 www.nps.gov/nr/twhp/wwwlps/lessons/133semo/133facts1.htm.

News One Staff. "Shame! 96-Year-Old Woman: Voting Now More Difficult Than During Jim Crow" *NewsOne*, October, 10, 2011. Available at http://newsone.com/1575525/voting-now-more-difficult-than-during-jim-crow/.

Northwest Austin Municipal Utility District No. 1 v. Holder. 557 U.S. 193 (2009). Retrieved May 4, 2013 at www.naacpldf.org/files/case_issue/Shelby-County-Alabama-v-Holder-Q%26A.pdf.

Oregon v. Mitchell, 400 U.S. 112 (1970).

Parker, Frank. *Black Votes Count: Political Empowerment in Mississippi After 1965*. First edition. Chapel Hill: The University of North Carolina Press, 1990.

Partidge, Elizabeth. *Marching for Freedom: Walk together Children and Don't You Grow Weary*. First edition. New York: Viking Juvenile, 2009.

Pease, Donald E. *The New American Exceptionalism*. Minneapolis: University of Minnesota Press, 2009.

Peck, J. "Constitution fails its roots, prof says: Wayne Flynt traces past of state document." *Huntsville Times* (Huntsville, AL) www.al.com/search/index.ssf?/base/news/1098954973277921.xml?huntsvilletimes?nlocal.

Perlman, Bill. Interviewed by the author via telephone, audio recording, December 19, 2012.

Phull, Hardeep. *Story behind the Protest Song: A Reference Guide to the 50 Songs That Changed the 20th century*. First edition. Westport: Greenwood Publishing Group, 2008.

Poletta, Francesssca. *Freedom Is an Endless Meeting: Democracy in American Social Movements*. Chicago: University of Chicago Press, 2002.

Quinton, Nicholas, and Gerald R. Webster. "Electoral Alignments and Place-Based Cleavages in Statewide Votes in Alabama." In *Revitalizing Electoral Geography*, edited by Barney Warf, and Jonathan Leib, 195–218. Farnham, UK: Ashgate Publishing Limited, 2011.

Raines, Howell. *My Soul is Rest: Movement Day in the Deep South Remembered*. New York: Putnam, 1977.

Reagon, Bernice Johnson. "Ella's Song." Flying Fish label, 1963.

Reed, Roy. "Wounded Negro dies in Alabama," *The New York Times* (New York, NY). February 27, 1965.

Reese, Frederick D. Interview by author, audio recording. February 9, 2013.

Reese, Frederick D. Interview, National Voting Rights Museum and Institute Archives, NVRMI 2004–2007.

Reynolds v. Sims, 377 U.S. 533 (1964).

Ritterhouse, Jennifer. *Growing up Jim Crow: How Black and White Southern Children Learned Race*. Chapel Hill: University of North Carolina Press, 2006.

Roberts, Gene, and Hank Klibanoff. *The Race Beat: The Press, the Civil Rights Struggle, and the Awakening of a Nation*. New York: Vintage, 2007.

Robnett, Belinda. "We Don't Agree: Collective Identity Justification Work in Social Movement Organizations." *Research in Social Movements, Conflicts, and Change* 26: (2005): 380–388.

Rogers, Everett. *Diffusion of Innovations*. Fifth edition. New York: Free Press, 2001.

Roosevelt, Franklin Delano. "The Four Freedoms Speech." January 6, 1941, http://docs.fdrlibrary.marist.edu/od4frees.html.

Sales, Ruby. Interview conducted by Blackside, Inc. on December 12, 1988, for Film and Media Archive, Henry Hampton Collection. "*Eyes on the Prize II: America at the Crossroads 1965 to 1985*." Washington University Libraries, 1988.

Sales, Ruby. "Growing Up in the Black Church." Interview Excerpts. www.veteransofhope.org/veteran/ruby-sales.

Sales, Ruby Nell. "Oral History/Interview Ruby Nell Sales," Interview by Jean Wiley and Bruce Hartford for Veterans of the Civil Rights Movement Oral History Project, September 2005. www.crmvet.org/nars/ruby sale.htm.

Santoro, Wayne A. "The Civil Rights Movement and the Right to Vote: Black Protest, Segregationist Violence and the Audience." *Social Forces* 86:4 (June 2008): 1340–1414. http://0search.ebscohost.com.umiss.lib.olemiss.edu/login.aspx?direct=true&db=sih&AN=32796428&site=ehost-live&scope=site.

Seeger, Pete, and Bob Reiser. *Everybody Says Freedom: A History of the Civil Rights Movement in Songs and Pictures*. New York: W.W. Norton & Company, 1989.

Shelby County, Alabama v. Eric Holder, Jr., No. 12-96, slip op. (U.S. Supreme Ct., June 25, 2013).

Sikora, Frank. *Until Justice Rolls Down: The Birmingham Church Bombing Case*. Tuscaloosa: University of Alabama Press, 1991.

Slevin, James, "*Time-Space*." *Blackwell Encyclopedia of Sociology*, edited by George Ritzer (2007) DOI:10.1111/b.9781405124331.2007.x.

Smith v. Allwright, 321 U.S. 649 (1944).

Social Science Data Analysis Network (SSDAN). "Trends in Voter Turnout." SSDAN Report. Accessed May 6, 2013. www.ssdan.net/sites/default/files/briefs/vtbrief.pdf.

South Carolina v. Katzenbach 383 U.S. 301 (1966).

Spigner, Charles. "Jimmy Lee Jackson." *Encyclopedia of Alabama.* Accessed January 13, 2013. www.encyclopediaofalabama.org/face/Article.jsp?id=h-2011.

Stanton, Mary. *From Selma to Sorrow: The Life and Death of Viola Liuzzo.* Athens: University of Georgia Press, 2000.

"The State of the South 1872," *The Nation: A Weekly Journal* 14 (New York: E.L. Godkin & Co. Publishers, 1872.) 197–198.

Stewart, John Craig. *The Governors of Alabama.* Gretna, LA: Pelican Publishing Company, 1975.

Suitts, Steve. "Voting Rights, the Supreme Court, and the Persistence of Southern History." *Southern Spaces.* Accessed June 4, 2013. http://southernspaces.org/2013?voting-rights-supreme-court-and-persistence-southern-history.

Summerlin, Donnie. "Samuel Younge Jr." *Encyclopedia of Alabama.* Accessed September 2, 2008. www.encyclopediaofalabama.org/face/Article.jsp?id+h-1669.

Sundquist, Eric J. *King's Dream: The Legacy of Martin Luther King Jr.'s I Have a Dream Speech.* New Haven, CT: Yale University Press, 2009.

Taylor, Paul. "The Growing Electoral Clout of Blacks is Driven by Turnout, Not Demographics." *Pew Research Social and Demographic Trends Report,* Pew Research Center, Washington DC, December 26, 2012. www.pewsocialtrends.org/2012/12/26/the-growing-electoral-clout-of-blacks-is-driven-by-turnout-not-demographics/.

Teel, Leonard Ray. *Ralph Emerson McGill: Voice of the Southern Conscience.* Knoxville: University of Tennessee Press, 2001.

Tilly, Charles. "Historical Sociology." In *Current Perspectives in Social Theory,* edited by Scott G. McNall, and Gary N. Howe. Vol. I. Greenwich, CT: JAI Press, 1980.

Tilly, Charles. "Social Movements and National Politics." In *Statemaking and Social Movements,* edited by Charles Bright and Susan Friend Harding, 297–317. Ann Arbor: University of Michigan Press, 1984.

Tilly, Charles. "Three Visions of History and Theory." *History and Theory* 46:2 (2007): 299–307.

Tiryakian, Edward A. "Emile Durkheim and Social Change" in *The Blackwell Encyclopedia of Sociology,* edited by George Ritzer, Hoboken, NJ: Blackwell, 2007.

Tuan, Yi-Fu and Steven Hoelscher Tuan. *Space and Place: The Perspective of Experience.* Minneapolis: University of Minnesota Press, 2001.

Tuch, Steven A., and Jack K. Martin. "Regional Differences in Whites' Racial Policy Attitudes." In *Racial Attitudes in the 1990s: Continuity and Change.* Westport, CT: Praeger Publishers, 1997.

Tullos, Allen M. "The Black Belt." *Southern Spaces,* April 19, 2004. Available at www.southernspaces.org/2004/black-belt.

Uphoff, Norman, and C. M. Wijayaratna. "Demonstrated Benefits from Social Capital: The Productivity of Farmer Organizations in Gal Oya, Sri Lanka." *World Development* 28: (2000): 1875–1890.

U.S. Census Bureau. 2010 Census. Available at www.al.com/census/index.ssf.

U.S. Commission on Civil Rights. "The Voting Rights Act: Ten Years Later." January 1975.

Valentino, Nicholas A., and David O. Sears. "Old Times There are Not Forgotten: Race and Partisan Realignment in the Contemporary South." *American Journal of Political Science* 49:3 (2005): 672-688.

Valeriani, Richard. Interview conducted by Blackside, Inc. on December 10, 1985, for *Eyes on the Prize: America's Civil Rights Years (1954–1965).* Washington University Libraries, Film and Media Archive, Henry Hampton Collection, 1985.

Vaughn, Wally, and Hattie Campbell Davis, Eds. *The Selma Campaign 1963–1965: The Decisive Battle of the Civil Rights Movement.* Dover, MA: The Majority Press, Inc., 2006.

Walker, Samuel. Interview by author, audio recording. Selma, AL. July 11, 2012.

Walton Jr., Hanes, and Robert Smith. *American Politics and the African-American Quest for Universal Freedom.* New York: Longman, Inc., 2003.

Waters, Ronald W. *Black Presidential Politics in America: A Strategic Choice.* New York: State University of New York (SUNY) Press, 1988.

Watson, Bruce. *Freedom Summer: The Savage Season of 1964 That Made Mississippi Burn and Made America a Democracy.* New York: Penguin Books, 2011.

Webster, Gerald R., and Nicholas Quinton. "The Electoral Geographies of Two Segregationist ("Jim Crow") Referenda in Alabama." *Political Geography* 29: (2010): 370–380.

Wesberry v. Sanders, 376 U.S. 1 (1964).

Wilkerson, Isabel. *The Warmth of Other Suns: The Epic Story of America's Great Migration.* Reprint edition. New York: Vintage, 2011.

Williams, Juan. *Eyes on the Prize: America's Civil Rights Years, 1954–1965.* New York: Viking Penguin, Inc., 1987.

Williams, Michael Vinson. *Medgar Evers: Mississippi Martyr.* Fayetteville: University of Arkansas Press, 2011.

Wilson, Theodore B. *The Black Codes of the South.* Tuscaloosa: University of Alabama Press, 1965.

Wimberley, Ronald C. and Libby V. Morris. *The Southern Black Belt: A National Perspective.* Lexington, KY: TVA Rural Studies, 1997.

Woodham, Rebecca. "Lowndes County Freedom Organization." *Encyclopedia of Alabama.* Accessed September 24, 2008. www.encyclopediaofalabama.org/face/Article.jsp?id=h-1781.

Woodham, Rebecca. "Jonathan Myrick Daniels." *Encyclopedia of Alabama.* Accessed September 24, 2008.

Woodward, C. Vann. Foreword by William E. Leuchtenburg. *The Burden of Southern History.* Updated third edition. Baton Rouge: Louisiana State University Press, 2008.

Woodward, C. Vann. *The Strange Career of Jim Crow*. Commemorative edition. New York: Oxford University Press, 2001.

Yeats, William Butler. "The Second Coming." In *Michael Robartes and the Dancer*. Whitefish: Kessinger Publishing, Reprint edition. 2003.

Zinn, Howard. "Registration in Alabama," *New Republic* 149: October 26, 1963.

Zinn, Howard. "Alabama: Freedom Day in Selma (from SNCC: The New Abolitionists)." In *The Zinn Reader: Writings on Disobedience and Democracy*. First edition. New York: Seven Stories Press, 1997.

Index

1876 presidential election 112–113
1941 State of the Union address 157–164;
  see also Four Freedoms speech
  (Roosevelt)
1964 presidential election 67
2000 presidential election 129
2008 presidential election 123, 131
2012 presidential election 134

ABC News 40
Achebe, Chinua 56
Adegbile, Debo 13–14, 111, 115, 121
African liberation 64
Alabama: Black Belt; electorate 126–127;
  Montgomery, history 1–2; social change
  22–50; Tuskegee Institute 82–84,
  91–92; voter registration 65, 118–120;
  see also Gomillion, Charles, Lowndes
  County, Alabama
Alexander, Michelle 131
Algeria 64
American exceptionalism 15–16
American Promise Speech (Johnson) 43,
  165–173
American South *see* Southern states
Arkansas 59
Ashmore, Harry 52–53
Avery, Annie Pearl 31, 39–40, 61, 87–88,
  93–95

Baker, Ella 42, 87–89
Belafonte, Harry 47

Bevel, James 34
Bhabha, Homi 51
Black Belt: history 26; social change in
  22–50
black voters *see* voter; voting age, voting
  rights, Voting Rights Act
Bland, Joanne 36–37, 38, 47, 86
Bloody Sunday (March 7, 1965) 1, 11,
  35–41, 49, 62
Branch, Taylor 28, 61
Brown v. The Board of Education of
  Topeka Kansas 58–59
Bureau of Refugees, Freedmen, and
  Abandoned Lands 3
buses 60
Bush, George W. 124, 130
Bush, Jeb 130

Carmichael, Stokely (aka Kwame Ture) 26
Chaney, James 42
change agents 48
"A Change is Gonna Come" (Cooke) 22,
  24
Chestnut, J.L. 22
children 79–81, 92–93
churches 80, 95–97, 103–104, 106
Citizens' Councils 71–72
Civil Rights Acts: 1957 56, 63; 1960 56,
  63; 1964 32, 56, 67, 74
civil rights movement: Alabama Black Belt
  22–50; children's role 79–81, 92–93;
  churches' role 80, 95–97, 103–104,

106; community collaborations 98–101; family influences 86, 87; individual sacrifice 101–103; local collaborations 98–101; martyrs 101–103; news reports 55; non-violence/violence debate 24–25; parental role 86, 87, 89; political rights comparison 128; Selma Campaign 6–15; teachers' role 89–91; terminology 7; voting rights protection 53–77; women's role 103–108

Clark, Jim 35, 37, 38–39, 69, 70–71, 75, 105

Clark, Kenneth and Mamie 59

Cloud, John 36

Cobb, Charles 27, 89

Coleman, James 133

Coleman, Tom 85

colleges 83–84; see also University . . .

Columbus, Georgia 81–82

Commission on Civil Rights 130

Compromise of 1877 30

Confederate flag 16

constitutional issues 17

Cooke, Sam 22, 24

Cooper, Annie 104–106

Courageous Eight 100

The Crisis (NAACP magazine) 4

critical mass 111

Dallas County Voters League (DCVL) 31, 32, 100

Daniels, Jonathan 50, 84, 85, 102

Danville, Virginia 74

decolonization 64

decoy demonstrations 94

democracy 9, 127–135

Democratic Party 67

Dickinson, William 45

Diffusion of Innovations Theory 10, 12, 53, 135–136; adopter categories 28–29, 54; change agents 48; innovators 50; knowledge/persuasion phase 55; rate of diffusion 54–55; time variable 54

disenfranchisement, Florida 129–131

district line redrawing 125–126

Dittmer, John 73, 98

doll experiments 59; see also Clark, Kenneth and Mamie

DuBois, W.E.B. 3, 81; "double consciousness" 81, 104, 196

economic intimidation/oppression 71–76, 84, 99–100, 101, 104–105

Edmund Pettus Bridge 37, 38

education: racial segregation 58–59

Eisenhower, Dwight D. 63

Election Assistance Commission 131

electorate, racial/ethnic composition 122

employment, racial segregation 74

Evers, Medgar 6, 61

Fager, Charles 7–8

family influences 86, 87

Fanon, Frantz 64

Faulkner, William 110

FBI 34, 107, 108

felons 130, 131–132

Fifteenth Amendment 11, 30, 57, 113, 143

First Unitarian Universalist Church 106

Fleming, Cynthia 98, 99

Florida 129–131

food assistance 73

Forman, James 64, 74, 75, 76, 86–87

Forrest, Nathan Bedford 1, 135

Fort Benning, Georgia 81

Four Freedoms speech (Roosevelt) 4–5, 157–164

Fourteenth Amendment 141–142

franchise see voting rights; Voting Rights Act

Franklin, John Hope 113

Freedmen's Bureau see Bureau of Refugees, Freedmen, and Abandoned Lands

freedom 2–6

Freedom Days 75–76

Freedom Riders 60, 72, 94

Freedom Singers 96

Fukuyama, Francis 133

Gaston Motel, Birmingham, Alabama 94

Gee's Bend, Wilcox County, Alabama 99

Georgia 81–82

Ginsburg, Justice 18

Gomillion, Charles 92, 197

Goodman, Andrew 42
Gore, Al 130
Gould, Jack 60
Greenwood, Mississippi 73

Hall, David 46
Hamer, Fannie Lou 53, 57, 64, 67
Hare, James 100
Harlem, New York 62
Harris, Katherine 130
Hayes–Tilden compromise 112–113
Highway 80 46
historical sociology 9
Holder, Eric 17–18
Hoover, J. Edgar 107
hypodermic theory of media 101–102

"I Have a Dream" speech (King) 66
illegal voting charges 129
impression management 70
Innovations Theory see Diffusion of
    Innovations Theory
interpersonal communication 41
Isaac, Larry 6, 60–61

Jackson, Jimmie Lee 32–34, 43, 102
Jeffries, Hasan Kwame 21, 31
Jenkins, Lummie 98–99
Johnson, Frank M. 43, 44
Johnson, Lyndon B. 1, 41–42, 43, 77,
    111, 112, 165–173
Judgment at Nuremberg (film) 40

Kellstedt, Paul 51
Kennedy, John F. 56, 62, 65
Keyssar, Alexander 110
King, Martin Luther, Jr. 35, 41, 48,
    49, 50, 76–77; "I Have a Dream"
    speech 66; "Letter from a
    Birmingham Jail" 98
Klibanoff, Hank 52
knowledge, diffusion decision process 55
Ku Klux Klan (KKK) 62, 71, 107, 108

Lafayette, Bernard 65, 99
Lafayette, Colia 75
Lazarsfeld, Paul 101–102
Lee, Harper 45

Legal Defense and Educational Fund
    (LDF) 43–44, 58, 64
legal structures 63–71
legislation see Civil Rights Act; Voting
    Rights Act
"Letter from a Birmingham Jail" (King) 98
Lewis, John 36, 37, 130, 131
Lincoln, Abraham 72–73
Little Rock, Arkansas 59
Liuzzo, Viola 48, 102, 103, 106–108
local collaborations 98–101
Loewen, James 19
Los Angeles 61
Louisiana 113, 116, 118–120, 123, 158
Lowndes County, Alabama: civil rights
    impact 138; economic oppression 84,
    99–100, 101; Selma to Montgomery
    march 46, 47, 48–49; sharecropper
    displacement 99–100, 101; voter
    registration 27–28, 31
Lowndes County Freedom Organization
    (LCFO) 100

McAdam, Doug 6
McCrary, Peyton 117–118
McGill, Ralph 58–59; see also "One Day it
    Will Be Monday"
macro-level analyses 8
Malcolm X 62
Mall, Clara 137
the March see Selma to Montgomery
    march
Marion march 33–34
Marshall, Thurgood 60
martyrs of civil rights movement 101–103
mass meetings 96–97
media: civil rights coverage 40–41, 55,
    59–60; hypodermic theory 101–102;
    television 40
meetings 96–97
micro-level analyses 8
middle class 99
Mississippi: black voter turnout 118;
    economic intimidation tactics 73; voter
    registration 118–120
Mississippi Freedom Democratic Party
    (MFDP) 66–67
Mississippi Freedom Summer project 66

Montgomery, Alabama: history 1–2
Moses, Robert 89
Moss, Alfred 113
Moton, Leroy 48, 107
Moyers, Bill 41–42
Murphy, Matthew Hobson, Jr. 108
music 3, 22, 47, 80, 95–96, 104

National Association for the
    Advancement of Colored People
    (NAACP) 4, 58, 129
Native Americans 2
New Deal programs 2–3
news reports 55, 59–60, 101–102; see also
    media
New York 62
non-violence policy 24–25, 60–61
Norton, Eleanor Holmes 17

Obama, Barack 123–125
"O Freedom" (song) 3
"One Day it Will Be Monday" (Ralph
    McGill editorial) 58, 191
opinion leaders 55, 79, 103
"outside agitators" argument 98, 107

parents 80, 86, 87, 89
parietals 83–84
Partridge, Elizabeth 22
Patterson, John 68–69
Perdue, Sonny 124
Perlman, Bill 86–87, 96
police brutality 62; see also Clark, Jim;
    violence
political/legal structures 63–71
political rights 128
polling sites 130
posters 23
Powell, Fay Bellamy 103
Powell, James 62
Prairie View A & M University 128–129
preclearance, voter ID laws 131
Prince Edward County, Virginia 58
prisoners 130, 131–132

racial bloc voting 120
racial segregation: challenges to 60;
    employment 74; public opinion survey
52; "redemption" process 57; schools
    58–59; Wallace's policy 68–70
racism 19, 42, 51–53
Reagan, Ronald 110
Reagon, Bernice Johnson 3, 104
Reconstruction era 29–30, 113; see also
    Fourteenth Amendment
Redemption 57
redistricting process 125–126
Reeb, James 42, 43, 62–63, 102
Reese, F.D. 90, 91, 96–97
Register to Vote poster 23
religious communities see churches
riots 62, 64; see also violence
Roberts, Gene 52
Rochester, New York 62
Rogers, Everett 10, 12, 28–29, 48, 50,
    54, 55
Roosevelt, Franklin D. 4–5, 157–164
Rowe, Gary Thomas 108

Sales, Ruby Nell 24–25, 79, 80–90, 108,
    137, 138
Sanders, Rose (Faya Toure) 14–15
schools, racial segregation 58–59
Schwerner, Michael "Mickey" 42, 66
segregation see racial segregation
self-defense 61
self-presentation 70
Selma, Alabama: civil rights movement
    6–15, 26–29; death of Jimmie Lee
    Jackson 32–34, 43; economy 74; history
    1; voter registration 75
Selma to Montgomery March 7, 34,
    44–49
Selma to Montgomery (pamphlet) 27
Selma Times–Journal article 173–177
"separate but equal" policy 58, 59
separation of powers 66
sexual orgies allegation, Selma to
    Montgomery march 45–46
sharecroppers 26, 73, 84, 99–100, 101
Shelby County, Alabama v. Holder 13–14,
    16–17, 125
slavery 26
social capital 133–134
social change 8, 10–11
social innovations 53–54

social integration 58; *see also* racial
    segregation
social movements, definition 78–79
social networks 102–103, 136–137
Social Science Data Analysis Network
    (SSDAN) 132
social unrest 58–63; *see also* violence
socio-historical approach 9
songs 3, 22, 47, 80, 95–96, 104
South Carolina 131
Southern Christian Leadership Conference
    (SCLC): SNCC relationship 60–61;
    voting rights campaign 32, 76
Southern Spaces (Internet journal) 19
Southern states: black subjugation 57–58;
    distinctiveness 15, 16, 123; economic
    oppression 71–76; "outside agitators"
    argument 98, 107; racial attitudes
    51–53; Redemption 57; resistance to
    black civil rights 56, 63, 65–66;
    "separate but equal" policy 58, 59;
    "states rights" 65–66; violence towards
    black people 71
Stanton, Mary 45
"Stars for Freedom Rally" 47
"states rights" 65–66
Student Nonviolent Coordinating
    Committee (SNCC) 31–32, 41, 64,
    74, 76–77; Avery's work for 94;
    relations with other civil rights groups
    67–68; Sales' work for 84; SCLC
    relationship 60–61; women in 103;
    young people 24
students 83–84, 91–92; *see also* University
Suitts, Steve 19
Supreme Court 17–18, 113, 124, 125, 130

teachers 89–91
tear gas 37
television 40
Tenth Amendment 66
terminology 7
Texas 128, 129
theoretical frameworks 9–10
Tilly, Charles 78–79
time-space connections, social change 11
To Kill a Mockingbird (Lee) 45
Toure, Faya *see* Sanders, Rose

Toure, Sekou 64
Ture, Kwame (aka Stokely Carmichael) 26
Turnaround Tuesday march 39, 41–44
Tuskegee Institute, Alabama 82–84, 91–92
Twenty-sixth Amendment 127, 128

United States: racial/ethnic composition of
    electorate 122; *see also* Southern states;
    U.S. Constitutional Amendments
University of Alabama 60, 68
University of Georgia 64
University of Mississippi 61

Valeriani, Richard 33–34, 40
Vancour, Sander 52, 53
violence: Annie Cooper's beating 105;
    Bloody Sunday 35–41; Los Angeles 61;
    Marion march 33–34; martyrs of civil
    rights movement 101–103; riots 62, 64;
    white on white violence 42–43, 137;
    see also non-violence policy
Virginia 58, 74
Vivian, C.T. 33
voter: dilution 120–121, 126, 136;
    discrimination 120–122;
    disenfranchisement 129–131;
    identification laws 131; registration
    27–28, 31, 65, 75, 118–121, 128;
    records 116–117; turnout 118, 132–135
voting age 127–128
voting rights: American values 110;
    barriers 31, 32, 128; consensus
    formation 53–77; exercise of 53;
    extensions 127; felons 131–132;
    infringement claims 20; post-
    Reconstruction era 30–32; prisoners
    131–132; protection for 20, 24, 53–77;
    Reconstruction era 29–30; Register to
    Vote poster 23; restrictions 128,
    131–132
Voting Rights Act (1965) 11, 111, 112,
    114–125; bailout provisions 117;
    coverage formula 18; legacy 135; place-
    based issues 122–127; reforms 20;
    Section 2 115, 121, 125; Section 4
    16–17, 18, 19–20; Section 5 13–15, 17,
    18, 115–117, 121, 124, 125; transcript
    144–156

Walker, Sam 27, 89, 92–93, 95, 134–135
Wallace, George 35, 43, 48, 62, 68–70
Waller County, Texas 128, 129
White Citizens' Councils 71–72
white primaries 113, 114
white voters: population percentage 126;
    support for Obama 123–125
Wilcox County, Alabama 98–99
Wilkins, Collie Leroy 108
Wilkins, Roy 67

Williams, Hosea 36
women: civil rights movement role
    103–108; voting rights 127
Woodward, C. Vann 15, 123
World Wars 4–5

Younge, Samuel 83, 103
young people 24; see also children

Zinn, Howard 75